BEST HOME PLANS

Two-Story Living

FRONT ELEVATION

Covered front porch lends instant appeal to this charming two-story home, reminiscent of a classic farmhouse. See plan GL-2161 on page 135.

Sunset Publishing Corporation ■ **Menlo Park, California**

SUNSET BOOKS
President and Publisher:
  Susan J. Maruyama
Director, Finance & Business
  Affairs: Gary Loebner
Director, Manufacturing & Sales
  Service: Lorinda Reichert
Western Regional Sales Director:
  Richard A. Smeby
Eastern Regional Sales Director:
  Richard M. Miller
Editorial Director:
  Kenneth Winchester
Coordinating Editor:
  Linda J. Selden
Contributing Editor:
  Don Vandervort

**SUNSET PUBLISHING
CORPORATION**
Chairman: Robert L. Miller
President/Chief Executive
  Officer: Robin Wolaner
Chief Financial Officer:
  James E. Mitchell
Circulation Director:
  Robert I. Gursha
Editor, Sunset Magazine:
  William R. Marken

Photographers: Mark Englund/
HomeStyles: 4, 5; Philip Harvey:
10 top, back cover; Stephen
Marley: 11 top left and right; Russ
Widstrand: 10 bottom; Tom Wyatt:
11 bottom.

Cover: Pictured is plan R-2083
on page 144. Cover design by
Naganuma Design & Direction.
Photography by Mark Englund/
HomeStyles.

First printing August 1994
Copyright © 1994, Sunset Publishing
Corporation, Menlo Park, CA 94025.
First edition. All rights reserved, including
the right of reproduction in whole or in part
in any form.

ISBN 0-376-01135-1.
Library of Congress Catalog Card Number:
94-66503.
Printed in the United States.

 printed on recycled paper

A Dream Come True

Planning and building a house is one of life's most creative
and rewarding challenges. Whether you're seriously considering building a new home or you're just dreaming about
it, this book offers a wealth of inspiration and information
to help you get started.

On the following pages, you'll learn how to plan and
manage a home-building project—and how to ensure its
success. Then you'll discover more than 200 proven home
plans, designed for families just like yours by architects
and professional designers. Peruse the pages and study the
floor plans; you're sure to find a home that's just right for
you. When you're ready to order blueprints, you can simply call or mail in your order, and you'll receive the plans
within days.

Enjoy the adventure!

Contents

Although designed for a narrow lot, this contemporary two-story offers plenty of elbow room, thanks to its open-plan design. See plan R-2052 on page 130.

Your Multi-Level Best

When it comes to value, two-story homes are unbeatable. A multi-story house takes advantage of every square inch of lot space, allows twice the space beneath a given size of roof, and can provide a natural separation between living areas and sleeping rooms. Moreover, a second story gives a house a substantial profile, often capturing views that a single-level dwelling would miss.

In this book, you'll find a wealth of proven two-story home plans, created by some of America's foremost architects and designers. A range of styles is presented, from classic traditional homes to striking contemporary houses, and from country charmers to affordable starters.

The two keys to success in building are capable project management and good design. The next few pages will walk you through some of the most important aspects of project management: you'll find an overview of the building process, directions for selecting the right plan and getting the most from it, and methods for successfully working with a builder and other professionals.

The balance of the book presents professionally designed stock plans. Once you find a plan that will work for you—perhaps with a few modifications made later to personalize it for your family—you can order construction blueprints for a fraction of the cost of a custom design, a savings of many thousands of dollars (see pages 12–15 for information on how to order).

Transom windows above the arched entry flood the interior of this distinctive home with natural light. The entry, living room, and dining room all have vaulted ceilings. The master suite, located on the second floor, includes a sitting area with a bay window and a roomy walk-in closet. See plan CDG-2007 on page 175.

Spacious country-style home is given grand street presence by a side-approach three-car garage at one end. The upstairs boasts four bedrooms, a second family room, and space for a loft, extra bedroom, and bath above the garage. See plan AX-91310 on page 201.

Stylish two-story offers clean, well-balanced lines. The living area and master suite are on the main floor. The unobtrusive second story contains two additional bedrooms and a bath. See plan AX-97144 on page 100.

Designed for family living, this traditional two-story offers an open-plan kitchen, breakfast nook, and family room downstairs and three bedrooms plus a master suite upstairs. See plan FB-1744-L on page 71.

The Art of Building

As you embark on your home-building project, think of it as a trip—clearly not a vacation but rather an interesting, adventurous, at times difficult expedition. Meticulous planning will make your journey not only far more enjoyable but also much more successful. By careful planning, you can avoid—or at least minimize—some of the pitfalls along the way.

Start with realistic expectations of the road ahead. To do this, you'll want to gain an understanding of the basic house-building process, settle on a design that will work for you and your family, and make sure your project is actually doable. By taking those initial steps, you can gain a clear idea of how much time, money, and energy you'll need to invest to make your dream come true.

The Building Process

Your role in planning and managing a house-building project can be divided into two parts: prebuilding preparation and construction management.

■ **Prebuilding preparation.** This is where you should focus most of your attention. In the hands of a qualified contractor whose expertise you can rely on, the actual building process should go fairly smoothly. But during most of the prebuilding stage, you're generally on your own. Your job will be to launch the project and develop a talented team that can help you bring your new home to fruition.

When you work with stock plans, the prebuilding process usually goes as follows:

First, you research the general area where you want to live, selecting one or more possible home sites (unless you already own a suitable lot). Then you choose a basic house design, with the idea that it may require some modification. Finally, you analyze the site, the design, and your budget to determine if the project is actually attainable.

If you decide that it is, you purchase the land and order blue-prints. If you want to modify them, you consult an architect, designer, or contractor. Once the plans are finalized, you request bids from contractors and arrange any necessary construction financing.

After selecting a builder and signing a contract, you (or your contractor) then file the plans with the building department. When the plans are approved, often several weeks—or even months—later, you're ready to begin construction.

■ **Construction management.** Unless you intend to act as your own contractor, your role during the building process is mostly one of quality control and time management. Even so, it's important to know the sequence of events and something about construction methods so you can discuss progress with your builder and prepare for any important decisions you may need to make along the way.

Decision-making is critical. Once construction begins, the builder must usually plunge ahead, keeping his carpenters and subcontractors progressing steadily. If you haven't made a key decision—which model bathtub or sink to install, for example—it can bring construction to a frustrating and expensive halt.

Usually, you'll make such decisions before the onset of building, but, inevitably, some issue or another will arise during construction. Being knowledgeable about the building process will help you anticipate and circumvent potential logjams.

Selecting a House Plan

Searching for the right plan can be a fun, interactive family experience—one of the most exciting parts of a house-building project. Gather the family around as you peruse the home plans in this book. Study the size, location, and configuration of each room; traffic patterns both inside the house and to the outdoors; exterior style; and how you'll use the available space. Discuss the pros and cons of the various plans.

Browse through pictures of homes in magazines to stimulate ideas. Clip the photos you like so you can think about your favorite options. When you visit the homes of friends, note special features that appeal to you. Also, look carefully at the homes in your neighborhood, noting their style and how they fit the site.

Mark those plans that most closely suit your ideals. Then, to narrow down your choices, critique each plan, using the following information as a guide.

■ **Overall size and budget.** How large a house do you want? Will the house you're considering fit your family's requirements? Look at the overall square footage and room sizes. If you have a hard time visualizing room sizes, measure some of the rooms in your present home and compare.

It's often better for the house to be a little too big than a little too small, but remember that every extra square foot will cost more money to build and maintain.

■ **Number and type of rooms.** Beyond thinking about the number of bedrooms and baths you want, consider your family's life-style and how you use space. Do you want both a family room and a living room? Do you need a formal dining space? Will you require some extra rooms, or "swing spaces," that can serve multiple purposes, such as a home office–guest room combination?

■ **Room placement and traffic patterns.** What are your preferences for locations of formal living areas, master bedroom, and children's rooms? Do you prefer a kitchen that's open to family areas or one that's private and out of the way? How much do you use exterior spaces and how should they relate to the interior?

Once you make those determinations, look carefully at the floor plan of the house you're considering to see if it meets your needs and if the traffic flow will be convenient for your family.

■ **Architectural style.** Have you always wanted to live in a Victorian farmhouse? Now is your chance to create a house that matches your idea of "home" (taking into account, of course, styles in your neighborhood). But don't let your preference for one particular architectural style dictate your home's floor plan. If the floor plan doesn't work for your family, keep looking.

■ **Site considerations.** Most people choose a site before selecting a plan—or at least they've zeroed in on the basic type of land where they'll situate their house. It sounds elementary, but choose a house that will fit the site.

When figuring the "footprint" of a house, you must know about any restrictions that will affect your home's height or proximity to the property lines. Call the local building department (look under city or county listings in the phone book) and get a very clear description of any restrictions, such as setbacks, height limits, and lot coverage, that will affect what you can build on the site (see "Working with City Hall," at right).

When you visit potential sites, note trees, rock outcroppings, slopes, views, winds, sun, neighboring homes, and other factors. All will impact on how your house works on a particular site.

Once you've narrowed down the choice of sites, consult an architect or building designer (see page 8) to help you evaluate how some potential houses will work on the sites you have in mind.

Is Your Project Doable?

Before you purchase land, make sure your project is doable. Although it's too early at this stage to pinpoint costs, making a few phone calls will help you determine whether your project is realistic. You'll be able to learn if you can afford to build the house, how long it will take, and what obstacles may stand in your way.

To get a ballpark estimate of cost, multiply a house's total square footage (of livable space) by the local average cost per square foot for new construction. (To obtain local averages, call a contractor, an architect, a realtor, or the local chapter of the National Association of Home Builders.) Some contractors may even be willing to give you a preliminary bid. Once you know approximate costs, speak to your lender to explore financing.

Working with City Hall

For any building project, even a minor one, it's essential to be familiar with building codes and other restrictions that can affect your project.

■ **Building codes,** generally implemented by the city or county building department, set the standards for safe, lasting construction. Codes specify minimum construction techniques and materials for foundations, framing, electrical wiring, plumbing, insulation, and all other aspects of a building. Although codes are adopted and enforced locally, most regional codes conform to the standards set by the national Uniform Building Code, Standard Building Code, or Basic Building Code. In some cases, local codes set more restrictive standards than national ones.

■ **Building permits** are required for home-building projects nearly everywhere. If you work with a contractor, the builder's firm should handle all necessary permits.

More than one permit may be needed; for example, one will cover the foundation, another the electrical wiring, and still another the heating equipment installation. Each will probably involve a fee and require inspections by building officials before work can proceed. (Inspections benefit *you,* as they ensure that the job is being done satisfactorily.) Permit fees are generally a percentage (1 to 1.5 percent) of the project's estimated value, often calculated on square footage.

It's important to file for the necessary permits. Failure to do so can result in fines or legal action against you. You can even be forced to undo the work performed. At the very least, your negligence may come back to haunt you later when you're ready to sell your house.

■ **Zoning ordinances,** particular to your community, restrict setbacks (how near to property lines you may build), your house's allowable height, lot coverage factors (how much of your property you can cover with structures), and other factors that impact design and building. If your plans don't conform to zoning ordinances, you can try to obtain a variance, an exception to the rules. But this legal work can be expensive and time-consuming. Even if you prove that your project won't negatively affect your neighbors, the building department can still refuse to grant the variance.

■ **Deeds and covenants** attach to the lot. Deeds set out property lines and easements; covenants may establish architectural standards in a neighborhood. Since both can seriously impact your project, make sure you have complete information on any deeds or covenants before you turn over a spadeful of soil.

It's a good idea to discuss your project with several contractors (see page 8). They may be aware of problems in your area that could limit your options—bedrock that makes digging basements difficult, for example. These conversations are actually the first step in developing a list of contractors from which you'll choose the one who will build your home.

Recruiting Your Home Team

A home-building project will interject you and your family into the building business, an area that may be unfamiliar territory. Among the people you'll be working with are architects, designers, landscapers, contractors, and subcontractors.

Design Help

A qualified architect or designer can help you modify and personalize your home plan, taking into account your family's needs and budget and the house's style. In fact, you may want to consider consulting such a person while you're selecting a plan to help you articulate your needs.

Design professionals are capable of handling any or all aspects of the design process. For example, they can review your house plans, suggest options, and then provide rough sketches of the options on tracing paper. Many architects will even secure needed permits and negotiate with contractors or subcontractors, as well as oversee the quality of the work.

Of course, you don't necessarily need an architect or designer to implement minor changes in a plan; although most contractors aren't trained in design, some can help you with modifications.

An open-ended, hourly-fee arrangement that you work out with your architect or designer allows for flexibility, but it often turns out to be more costly than working on a flat-fee basis. On a flat fee, you agree to pay a specific amount of money for a certain amount of work.

To find architects and designers, contact such trade associations as the American Institute of Architects (AIA), American Institute of Building Designers (AIBD), American Society of Landscape Architects (ASLA), and American Society of Interior Designers (ASID). Although many professionals choose not to belong to trade associations, those who do have met the standards of their respective associations. For phone numbers of local branches, check the Yellow Pages.

■ **Architects** are licensed by the state and have degrees. They're trained in all facets of building design and construction. Although some can handle interior design and structural engineering, others hire specialists for those tasks.

■ **Building designers** are generally unlicensed but may be accredited by the American Institute of Building Designers. Their backgrounds are varied: some may be unlicensed architects in apprenticeship; others are interior designers or contractors with design skills.

■ **Draftspersons** offer an economical route to making simple changes on your drawings. Like building designers, these people may be unlicensed architect apprentices, engineers, or members of related trades. Most are accomplished at drawing up plans.

■ **Interior designers,** as their job title suggests, design interiors. They work with you to choose room finishes, furnishings, appliances, and decorative elements. Part of their expertise is in arranging furnishings to create a workable space plan. Some interior designers are employed by architectural firms; others work independently. Financial arrangements vary, depending on the designer's preference.

Related professionals are kitchen and bathroom designers, who concentrate on fixtures, cabinetry, appliances, materials, and space planning for the kitchen and bath.

■ **Landscape architects, designers, and contractors** design outdoor areas. Landscape architects are state-licensed to practice landscape design. A landscape designer usually has a landscape architect's education and training but does not have a state license. Licensed landscape contractors specialize in garden construction, though some also have design skills and experience.

■ **Soils specialists and structural engineers** may be needed for projects where unstable soils or uncommon wind loads or seismic forces must be taken into account. Any structural changes to a house require the expertise of a structural engineer to verify that the house won't fall down.

Services of these specialists can be expensive, but they're imperative in certain conditions to ensure a safe, sturdy structure. Your building department will probably let you know if their services are required.

General Contractors

To build your house, hire a licensed general contractor. Most states require a contractor to be licensed and insured for worker's compensation in order to contract a building project and hire other subcontractors. State licensing ensures that contractors have met minimum training standards and have a specified level of experience. Licensing does not guarantee, however, that they're good at what they do.

When contractors hire subcontractors, they're responsible for overseeing the quality of work and materials of the subcontractors and for paying them.

■ **Finding a contractor.** How do you find a good contractor? Start by getting referrals from people you know who have built or remodeled their home. Nothing beats a personal recommendation. The best contractors are usually busily moving from one satisfied client to another prospect, advertised only by word of mouth.

You can also ask local real estate brokers and lenders or even your building inspector for names of qualified builders. Experienced lumber dealers are another good source of names.

In the Yellow Pages, look under "Contractors–Building, General"; or call the local chapter of the National Association of Home Builders.

■ **Choosing a contractor.** Once you have a list of names of prospective builders, call several of them. On the telephone, ask first whether they handle your type of job and can work within your schedule. If they can, arrange a meeting with each one and ask them to be prepared with references of former clients and photos of previous jobs. Better still, meet them at one of their current work sites so you can get a glimpse of the quality of their work and how organized and thorough they are.

Take your plan to the meeting and discuss it enough to request a rough estimate (some builders will comply, while others will be reluctant to offer a ballpark estimate, preferring to give you a hard bid based on complete drawings). Don't hesitate to probe for advice or suggestions that might make building your house less expensive.

Be especially aware of each contractor's personality and how well you communicate. Good chemistry between you and your builder is a key ingredient for success.

Narrow down the candidates to three or four. Ask each for a firm bid, based on the exact same set of plans and specifications. For the bids to be accurate, your plans need to be complete and the specifications as precise as possible, call-

ing out particular appliances, fixtures, floorings, roofing material, and so forth. (Some of these are specified in a stock-plan set; others are not.)

Call the contractors' references and ask about the quality of their work, their relationship with their clients, their promptness, and their readiness to follow up on problems. Visit former clients to check the contractor's work firsthand.

Be sure your final candidates are licensed, bonded, and insured for worker's compensation, public liability, and property damage. Also, try to determine how financially solvent they are (you can call their bank and credit references). Avoid contractors who are operating hand-to-mouth.

Don't automatically hire the contractor with the lowest bid if you don't think you'll get along well or if you have any doubts about the quality of the person's work. Instead, look for both the most reasonable bid and the contractor with the best credentials, references, terms, and compatibility with your family.

A word about bonds: You can request a performance bond that guarantees that your job will be finished by your contractor. If the job isn't completed, the bonding company will cover the cost of hiring another contractor to finish it. Bonds cost from 2 to 6 percent of the value of the project.

Your Building Contract

A building contract (see below) binds and protects both you and your contractor. It isn't just a legal document. It's also a list of the expectations of both parties. The best way to minimize the possibility of misunderstandings and costly changes later on is to write down every possible detail. Whether the contract is a standard form or one composed by you, have an attorney look it over before both you and the contractor sign it.

The contract should clearly specify all the work that needs to be done, including particular materials and work descriptions, the time schedule, and method of payment. It should be keyed to the working drawings.

A Sample Building Contract

Project and participants. Give a general description of the project, its address, and the names and addresses of both you and the builder.

Construction materials. Identify all construction materials by brand name, quality markings (species, grades, etc.), and model numbers where applicable. Avoid the clause "or equal," which allows the builder to substitute other materials for your choices. For materials you can't specify now, set down a budget figure.

Time schedule. Include both start and completion dates and specify that work will be "continuous." Although a contractor cannot be responsible for delays caused by strikes and material shortages, your builder should assume responsibility for completing the project within a reasonable period of time.

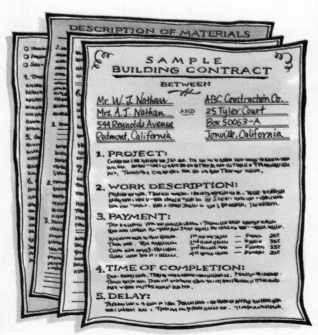

Work to be performed. State all work you expect the contractor to perform, from initial grading to finished painting.

Method and schedule of payment. Specify how and when payments are to be made. Typical agreements specify installment payments as particular phases of work are completed. Final payment is withheld until the job receives its final inspection and is cleared of all liens.

Waiver of liens. Protect yourself with a waiver of liens signed by the general contractor, the subcontractors, and all major suppliers. That way, subcontractors who are not paid for materials or services cannot place a lien on your property.

Personalizing Stock Plans

The beauty of buying stock plans for your new home is that they offer tested, well-conceived design at an affordable price. And stock plans dramatically reduce the time it takes to design a house, since the plans are ready when you are.

Because they were not created specifically for your family, stock plans may not reflect your personal taste. But it's not difficult to make revisions in stock plans that will turn your home into an expression of your family's personality. You'll surely want to add personal touches and choose your own finishes.

Ideally, the modifications you implement will be fairly minor. The more extensive the changes, the more expensive the plans. Major changes take valuable design time, and those that affect a house's structure may require a structural engineer's approval.

If you anticipate wholesale changes, such as moving a number of bearing walls or changing the roofline significantly, you may be better off selecting another plan. On the other hand, reconfiguring or changing the sizes of some rooms can probably be handled fairly easily.

Some structural changes may even be necessary to comply with local codes. Your area may have specific requirements for snow loads, energy codes, seismic or wind resistance, and so forth. Those types of modifications are likely to require the services of an architect or structural engineer.

Plan Modifications

Before you pencil in any changes, live with your plans for a while. Study them carefully—at your building site, if possible. Try to picture the finished house: how rooms will interrelate, where the sun will enter and at what angle, what the view will be from each window. Think about traffic patterns, access to rooms, room sizes, window and door locations, natural light, and kitchen and bathroom layouts.

Typical changes might involve adding windows or skylights to

bring in natural light or capture a view. Or you may want to widen a hallway or doorway for roomier access, extend a room, eliminate doors, or change window and door sizes. Perhaps you'd like to shorten a room, stealing the gained space for a large closet. Look closely at the kitchen; it's not difficult to reconfigure the layout if it makes the space more convenient for you.

Above all, take your time—this is your home and it should reflect your taste and needs. Make your changes now, during the planning stage. Once construction begins, it will take crowbars, hammers, saws, new materials, and, most significantly, time to alter the plans. Because changes are not part of your building contract, you can count on them being expensive extras once construction begins.

Specifying Finishes

One way to personalize a house without changing its structure is to substitute your favorite finishes for those specified on the plan.

Would you prefer a stuccoed exterior rather than the wood siding shown on the plan? In most cases, this is a relatively easy change. Do you like the look of a wood shingle roof rather than the composition shingles shown on the plan? This, too, is easy. Perhaps you would like to change the windows from sliders to casements, or upgrade to high-efficiency glazing. No problem. Many of those kinds of changes can be worked out with your contractor.

Inside, you may want hardwood where vinyl flooring is shown. In fact, you can—and should—choose types, colors, and styles of floorings, wall coverings, tile, plumbing fixtures, door hardware, cabinetry, appliances, lighting fixtures, and other interior details, for it's these materials that will personalize your home. For help in making selections, consult an architect or interior designer (see page 8).

Each material you select should be spelled out clearly and precisely in your building contract.

Finishing touches can transform a house built from stock plans into an expression of your family's taste and style. Clockwise, from far left: Colorful tilework and custom cabinetry enliven a bathroom (Design: Osburn Design); highly organized closet system maximizes storage space (Architect: David Jeremiah Hurley); low-level deck expands living space to outdoor areas (Landscape architects: The Runa Group, Inc.); built-ins convert the corner of a guest room into a home office (Design: Lynn Williams of The French Connection); French country cabinetry lends style and old-world charm to a kitchen (Design: Garry Bishop/Showcase Kitchens).

What the Plans Include

Complete construction blueprints are available for every house shown in this book. Clear and concise, these detailed blueprints are designed by licensed architects or members of the American Institute of Building Designers (AIBD). Each plan is designed to meet standards set down by nationally recognized building codes (the Uniform Building Code, Standard Building Code, or Basic Building Code) at the time and for the area where they were drawn.

Remember, however, that every state, county, and municipality has its own codes, zoning requirements, ordinances, and building regulations. Modifications may be necessary to comply with such local requirements as snow loads, energy codes, seismic zones, and flood areas.

Although blueprint sets vary depending on the size and complexity of the house and on the individual designer's style, each set may include the elements described below and shown at right.

■ **Exterior elevations** show the front, rear, and sides of the house, including exterior materials, details, and measurements.

■ **Foundation plans** include drawings for a full, partial, or daylight basement, crawlspace, pole, pier, or slab foundation. All necessary notations and dimensions are included. (Foundation options will vary for each plan. If the plan you choose doesn't have the type of foundation you desire, a generic conversion diagram is available.)

■ **Detailed floor plans** show the placement of interior walls and the dimensions of rooms, doors, windows, stairways, and similar elements for each level of the house.

■ **Cross sections** show details of the house as though it were cut in slices from the roof to the foundation. The cross sections give the home's construction, insulation, flooring, and roofing details.

■ **Interior elevations** show the specific details of cabinets (kitchen, bathroom, and utility room), fireplaces, built-in units, and other special interior features.

■ **Roof details** give the layout of rafters, dormers, gables, and other roof elements, including clerestory windows and skylights. These details may be shown on the elevation sheet or on a separate diagram.

■ **Schematic electrical layouts** show the suggested locations for switches, fixtures, and outlets. These details may be shown on the floor plan or on a separate diagram.

■ **General specifications** provide instructions and information regarding excavation and grading, masonry and concrete work, carpentry and woodwork, thermal and moisture protection, drywall, tile, flooring, glazing, and caulking and sealants.

Other Helpful Building Aids

In addition to the construction information on every set of plans, you can buy the following guides.

■ **Reproducible blueprints** are helpful if you'll be making changes to the stock plan you've chosen. These blueprints are original line drawings produced on erasable, reproducible paper for the purpose of modification. When alterations are complete, working copies can be made.

■ **Itemized materials list** details the quantity, type, and size of materials needed to build your home. (This list is extremely helpful in obtaining an accurate construction bid. It's not intended for use to order materials.)

■ **Mirror-reverse plans** are useful if you want to build your home in the reverse of the plan that's shown. Because the lettering and dimensions read backwards, be sure to buy at least one regular-reading set of blueprints.

■ **Description of materials** gives the type and quality of materials suggested for the home. This form may be required for obtaining FHA or VA financing.

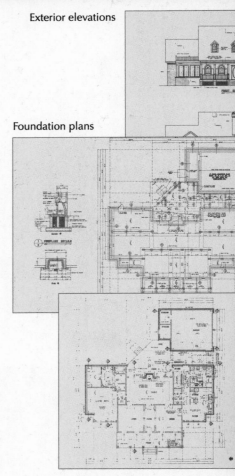

Exterior elevations

Foundation plans

Detailed floor plans

■ **How-to diagrams** for plumbing, wiring, solar heating, framing and foundation conversions show how to plumb, wire, install a solar heating system, convert plans with 2 by 4 exterior walls to 2 by 6 construction (or vice versa), and adapt a plan for a basement, crawlspace, or slab foundation. These diagrams are not specific to any one plan.

NOTE: Due to regional variations, local availability of materials, local codes, methods of installation, and individual preferences, detailed heating, plumbing, and electrical specifications are not included on plans. The duct work, venting, and other details will vary, depending on the heating and cooling system you use and the type of energy that operates it. These details and specifications are easily obtained from your builder or local supplier.

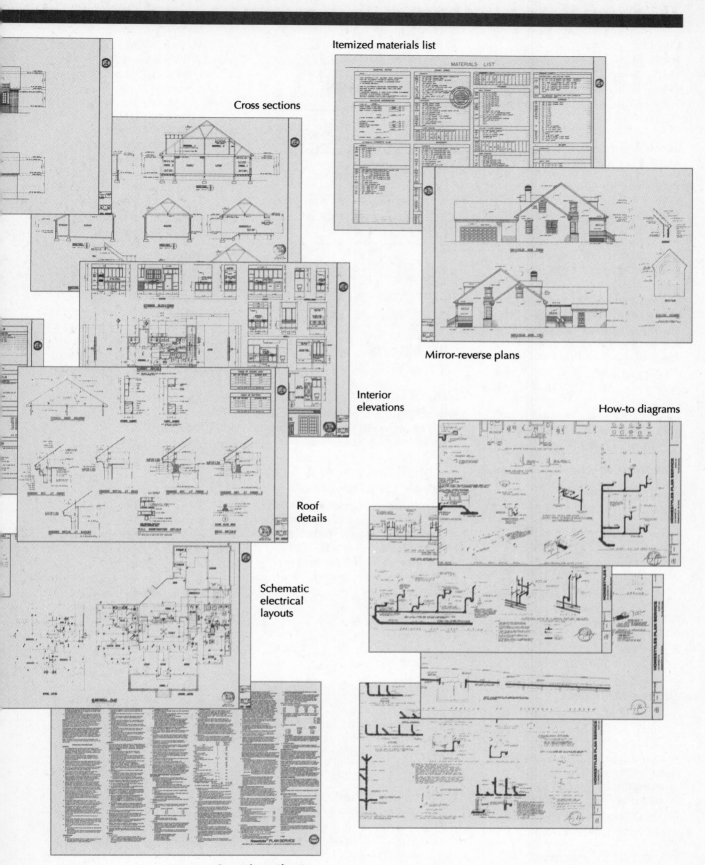

Itemized materials list

Cross sections

MATERIALS LIST

Mirror-reverse plans

Interior
elevations

How-to diagrams

Roof
details

Schematic
electrical
layouts

General specifications

Before You Order

Once you've chosen the one or two house plans that work best for you, you're ready to order blueprints. Before filling in the form on the facing page, note the information that follows.

How Many Blueprints Will You Need?

A single set of blueprints will allow you to study a home design in detail. You'll need more for obtaining bids and permits, as well as some to use as reference at the building site. If you'll be modifying your home plan, order a reproducible set (see page 12).

Figure you'll need at least one set each for yourself, your builder, the building department, and your lender. In addition, some subcontractors—foundation, plumber, electrician, and HVAC—may also need at least partial sets. If they do, ask them to return the sets when they're finished. The chart below can help you calculate how many sets you're likely to need.

Blueprint Checklist

_____ Owner's set(s)

_____ **Builder usually requires at least three sets: one for legal documentation, one for inspections, and a minimum of one set for subcontractors.**

_____ **Building department requires at least one set. Check with your local department before ordering.**

_____ **Lending institution usually needs one set for a conventional mortgage, three sets for FHA or VA loans.**

_____ **TOTAL SETS NEEDED**

Blueprint Prices

The cost of having an architect design a new custom home typically runs from 5 to 15 percent of the building cost, or from $5,000 to $15,000 for a $100,000 home. A single set of blueprints for the plans in this book ranges from $250 to $535, depending on the house's size. Working with these drawings, you can save enough on design fees to add a deck, a swimming pool, or a luxurious kitchen.

Pricing is based on "total finished living space." Garages, porches, decks, and unfinished basements are not included.

Price Code (Size)	1 Set	4 Sets	7 Sets	Reproducible Set
A (under 1,500 sq. ft.)	$250	$295	$325	$425
B (1,500-1,999 sq. ft.)	$285	$330	$360	$460
C (2,000-2,499 sq. ft.)	$320	$365	$395	$495
D (2,500-2,999 sq. ft.)	$355	$400	$430	$530
E (3,000-3,499 sq. ft.)	$390	$435	$465	$565
F (3,500-3,999 sq. ft.)	$425	$470	$500	$600
G (4,000 sq. ft. and up)	$460	$505	$535	$635

Building Costs

Building costs vary widely, depending on a number of factors, including local material and labor costs and the finishing materials you select. For help estimating costs, see "Is Your Project Doable?" on page 7.

Foundation Options & Exterior Construction

Depending on your site and climate, your home will be built with a slab, pier, pole, crawlspace, or basement foundation. Exterior walls will be framed with either 2 by 4s or 2 by 6s, determined by structural and insulation standards in your area. Most contractors can easily adapt a home to meet the foundation and/or wall requirements for your area. Or ask for a conversion how-to diagram (see page 12).

Service & Blueprint Delivery

Service representatives are available to answer questions and assist you in placing your order. Every effort is made to process and ship orders within 48 hours.

Returns & Exchanges

Each set of blueprints is specially printed and shipped to you in response to your specific order; consequently, requests for refunds cannot be honored. However, if the prints you order cannot be used, you may exchange them for another plan from any Sunset home plan book. For an exchange, you must return all sets of plans within 30 days. A nonrefundable service charge will be assessed for all exchanges; for more information, call the toll-free number on the facing page. Note: Reproducible sets cannot be exchanged.

Compliance with Local Codes & Regulations

Because of climatic, geographic, and political variations, building codes and regulations vary from one area to another. These plans are authorized for your use expressly conditioned on your obligation and agreement to comply strictly with all local building codes, ordinances, regulations, and requirements, including permits and inspections at time of construction.

Architectural & Engineering Seals

With increased concern about energy costs and safety, many cities and states now require that an architect or engineer review and "seal" a blueprint prior to construction. To find out whether this is a requirement in your area, contact your local building department.

License Agreement, Copy Restrictions & Copyright

When you purchase your blueprints, you are granted the right to use those documents to construct a single unit. All the plans in this publication are protected under the Federal Copyright Act, Title XVII of the United States Code and Chapter 37 of the Code of Federal Regulations. Each designer retains title and ownership of the original documents. The blueprints licensed to you cannot be used by or resold to any other person, copied, or reproduced by any means. The copying restrictions do not apply to reproducible blueprints. When you buy a reproducible set, you may modify and reproduce it for your own use.

Blueprint Order Form

Complete this order form in just three easy steps. Then mail in your order or, for faster service, call toll-free.

1. Blueprints & Accessories

BLUEPRINT CHART

Price Code	1 Set	4 Sets	7 Sets	Reproducible Set*
A	$250	$295	$325	$425
B	$285	$330	$360	$460
C	$320	$365	$395	$495
D	$355	$400	$430	$530
E	$390	$435	$465	$565
F	$425	$470	$500	$600
G	$460	$505	$535	$635

Prices subject to change

*A reproducible set is produced on erasable paper for the purpose of modification. It is only available for plans with prefixes AG, AGH, AH, AHP, APS, AX, B, C, CAR, CPS, DD, DW, E, EOF, FB, GL, GML, GSA, H, HFL, J, K, KLF, LMB, LRD, M, NW, OH, PH, PI, PM, S, SDG, THD, UDG, V.

Mirror-Reverse Sets: $40 surcharge. From the total number of sets you ordered above, choose the number you want to be reversed. *Note: All writing on mirror-reverse plans is backwards. Order at least one regular-reading set.*

Itemized Materials List: One set $40; each additional set $10. Details the quantity, type, and size of materials needed to build your home.

Description of Materials: Sold in a set of two for $40 (for use in obtaining FHA or VA financing).

Typical How-To Diagrams: One set $12.50; two sets $23; three sets $30; four sets $35. General guides on plumbing, wiring, and solar heating, plus information on how to convert from one foundation or exterior framing to another. *Note: These diagrams are not specific to any one plan.*

2. Sales Tax & Shipping

Determine your subtotal and add appropriate local state sales tax, plus shipping and handling (see chart below).

SHIPPING & HANDLING

	1–3 Sets	4–6 Sets/ Reproducible Set	7 or More Sets
U.S. Regular (4–6 working days)	$12.50	$15.00	$17.50
U.S. Express (2–3 working days)	$25.00	$27.50	$30.00
Canada Regular (2–3 weeks)	$12.50	$15.00	$17.50
Canada Express (4–6 working days)	$25.00	$30.00	$35.00
Overseas/Airmail (7–10 working days)	$50.00	$60.00	$70.00

3. Customer Information

Choose the method of payment you prefer. Include check, money order, or credit card information, complete name and address portion, and mail to:

Sunset/HomeStyles Plan Service
P.O. Box 50670
Minneapolis, MN 55405

FOR FASTER SERVICE
CALL 1-800-547-5570

SS09

COMPLETE THIS FORM

Plan Number _____ **Price Code** _____

Foundation _____
(Review your plan carefully for foundation options—basement, pole, pier, crawlspace, or slab. Many plans offer several options; others offer only one.)

Number of Sets: $_____
(See chart at left)
☐ One Set
☐ Four Sets
☐ Seven Sets
☐ One Reproducible Set

Additional Sets _____ $_____
($35 each)

Mirror-Reverse Sets _____ $_____
($40 surcharge)

Itemized Materials List $_____
Only available for plans with prefixes AH, AHP, APS*, AX, B*, C, CAR, CDG*, CPS, DD*, DW, E, FB, GSA, H, HFL, I, J, K, LMB*, LRD, N, NW*, P, PH, R, S, SD*, THD, U, UDG, VL.*Not available on all plans. Please call before ordering.

Description of Materials $_____
Only available for plans with prefixes AHP, C, DW, H, HFL, J, K, KY, LMB, N, P, PH, VL.

Typical How-To Diagrams $_____
☐ Plumbing   ☐ Wiring   ☐ Solar Heating   ☐ Foundation & Framing Conversion

SUBTOTAL $_____

SALES TAX $_____

SHIPPING & HANDLING $_____

GRAND TOTAL $_____

☐ Check/money order enclosed (in U.S. funds)
☐ VISA   ☐ MasterCard   ☐ AmEx   ☐ Discover

Credit Card # _____ **Exp. Date** _____

Signature _____

Name _____

Address _____

City _____ **State** ____ **Country** _____

Zip _____ **Daytime Phone** (____) _____

☐ Please check if you are a contractor.

Mail form to: Sunset/HomeStyles Plan Service
P.O. Box 50670
Minneapolis, MN 55405

Or Fax to: (612) 338-1626

FOR FASTER SERVICE
CALL 1-800-547-5570

SS09

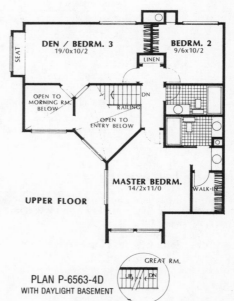

Photo courtesy of Piercy & Barclay Designers

Quality Design for a Narrow, Sloping Lot

Multi-pitched rooflines, custom window treatments and beveled board siding add a distinctive facade to this two-level home of only 1,516 sq. ft. Its slim 34' width allows it to fit nicely on a narrow lot while offering ample indoor and outdoor living areas.

The enclosed entry courtyard is a pleasant area for al fresco breakfasts or spill-over entertaining. The wide, high-ceilinged entry hall opens directly into the sweeping Great Room and dining area. This room is warmed by a large fireplace and has a door to a large wood deck. Also off the entry hall is the morning room with a vaulted ceiling and a matching arched window overlooking the courtyard. A half-bath and utility room is on the other side of the entry.

An open-railed stairway leads from the entry to the bedrooms on the second level. The master suite has a high dormer with peaked windows, a walk-in closet and a private bathroom. The larger of the other bedrooms could be used as a den, and it also overlooks the morning room and entry hall. If additional room is required, this plan is available with a daylight basement.

**NOTE:
The above photographed home may have been modified by the homeowner. Please refer to floor plan and/or drawn elevation shown for actual blueprint details.

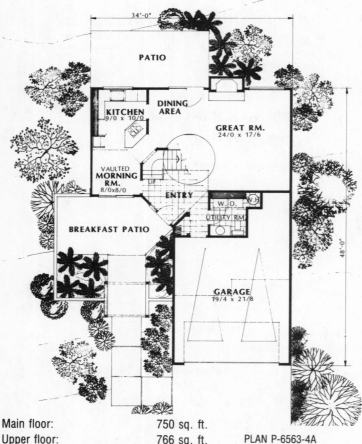

PLAN P-6563-4A
WITHOUT BASEMENT

PLAN P-6563-4D
WITH DAYLIGHT BASEMENT

Main floor:	750 sq. ft.
Upper floor:	766 sq. ft.
Total living area:	1,516 sq. ft.
Basement level:	809 sq. ft.

Blueprint Price Code B

TO ORDER THIS BLUEPRINT,
CALL TOLL-FREE 1-800-547-5570

Plans P-6563-4A & -4D

PRICES AND DETAILS
ON PAGES 12-15

Compact Home Offers Soaring Living Room Ceiling

Main floor: 780 sq. ft.
Upper floor: 317 sq. ft.

Total living area: 1,097 sq. ft.
(Not counting basement or garage)

Basement level: 780 sq. ft.

PLAN P-6543-2A
WITHOUT BASEMENT
(CRAWLSPACE FOUNDATION)

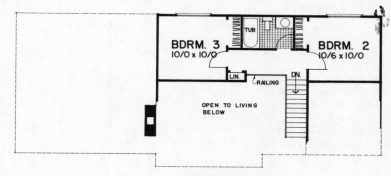

UPPER FLOOR

PLAN P-6543-2D
WITH DAYLIGHT BASEMENT

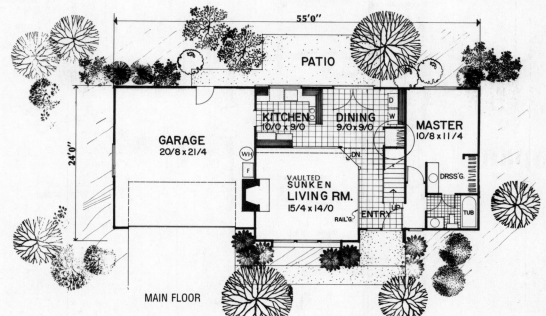

MAIN FLOOR

Blueprint Price Code A

Plans P-6543-2A & -2D

Open Design in Compact Traditional

- An instant feeling of spaciousness and openness is created in this hospitable home with a vaulted Great Room and open-railed stairway.
- Additional appeal comes from a wood-burning fireplace, visible from the adjoining kitchen and dining area.
- The spacious kitchen has a pantry and attached walk-in laundry room.
- The main-level master bedroom is well isolated from the living areas, yet easily accessible to the children's bedrooms on the upper level.

UPPER FLOOR

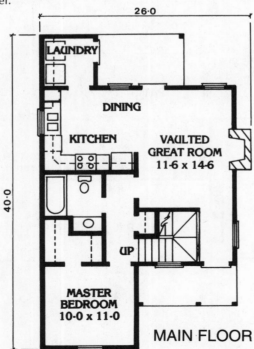

MAIN FLOOR

Plan V-1098	
Bedrooms: 3	**Baths: 2**
Space:	
Upper floor	396 sq. ft.
Main floor	702 sq. ft.
Total Living Area	**1,098 sq. ft.**
Exterior Wall Framing	2x6
Foundation options:	
Crawlspace	
(Foundation & framing conversion diagram available—see order form.)	
Blueprint Price Code	**A**

TO ORDER THIS BLUEPRINT, CALL TOLL-FREE 1-800-547-5570

Plan V-1098

PRICES AND DETAILS ON PAGES 12-15

A-Frame Offers Options

In this versatile A-frame, the main floor is the same in all versions, and includes one bedroom. The upper floor gives you a choice of one large bedroom or two smaller ones.

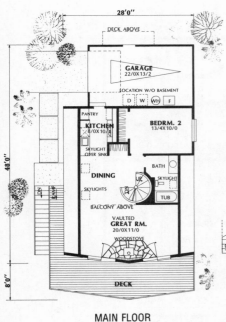

28'0"

DECK ABOVE

GARAGE
22/0X 13/2

LOCATION W/O BASEMENT

D W WH F

PANTRY

KITCHEN
8/0X 10/4

BEDRM. 2
13/4X 10/0

SKYLIGHT OVER SINK

DINING

BATH

48'0"

SKYLIGHTS

UP

BALCONY ABOVE

TUB

VAULTED
GREAT RM.
20/0X 11/0

WOODSTOVE

8'0"

DECK

MAIN FLOOR

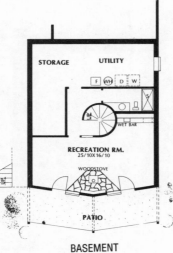

STORAGE

UTILITY

F WH D W

DN

WET BAR

RECREATION RM.
25/10X 16/10

WOODSTOVE

PATIO

BASEMENT

DECK

VAULTED
MASTER
10/0X 16/0

STORAGE

STORAGE

VAULTED
BATH

SKYLIGHT

LIN

SPA

STORAGE

SKYLIGHTS

DN

BALCONY RAILING

OPEN TO GREAT RM. BELOW

UPPER FLOOR
PLAN P-530-5A
WITH CRAWLSPACE

PLAN P-530-5D
WITH BASEMENT

DECK

VAULTED
BEDRM. 1
10/0X 12/0

STORAGE

STORAGE

LIN

TUB

VAULTED
BEDRM. 3
8/0X 10/0

SKYLIGHT

STORAGE

SKYLIGHTS

DN

BALCONY RAILING

OPEN TO GREAT RM. BELOW

UPPER FLOOR
PLAN P-530-2A
WITH CRAWLSPACE

PLAN P-530-2D
WITH BASEMENT

Upper floor:	400 sq. ft.
Main floor:	761 sq. ft.
Total living area: (Not counting basement or garage)	1,161 sq. ft.
Basement:	938 sq. ft.
Total living area with daylight basement:	2,099 sq. ft.

Blueprint Price Code C With Basement
Blueprint Price Code A Without Basement

Compact Three-Bedroom

- Both openness and privacy are possible in this economical three-bedroom home design.
- The bright living room boasts a 17-ft. vaulted ceiling, a warming fireplace and a corner window. A high clerestory window lets in additional natural light.
- The modern, U-shaped kitchen features a handy corner pantry and a versatile snack bar.
- The adjacent open dining area provides access to a backyard deck through sliding glass doors.
- A lovely corner window brightens the secluded master bedroom, which also includes a roomy walk-in closet and private access to a compartmentalized hall bath.
- Upstairs, two good-sized bedrooms share a second split bath.

Plan B-101-8501

Bedrooms: 3	Baths: 2
Living Area:	
Upper floor	400 sq. ft.
Main floor	846 sq. ft.
Total Living Area:	**1,246 sq. ft.**
Garage	400 sq. ft.
Standard basement	846 sq. ft.
Exterior Wall Framing:	2x4

Foundation Options:

Standard basement

(All plans can be built with your choice of foundation and framing. A generic conversion diagram is available. See order form.)

BLUEPRINT PRICE CODE: A

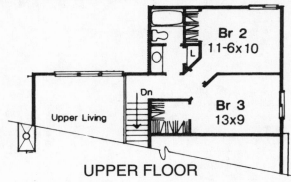

UPPER FLOOR

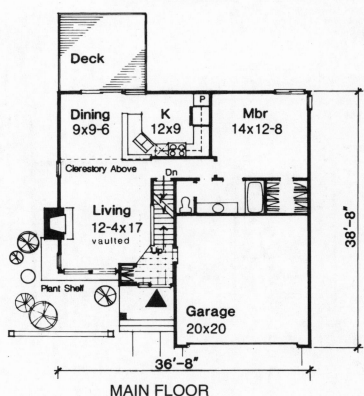

MAIN FLOOR

TO ORDER THIS BLUEPRINT, CALL TOLL-FREE 1-800-547-5570

Plan B-101-8501

PRICES AND DETAILS ON PAGES 12-15

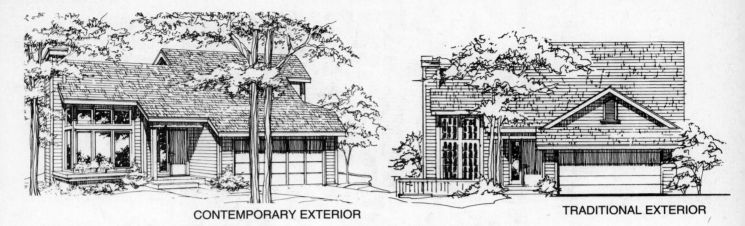

CONTEMPORARY EXTERIOR

TRADITIONAL EXTERIOR

Economical Attraction

- This great-looking three-bedroom home is as economical as it is attractive. Two exterior styles (both are included in the blueprints) offer you the choice of a bold contemporary look or a more traditional facade.
- The exciting space-saving floor plan incorporates an open living area and a main-floor master suite with a dual-access bath.
- The vaulted living room is brightened by tall windows and warmed by a fireplace. A clerestory window lies between the living room and the dining room, which has sliding glass doors to a rear deck. The kitchen features an angled sink set into a snack bar.
- Upstairs, the balcony hall overlooks the living room. Two nice-sized bedrooms, one of which has a walk-in closet, and a full bath are found here.

Plan B-8323

Bedrooms: 3	Baths: 2
Living Area:	
Upper floor	400 sq. ft.
Main floor	846 sq. ft.
Total Living Area:	**1,246 sq. ft.**
Standard basement	846 sq. ft.
Garage	400 sq. ft.
Exterior Wall Framing:	2x4

Foundation Options:

Standard basement

(All plans can be built with your choice of foundation and framing. A generic conversion diagram is available. See order form.)

BLUEPRINT PRICE CODE:	**A**

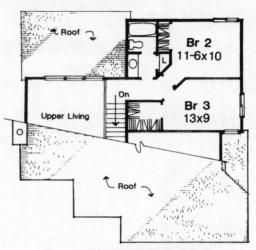

UPPER FLOOR

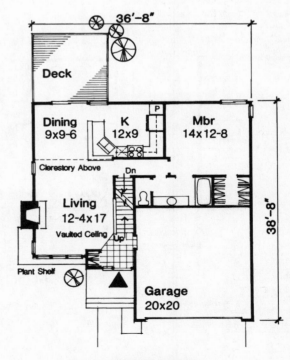

MAIN FLOOR

Sun-Soaked Leisure Home

- This eye-catching leisure home is accented with vertical and diagonal siding and soaked in sunlight from dynamic clerestory windows.
- A generous amount of living space and three bedrooms are neatly packaged to maximize the home's square footage.
- The exciting Great Room covers half of the main floor and is open to the upper floor. A dramatic woodstove serves as the focal point of the room, which adjoins the dining area, the kitchen and a large deck. This entire area is enhanced by a 16½-ft. vaulted ceiling and clerestory windows.
- The main-floor master bedroom offers two closets and a nearby bath. A nice laundry room is just off the entrance.
- The upper floor includes two more bedrooms that are separated by a full bath. The balcony hall provides a dramatic view to the rooms below.

Plan P-520-D

Bedrooms: 3	Baths: 2
Living Area:	
Upper floor	448 sq. ft.
Main floor	823 sq. ft.
Total Living Area:	**1,271 sq. ft.**
Garage/Shop	702 sq. ft.
Exterior Wall Framing:	2x6

Foundation Options:

Daylight basement
(All plans can be built with your choice of foundation and framing. A generic conversion diagram is available. See order form.)

BLUEPRINT PRICE CODE: A

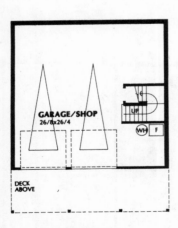

DAYLIGHT BASEMENT

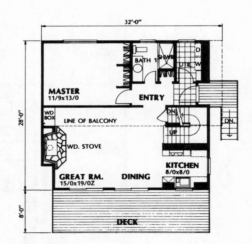

MAIN FLOOR

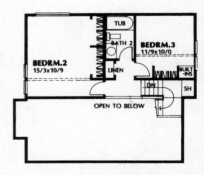

UPPER FLOOR

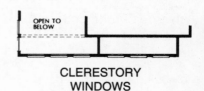

CLERESTORY WINDOWS

Plan P-520-D

PRICES AND DETAILS ON PAGES 12-15

Fancy Country Styling

- With a covered front porch and gables above, this affordable two-story home fancies country styling.
- Off the lovely covered porch is a soaring entry, open to the upper level and featuring an angled stairway focal point.
- A large living area with a fireplace and a patio view adjoins the dining room, which opens to the outdoors.
- Convenient main-floor laundry facilities and a half-bath are located near the garage entrance.
- The upper level includes a master bedroom with a private bath, a walk-in closet and an 11-ft.-high vaulted ceiling. Another full bath with a dual-sink vanity serves the two secondary bedrooms.

Plan AG-1201

Bedrooms: 3	Baths: 2½
Living Area:	
Upper floor	668 sq. ft.
Main floor	620 sq. ft.
Total Living Area:	**1,288 sq. ft.**
Standard basement	620 sq. ft.
Garage	420 sq. ft.
Exterior Wall Framing:	2x4

Foundation Options:

Standard basement

(All plans can be built with your choice of foundation and framing. A generic conversion diagram is available. See order form.)

BLUEPRINT PRICE CODE:	**A**

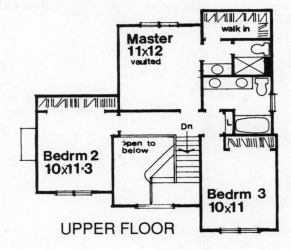

UPPER FLOOR

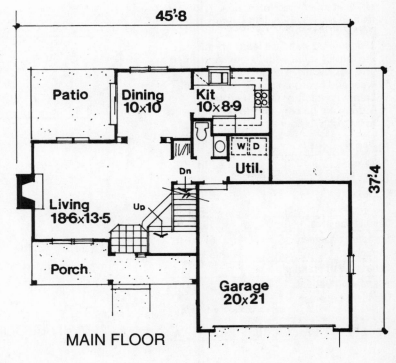

MAIN FLOOR

Striking Stone Chimney

- With tall windows and a rustic stone chimney, the striking facade of this home demands attention.
- The sheltered entry leads into a raised foyer, which steps down to the sunny living room and its dramatic 16-ft. vaulted ceiling.
- A handsome fireplace warms the living room and the adjoining dining room, which offers access to an inviting deck.
- A cozy breakfast nook is included in the efficient, open-design kitchen. A special feature is the convenient pass-through to the dining room.
- A skylighted staircase leads upstairs to the master suite, with its private bath and large walk-in closet.
- A second bedroom shares another full bath with a loft or third bedroom.
- A dramatic balcony overlooks the living room below.

Plan B-224-8512

Bedrooms: 2+	Baths: 2½
Living Area:	
Upper floor	691 sq. ft.
Main floor	668 sq. ft.
Total Living Area:	**1,359 sq. ft.**
Standard basement	668 sq. ft.
Garage	458 sq. ft.
Exterior Wall Framing:	2x4

Foundation Options:

Standard basement

(All plans can be built with your choice of foundation and framing. A generic conversion diagram is available. See order form.)

BLUEPRINT PRICE CODE: A

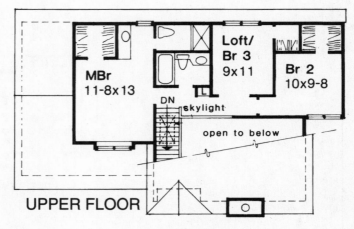

UPPER FLOOR

MBr 11-8x13
Loft/ Br 3 9x11
Br 2 10x9-8
DN
skylight
open to below

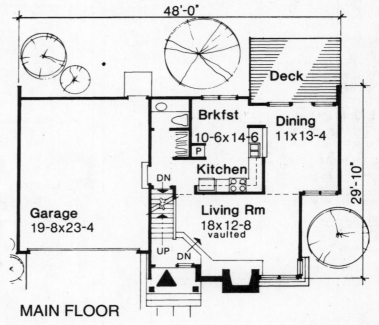

MAIN FLOOR

48'-0"
29'-10"
Deck
Brkfst 10-6x14-6
Dining 11x13-4
Kitchen
Garage 19-8x23-4
Living Rm 18x12-8 vaulted
DN
UP
DN

Comfort on a Narrow Lot

- With its narrow width of only 24 ft., this home is well suited for zero-lot developments or duplex construction.
- The covered entry opens to an efficient foyer that leads traffic into the living room or the family room. Also note the convenient powder room off the entry.
- The unique living room contains an impressive fireplace and a 16-ft. vaulted ceiling. The adjoining family room provides additional entertainment space, with sliding glass doors that lead to a corner patio.
- The kitchen is efficient and open, with a laundry area conveniently close.
- Upstairs, the master bedroom includes a generous-sized walk-in closet and a private bath. A railing offers views of the living room below.
- Two secondary bedrooms share a second full bath.

Plan H-1427-1A

Bedrooms: 3	Baths: 2½
Living Area:	
Upper floor	755 sq. ft.
Main floor	655 sq. ft.
Total Living Area:	**1,410 sq. ft.**
Garage	404 sq. ft.
Exterior Wall Framing:	2x4

Foundation Options:

Crawlspace
(All plans can be built with your choice of foundation and framing. A generic conversion diagram is available. See order form.)

BLUEPRINT PRICE CODE:	**A**

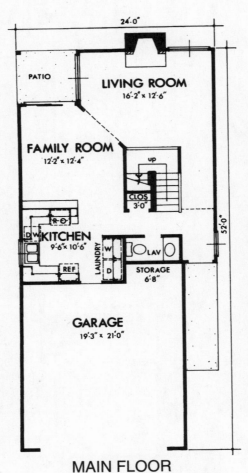

MAIN FLOOR

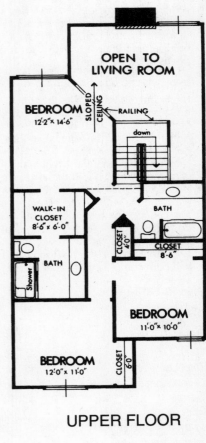

UPPER FLOOR

Authentic Charm

- A covered front porch, decorative trim and shuttered windows lend authentic charm to this space-efficient home.
- The main living areas are oriented around stairways that access the basement and the upper floor. The spacious family room shows off a dramatic central fireplace and an array of glass, including a French door that opens to the backyard.
- The nice-sized kitchen is conveniently nestled between the sunny breakfast room and the formal dining room. The breakfast room features a 10-ft. vaulted ceiling and two walls of glass.
- A laundry closet is neatly positioned to one side of the breakfast room, where it is handy from both the kitchen and the garage entrance. A half-bath is nearby.
- Upstairs, the deluxe master bedroom offers a huge walk-in closet and a 9-ft. tray ceiling. The luxurious master bath hosts a 13-ft. vaulted ceiling, an oval spa tub and a separate shower.
- Two more good-sized bedrooms and a hall bath complete the upper floor.

Plan FB-5013-LYNW

Bedrooms: 3	Baths: 2½
Living Area:	
Upper floor	681 sq. ft.
Main floor	771 sq. ft.
Total Living Area:	**1,452 sq. ft.**
Daylight basement	771 sq. ft.
Garage	420 sq. ft.
Storage	20 sq. ft.
Exterior Wall Framing:	2x4

Foundation Options:

Daylight basement

(All plans can be built with your choice of foundation and framing. A generic conversion diagram is available. See order form.)

BLUEPRINT PRICE CODE: **A**

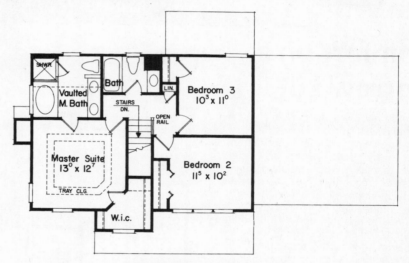

UPPER FLOOR

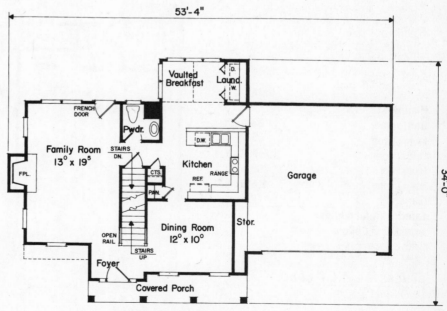

MAIN FLOOR

Plan FB-5013-LYNW

PRICES AND DETAILS
ON PAGES 12-15

Pleasantly Peaceful

- The covered front porch of this lovely two-story traditional home offers a pleasant and peaceful welcome.
- Off the open foyer is an oversized family room, drenched with sunlight through a French door and surrounding windows. A handsome fireplace adds further warmth.
- The neatly arranged kitchen is conveniently nestled between the formal dining room and the sunny breakfast room. A pantry and a powder room are also within easy reach.
- A stairway off the family room accesses the upper floor, which houses three bedrooms. The isolated master bedroom features a 10-ft. tray ceiling, a huge walk-in closet and a private bath offering a vaulted ceiling, an oval garden tub and a separate shower.
- The two secondary bedrooms share another full bath.

Plan FB-1466

Bedrooms: 3	Baths: 2½
Living Area:	
Upper floor	703 sq. ft.
Main floor	763 sq. ft.
Total Living Area:	**1,466 sq. ft.**
Daylight basement	763 sq. ft.
Garage	426 sq. ft.
Storage	72 sq. ft.
Exterior Wall Framing:	2x4

Foundation Options:
Daylight basement
Crawlspace
(All plans can be built with your choice of foundation and framing. A generic conversion diagram is available. See order form.)

BLUEPRINT PRICE CODE:	A

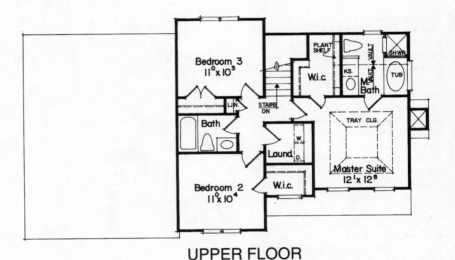

UPPER FLOOR

Bedroom 3 11⁰ x 10³
Bedroom 2 11⁰ x 10⁴
W.i.c.
Bath
LIN.
STAIRS DN
Laund.
W. D.
PLANT SHELF
W.i.c.
M. Bath
KS
VAULT
SHWR
TUB
TRAY CLG.
Master Suite 12¹ x 12⁶

MAIN FLOOR

52'-4"
30'-0"

Storage
Garage
Powder
PAN.
Breakfast
STAIRS UP
FRENCH DOOR
Kitchen
RANGE
D.W.
REF.
COATS
STAIRS DN
Family Room 15⁰ x 19⁶
FPL.
Dining Room 11⁰ x 11⁶
Covered Porch

Carefree and Comfortable

- A dramatic 17-ft.-high entry with an illuminating clerestory window and an overhead balcony highlights this home's open and carefree interior.
- The airy, spacious feeling continues into the adjoining den with corner windows and a 17-ft. vaulted ceiling.

- The central living room is warmed by a handsome fireplace. The adjacent dining room offers sliding glass doors to a backyard patio.
- The cozy country kitchen boasts a pantry and a high 10-ft. ceiling.
- Upstairs, the master suite features a spacious walk-in closet, which frees up additional wall space and allows for a flexible furniture arrangement.
- Measuring just 30 ft. wide, this home is well suited for a narrow lot.

Plan R-2097	
Bedrooms: 3	**Baths:** 2½
Living Area:	
Upper floor	698 sq. ft.
Main floor	768 sq. ft.
Total Living Area:	**1,466 sq. ft.**
Garage	410 sq. ft.
Exterior Wall Framing:	2x6
Foundation Options:	

Crawlspace
(All plans can be built with your choice of foundation and framing. A generic conversion diagram is available. See order form.)

BLUEPRINT PRICE CODE:	**A**

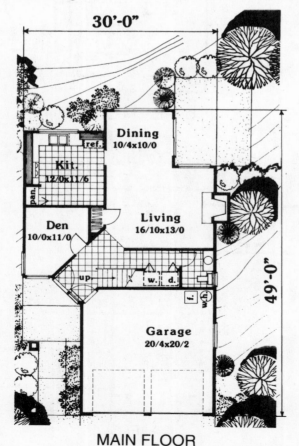

MAIN FLOOR

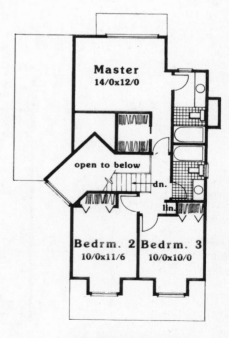

UPPER FLOOR

Plan R-2097

PRICES AND DETAILS ON PAGES 12-15

REAR VIEW

All Decked Out!

- All decked out to take full advantage of the outdoors, this stylish home is perfect for a scenic site.
- Entered through a front vestibule, the bright and open floor plan provides an ideal setting for casual lifestyles.
- The sunken living room features a handsome fireplace, a skylighted 19-ft. ceiling and three sets of sliding glass doors that open to an expansive backyard deck.
- The efficient kitchen has a sunny sink and a pass-through with bi-fold doors to the adjoining dining room.
- The main-floor bedroom has a walk-in closet and sliding glass doors to the deck. A half-bath is nearby.
- Upstairs, a railed balcony overlooks the living room. The smaller of the two bedrooms has private access to the bathroom and another deck.

Plan CAR-81007

Bedrooms: 2+	Baths: 1½
Living Area:	
Upper floor	560 sq. ft.
Main floor	911 sq. ft.
Total Living Area:	**1,471 sq. ft.**
Standard basement	911 sq. ft.
Exterior Wall Framing:	2x6

Foundation Options:

Standard basement

(All plans can be built with your choice of foundation and framing. A generic conversion diagram is available. See order form.)

BLUEPRINT PRICE CODE: A

UPPER FLOOR

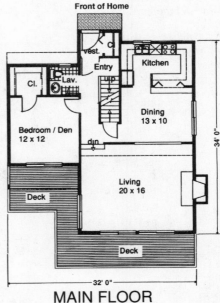

MAIN FLOOR

FRONT VIEW

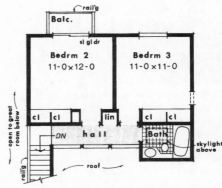

REAR VIEW

More for Less

- Big in function but small in square footage, this passive-solar plan can be built as a single-family home or as part of a multiple-unit complex.
- The floor plan flows visually from its open foyer to its high-ceilinged Great Room, where a high-efficiency fireplace is flanked by glass. Sliding glass doors open to a brilliant south-facing sun room that overlooks a backyard terrace.
- The eat-in kitchen has a pass-through to a bright dining area that opens to a nice side terrace.
- The master bedroom boasts a pair of tall windows, a deluxe private bath and two roomy closets.
- A handy laundry closet and a half-bath are located at the center of the floor plan, near the garage.
- Upstairs, a skylighted bath serves two more bedrooms, one with a private, rear-facing balcony.

Plan K-507-S

Bedrooms: 3	Baths: 2½
Living Area:	
Upper floor	397 sq. ft.
Main floor	915 sq. ft.
Sun room	162 sq. ft.
Total Living Area:	**1,474 sq. ft.**
Standard basement	915 sq. ft.
Garage	400 sq. ft.
Exterior Wall Framing:	2x4 or 2x6

Foundation Options:

Standard basement

Slab

(All plans can be built with your choice of foundation and framing. A generic conversion diagram is available. See order form.)

BLUEPRINT PRICE CODE:	**A**

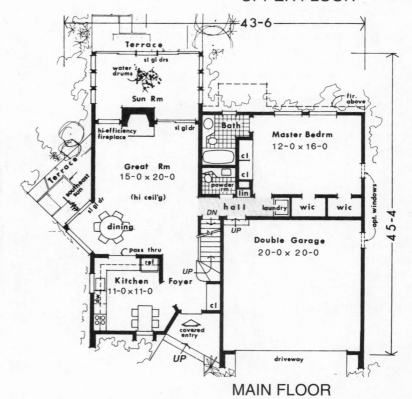

UPPER FLOOR

MAIN FLOOR

TO ORDER THIS BLUEPRINT, CALL TOLL-FREE 1-800-547-5570

Plan K-507-S

PRICES AND DETAILS ON PAGES 12-15

Attractive, Sunny Design

- This versatile plan features a striking exterior and numerous energy-saving extras, like passive-solar heating, glazed roof panels with adjustable shades, and operable skylights.
- An air-lock vestibule, which minimizes heat loss, leads into the spacious living room. This room has a stone fireplace, an operable clerestory window, a

14½-ft. sloped ceiling and sliding doors to the glass-roofed solar room.
- The adjacent dining room also has a sloped ceiling and offers sliding glass doors to a backyard terrace.
- The U-shaped kitchen features a laundry closet, a handy pantry and an eating bar for informal dining.
- The skylighted upper-floor hallway leads to the master suite, which offers a private balcony and a personal bath with a whirlpool tub.
- Two additional bedrooms, one with a bay window, share a second full bath.

Plan K-521-C	
Bedrooms: 3	**Baths:** 2½
Living Area:	
Upper floor	686 sq. ft.
Main floor	690 sq. ft.
Solar room	106 sq. ft.
Total Living Area:	**1,482 sq. ft.**
Standard basement	690 sq. ft.
Garage	437 sq. ft.
Exterior Wall Framing:	2x4 or 2x6

Foundation Options:

Standard basement
Slab
(All plans can be built with your choice of foundation and framing. A generic conversion diagram is available. See order form.)

BLUEPRINT PRICE CODE:	**A**

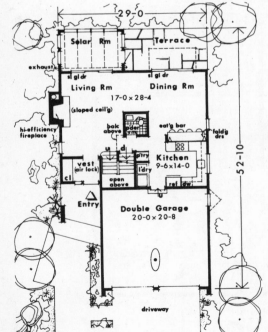

MAIN FLOOR

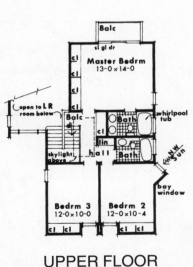

UPPER FLOOR

VIEW INTO LIVING ROOM AND SOLAR ROOM

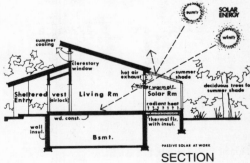

SECTION

Compact, Cozy, Inviting

- Full-width porches at the front and the rear of this home add plenty of space for outdoor living and entertaining.
- The huge, centrally located living room is the core of this three-bedroom home. The room features a corner fireplace, a 16-ft. sloped, open-beam ceiling and access to the back porch.
- The dining room combines with the kitchen to create an open, more spacious atmosphere. A long, central work island and a compact laundry closet are other space-saving features.
- The main-floor master suite offers a private bath with dual vanities and a large walk-in closet. Two additional bedrooms, a full bath and an intimate sitting area that overlooks the living room and entry are upstairs.
- A separate two-car garage is included with the blueprints.

Plan E-1421

Bedrooms: 3	Baths: 2
Living Area:	
Upper floor	561 sq. ft.
Main floor	924 sq. ft.
Total Living Area:	**1,485 sq. ft.**
Standard basement	924 sq. ft.
Exterior Wall Framing:	2x6

Foundation Options:
Standard basement
Crawlspace
Slab
(All plans can be built with your choice of foundation and framing. A generic conversion diagram is available. See order form.)

BLUEPRINT PRICE CODE: A

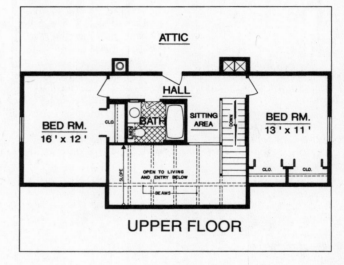

UPPER FLOOR

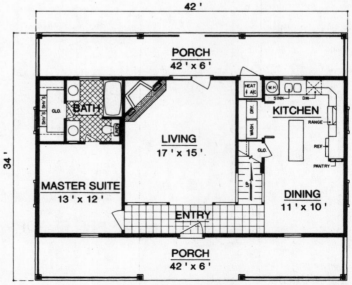

MAIN FLOOR

TO ORDER THIS BLUEPRINT, CALL TOLL-FREE 1-800-547-5570   Plan E-1421   **PRICES AND DETAILS ON PAGES 12-15**

Unique and Dramatic

- This home's unique interior and dramatic exterior make it perfect for a sloping, scenic lot.
- The expansive and impressive Great Room, warmed by a woodstove, flows into the island kitchen, which is completely open in design.
- The passive-solar sun room collects and stores heat from the sun, while offering a good view of the surroundings. Its ceiling rises to a height of 16 feet.
- Upstairs, a glamorous, skylighted master suite features an 11-ft. vaulted ceiling, a private bath and a huge walk-in closet.
- A skylighted hall bath serves the bright second bedroom. Both bedrooms open to the vaulted sun room below.
- The daylight basement adds a sunny sitting room, a third bedroom and a large recreation room.

Plans P-536-2A & -2D

Bedrooms: 2+	Baths: 2½-3½
Living Area:	
Upper floor	642 sq. ft.
Main floor	863 sq. ft.
Daylight basement	863 sq. ft.
Total Living Area:	**1,505/2,368 sq. ft.**
Garage	445 sq. ft.
Exterior Wall Framing:	2x6
Foundation Options:	**Plan #**
Daylight basement	P-536-2D
Crawlspace	P-536-2A

(All plans can be built with your choice of foundation and framing. A generic conversion diagram is available. See order form.)

BLUEPRINT PRICE CODE:	**B/C**

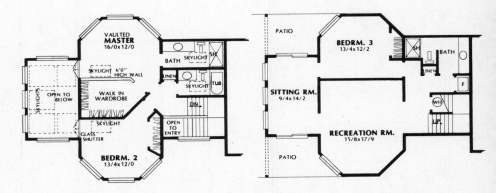

UPPER FLOOR   **DAYLIGHT BASEMENT**

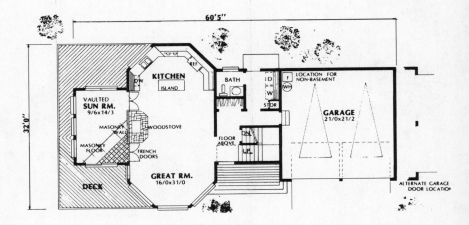

MAIN FLOOR

Private, Vaulted Master Retreat

- The highlight of this stylish contemporary design is undoubtedly the private master retreat on the upper floor. The spacious master bedroom boasts a 14-ft.-high vaulted ceiling, a private bath and two balconies that overlook the main entry and the breakfast nook.
- The living room is another haven for relaxation. The 16½-ft. vaulted ceiling and the inviting fireplace create a

dramatic but cozy atmosphere. The living room flows into the formal dining room for an open, airy effect.
- The compact kitchen and the bright breakfast nook merge at the back of the main floor. Both rooms overlook the patio and the backyard beyond. A handy pantry closet is nearby, next to the coat closet in the entry hall.
- A nice-sized laundry room, a hall bath and two bedrooms complete the home.
- If the basement foundation is preferred, the stairway would replace the storage closet between the laundry room and the nook, as pictured below.

Plans P-6490-2A & -2D	
Bedrooms: 3	**Baths:** 2
Living Area:	
Upper floor	345 sq. ft.
Main floor	1,173 sq. ft.
Total Living Area:	**1,518 sq. ft.**
Daylight basement	1,173 sq. ft.
Garage	458 sq. ft.
Exterior Wall Framing:	2x4
Foundation Options:	**Plan #**
Daylight basement	P-6490-2D
Crawlspace	P-6490-2A

(All plans can be built with your choice of foundation and framing. A generic conversion diagram is available. See order form.)

BLUEPRINT PRICE CODE:	**B**

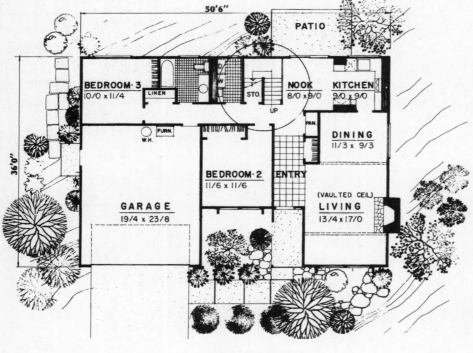

MAIN FLOOR

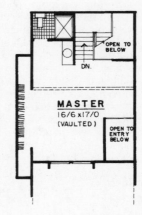

UPPER FLOOR

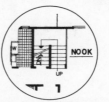

BASEMENT STAIRWAY LOCATION

TO ORDER THIS BLUEPRINT, CALL TOLL-FREE 1-800-547-5570 Plans P-6490-2A & -2D **PRICES AND DETAILS ON PAGES 12-15**

First floor:	871 sq. ft.
Second floor:	679 sq. ft.
Total living area:	1,550 sq. ft.
(Not counting garage)	

Country Cottage

An informal floor plan complements the Cape Code exterior of this 1,550 sq. ft. home. The master suite features a compartmentalized bath with dressing area and access to the centrally located utility room. The remainder of the 871 sq. ft. of heated living area on the main floor is divided between a Great Room with raised-hearth fireplace and an open L-shaped kitchen with eating area.

An additional 679 sq. ft. of heated living area on the upper floor consists of a second full bath with linen closet and two bedrooms with double closets. A screened-in side porch doubles as a breezeway connecting house and garage. Front porch, multi-paned windows, shutters and horizontal wood siding combine for a cozy, inviting look.

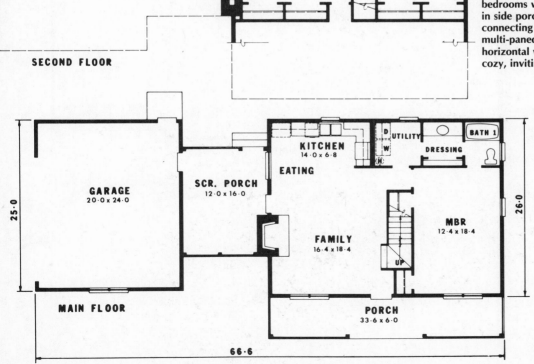

SECOND FLOOR

LINEN
BATH 2
BR 2 16·4 x 17·6
DN
BR 3 12·4 x 17·6

MAIN FLOOR

GARAGE 20·0 x 24·0
SCR. PORCH 12·0 x 16·0
KITCHEN 14·0 x 6·8
EATING
D W H
UTILITY
DRESSING
BATH 1
FAMILY 16·4 x 18·4
MBR 12·4 x 18·4
UP
PORCH 33·6 x 6·0
25·0
26·0
66·6

Blueprint Price Code B

Plan C-8018

PRICES AND DETAILS ON PAGES 12-15

Country Kitchen Centerpiece

- This charming home features a rustic combination of stone and wood, which is offset by two half-round windows in the attention-getting gables.
- The centerpiece of the floor plan is the spacious country kitchen, featuring ample work surfaces, a nice-sized eating area with built-in bookshelves and access to a large backyard deck.
- The formal dining area is highlighted by a dramatic three-sided fireplace that is shared with the adjoining living room. The living room is enhanced by a dramatic 17-ft. vaulted ceiling.
- A powder room and a deluxe laundry room are easily reached from all of the main-floor rooms as well as the garage.
- Upstairs, the master bedroom boasts a 12-ft. vaulted ceiling that reveals a plant shelf above the entrance to the private bath and the walk-in closet.
- The two smaller bedrooms are separated by a full bath. The front-facing bedroom features an arched window set into a high-ceilinged area.

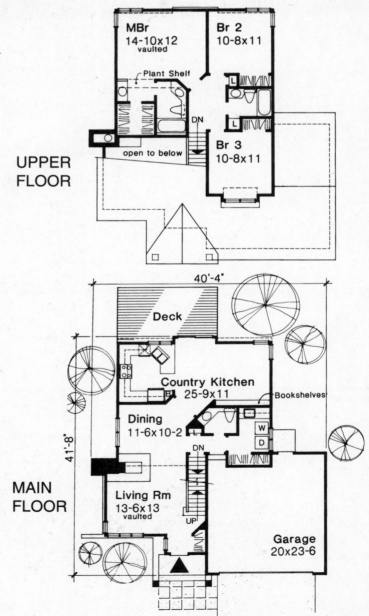

UPPER FLOOR

MAIN FLOOR

Plan B-87107

Bedrooms: 3	Baths: 2½
Living Area:	
Upper floor	722 sq. ft.
Main floor	834 sq. ft.
Total Living Area:	**1,556 sq. ft.**
Standard basement	834 sq. ft.
Garage	470 sq. ft.
Exterior Wall Framing:	2x4

Foundation Options:

Standard basement

(All plans can be built with your choice of foundation and framing. A generic conversion diagram is available. See order form.)

BLUEPRINT PRICE CODE:	**B**

TO ORDER THIS BLUEPRINT, CALL TOLL-FREE 1-800-547-5570

Plan B-87107

PRICES AND DETAILS ON PAGES 12-15

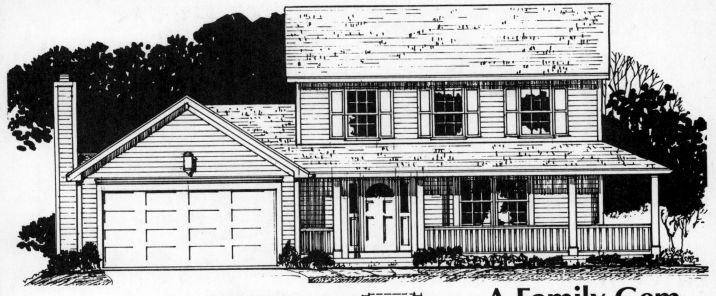

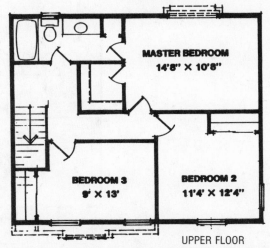

MASTER BEDROOM
14'8" × 10'8"

BEDROOM 3
9' × 13'

BEDROOM 2
11'4" × 12'4"

UPPER FLOOR

A Family Gem

- Flexibility and affordability make this traditional design a great family choice.
- The large family room, dinette and kitchen combine along the rear of the home to form a unique dining or entertaining solution.
- The dining and living rooms join to the right of the foyer for a more formal alternative.
- The upper-level master bedroom offers a walk-in closet and private access to the bathroom, also shared with the two secondary bedrooms.

Plan GL-1597

Bedrooms: 3	Baths: 1 ½
Space:	
Upper floor	672 sq. ft.
Main floor	925 sq. ft.
Total Living Area	**1,597 sq. ft.**
Basement	925 sq. ft.
Garage	413 sq. ft.
Exterior Wall Framing	2x6
Foundation options:	
Standard Basement	
(Foundation & framing conversion diagram available—see order form.)	
Blueprint Price Code	B

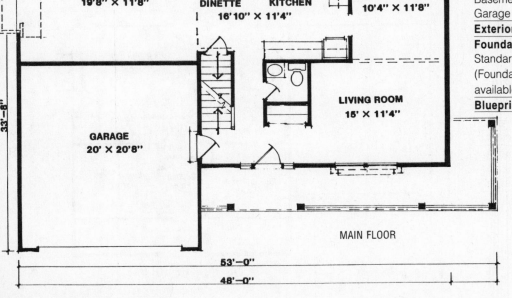

FAMILY ROOM
19'8" × 11'8"

DINETTE   KITCHEN
16'10" × 11'4"

DINING ROOM
10'4" × 11'8"

LIVING ROOM
15' × 11'4"

GARAGE
20' × 20'8"

33'—8"

53'—0"

48'—0"

MAIN FLOOR

Luxury and Livability

- Big on style, this modest-sized home features a quaint Colonial exterior and an open interior.
- The covered front porch leads to a two-story foyer that opens to the formal living and dining rooms. A coat closet, an attractive display niche and a powder room are centrally located, as is the stairway to the upper floor.
- The kitchen, breakfast nook and family room are designed so that each room has its own definition yet also functions as part of a whole. The angled sink separates the kitchen from the breakfast nook, which is outlined by a bay window. The large family room includes a fireplace.
- The upper floor has an exceptional master suite, featuring an 8-ft., 6-in. tray ceiling in the sleeping area and an 11-ft. vaulted ceiling in the spa bath.
- Two more bedrooms and a balcony hall add to this home's luxury and livability.

Plan FB-1600

Bedrooms: 3	Baths: 2½
Living Area:	
Upper floor	772 sq. ft.
Main floor	828 sq. ft.
Total Living Area:	**1,600 sq. ft.**
Daylight basement	828 sq. ft.
Garage	473 sq. ft.
Exterior Wall Framing:	2x4

Foundation Options:

Daylight basement
Crawlspace
Slab

(All plans can be built with your choice of foundation and framing. A generic conversion diagram is available. See order form.)

BLUEPRINT PRICE CODE:	B

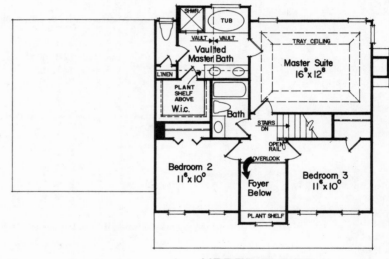

UPPER FLOOR

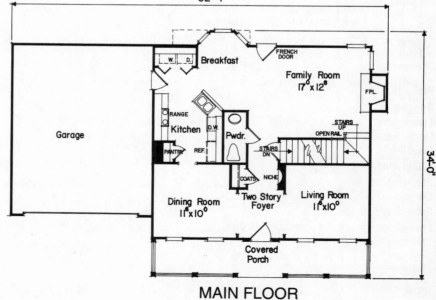

MAIN FLOOR

TO ORDER THIS BLUEPRINT, CALL TOLL-FREE 1-800-547-5570

Plan FB-1600

PRICES AND DETAILS ON PAGES 12-15

Either Choice Is a Winner

- Win either way in this charming home, offering a choice of two or three bedrooms on the upper floor.
- The L-shaped front porch greets visitors and leads to both the main entry and the service entry.
- The main entry is flanked by the living room and the stairway to the upper floor. The living room features a warm fireplace and a large bay window.
- The rear-oriented kitchen offers a sunny sink area, a pantry closet and a bayed breakfast nook that connects the kitchen to the family room.
- Sliding glass doors open from the family room to a backyard deck. An oversized laundry room and a half-bath are convenient to the family living area as well as to the service entry.
- Both upper floor plans include a master suite with a private bath, a second full bath and a railing overlooking the front entry below.

Plans H-1439-2D, -2E, -3D, -3E

Bedrooms: 2+	Baths: 2½
Living Area:	
Upper floor	678 sq. ft.
Main floor	940 sq. ft.
Total Living Area:	**1,618 sq. ft.**
Standard basement	940 sq. ft.
Garage	544 sq. ft.
Exterior Wall Framing:	2x6

Foundation Options:	2-bedroom	3-bedroom
Standard basement	H-1439-2E	H-1439-3E
Crawlspace	H-1439-2D	H-1439-3D

(All plans can be built with your choice of foundation and framing. A generic conversion diagram is available. See order form.)

BLUEPRINT PRICE CODE: B

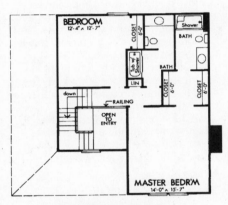

UPPER FLOOR
(with two bedrooms)

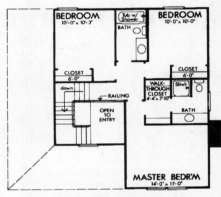

UPPER FLOOR
(with three bedrooms)

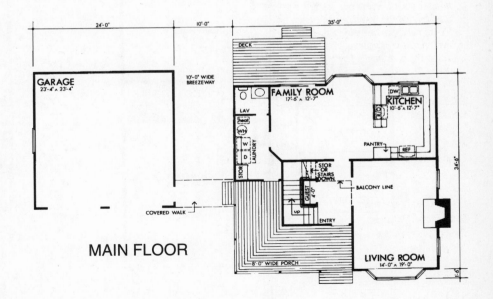

MAIN FLOOR

Modern Country Charm

- Charming window treatments, a covered porch and detailed railings give this modern home a country feeling.
- The inviting entry flows into the elegant living room, which features a 10-ft. ceiling and a striking corner fireplace.
- The sunny kitchen is built into a beautiful bay and easily serves the formal dining room.

- The spacious sunken family room enjoys bright windows and offers sliding glass doors to a backyard patio.
- A half-bath, a laundry/utility room and a storage area are conveniently located off the garage entrance.
- Upstairs, the master bedroom includes a private garden bath, a walk-in closet and a separate dressing area with a dual-sink vanity.
- Two additional upper-floor bedrooms share a full bath and a linen closet. Both rooms are enhanced by sizable closets and cozy window seats.

Plan NW-836	
Bedrooms: 3	**Baths:** 2½
Living Area:	
Upper floor	684 sq. ft.
Main floor	934 sq. ft.
Total Living Area:	**1,618 sq. ft.**
Garage	419 sq. ft.
Exterior Wall Framing:	2x6

Foundation Options:

Crawlspace
(All plans can be built with your choice of foundation and framing. A generic conversion diagram is available. See order form.)

BLUEPRINT PRICE CODE: B

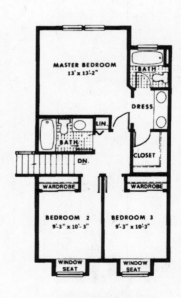

MAIN FLOOR

UPPER FLOOR

TO ORDER THIS BLUEPRINT, CALL TOLL-FREE 1-800-547-5570

Plan NW-836

PRICES AND DETAILS ON PAGES 12-15

Expandable Living Spaces!

- Expandable spaces make this attractive two-story a great choice for growing families. The formal dining room or the living room could be easily converted into a library or den, while the optional bonus room above the garage provides a host of possible uses.

- The nice-sized family room offers an inviting fireplace and access to the backyard. The sunny breakfast room is just a few steps away and adjoins an efficient L-shaped kitchen.

- The upper floor features a balcony hall that overlooks the two-story-high foyer. The master suite is dignified by a 9-ft. tray ceiling in the sleeping area and an 11½-ft. vaulted ceiling in the private bath with a corner spa tub. The large walk-in closet includes a linen closet and sports an overhead plant shelf.

- The bonus room, two more bedrooms, a convenient laundry closet and a full bath complete the upper floor.

Plan FB-1631

Bedrooms: 3+	Baths: 2½
Living Area:	
Upper floor	787 sq. ft.
Main floor	844 sq. ft.
Bonus room	340 sq. ft.
Total Living Area:	**1,971 sq. ft.**
Daylight basement	844 sq. ft.
Garage	460 sq. ft.
Exterior Wall Framing:	2x4

Foundation Options:
Daylight basement
(All plans can be built with your choice of foundation and framing. A generic conversion diagram is available. See order form.)

BLUEPRINT PRICE CODE:	**B**

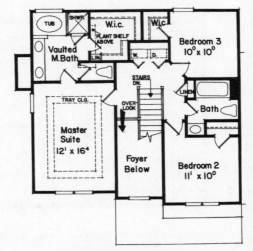

UPPER FLOOR

ALTERNATE UPPER FLOOR

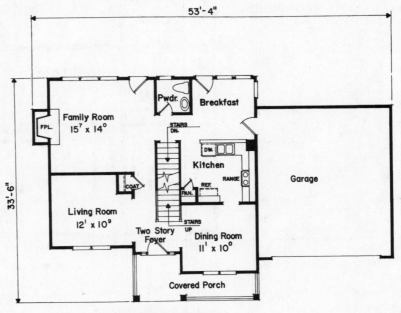

MAIN FLOOR

Front Porch Dresses Up Facade

- A covered front porch adorns the facade of this updated two-story.
- Opposite the foyer are the formal living and dining rooms.
- Oriented to the rear of the home are the family room with fireplace and skylights, the dinette and a U-shaped kitchen.
- A powder room and convenient main-floor washer/dryer intercept incoming traffic from the garage.
- Three generous-sized bedrooms occupy the upper floor.

UPPER FLOOR

W.I.C • BATH • BR. #3 11-0 X 11-6 • CLOS • BR. #1 12-0 X 16-6 • DN • CLOS • BR. 2 13-0 X 10-6

MAIN FLOOR

54-0 • 40-4

FAM. RM. 12-0 X 16-0 • DINETTE 9-0 X 10-0 • KIT. 11-0 X 12-0 • DW • PDR • LAUN • BC • MUD • CLOS • CLOS • REF • LIVING RM. 12-0 X 14-0 • FOYER • DINING RM. 12-0 X 12-0 • GARAGE 22-0 X 22-0 • PORCH

Plan A-2237-DS

Bedrooms: 3	**Baths:** 1 ½

Space:

Upper floor	672 sq. ft.
Main floor	972 sq. ft.
Total Living Area	**1,644 sq. ft.**
Basement	972 sq. ft.
Garage	484 sq. ft.
Exterior Wall Framing	**2x6**

Foundation options:

Standard Basement

(Foundation & framing conversion diagram available—see order form.)

Blueprint Price Code	**B**

Single-Level Conveniences

- This modern-day Cape Cod offers the convenience of single-level living with the secondary bedrooms and a separate bath located on the upper level.
- The open floor plan allows a view of the family room fireplace from the kitchen and the bayed dining area.
- Pocket doors between the family room and the living room provide the modest-sized home flexibility. They may be closed for a cozy, private sitting area or opened for frequent traffic flow or entertaining.
- The generous-sized master bedroom is convenient to the kitchen and the laundry room. It features a large walk-in closet and a private bath.
- Joining the two bedrooms on the upper level is a skylighted library loft that overlooks the foyer below. A larger alternate bath may replace the smaller bath, adding 48 sq. feet.

Plan GL-1654-P

Bedrooms: 3	Baths: 2½
Living Area:	
Upper floor	462 sq. ft.
Main floor	1,192 sq. ft.
Total Living Area:	**1,654 sq. ft.**
Standard basement	1,192 sq. ft.
Garage	448 sq. ft.
Exterior Wall Framing:	2x4

Foundation Options:

Standard basement
(All plans can be built with your choice of foundation and framing. A generic conversion diagram is available. See order form.)

BLUEPRINT PRICE CODE: B

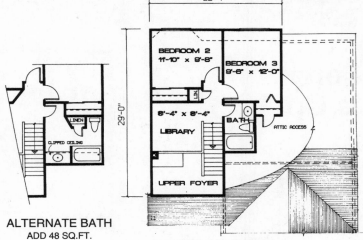

ALTERNATE BATH
ADD 48 SQ.FT.

UPPER FLOOR

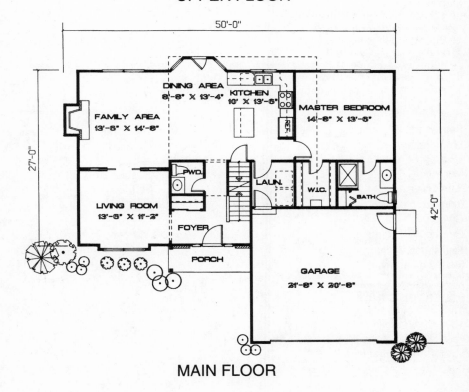

MAIN FLOOR

Smart Farmhouse

- This smart-looking farmhouse boasts a front wrapping porch, overlooked from the dining and living rooms.
- The two-story-high foyer reveals a decorative plant shelf and entry columns that accent and define these formal spaces.
- The informal living areas merge at the rear of the home and look out over the adjoining patio. The large family room shows off a big fireplace and shares a handy pass-through serving counter with the kitchen and the breakfast nook.
- A handy main-floor laundry closet is located off the kitchen.
- A nice-sized master bedroom with a TV niche and a private bath shares the upper floor with two additional bedrooms and a second bath.

Plan AG-9102

Bedrooms: 3	Baths: 2½
Living Area:	
Upper floor	769 sq. ft.
Main floor	910 sq. ft.
Total Living Area:	**1,679 sq. ft.**
Standard basement	910 sq. ft.
Garage	480 sq. ft.
Exterior Wall Framing:	2x6

Foundation Options:

Standard basement
(All plans can be built with your choice of foundation and framing. A generic conversion diagram is available. See order form.)

BLUEPRINT PRICE CODE: **B**

UPPER FLOOR

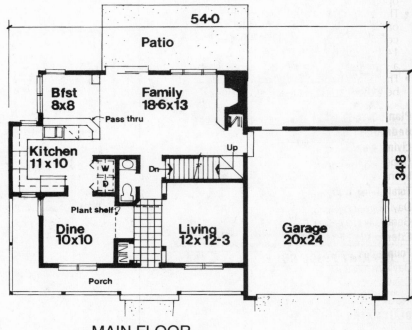

MAIN FLOOR

 TO ORDER THIS BLUEPRINT, CALL TOLL-FREE 1-800-547-5570   Plan AG-9102   **PRICES AND DETAILS ON PAGES 12-15**

Plenty of Presence

- A stucco facade complemented by fieldstone, a dramatic roofline and handsome keystones accenting the window treatments gives this home plenty of presence.
- Inside, the two-story foyer boasts an open stairway with a balcony overlook. Straight ahead, the huge family room is expanded by a 16½-ft. vaulted ceiling, plus a tall window and a French door that frame the fireplace.
- The adjoining dining room flows into the kitchen and breakfast room, which feature an angled serving bar, a bright window wall and a French door that opens to a covered patio.
- The main-floor master suite is the pride of the floor plan, offering a 10-ft. tray ceiling. The deluxe master bath has a 14-ft. vaulted ceiling, a garden tub and a spacious walk-in closet.
- The upper floor offers two more bedrooms, a full bath and attic space.

Plan FB-1681

Bedrooms: 3	Baths: 2½
Living Area:	
Upper floor	449 sq. ft.
Main floor	1,232 sq. ft.
Total Living Area:	**1,681 sq. ft.**
Daylight basement	1,232 sq. ft.
Garage and storage	435 sq. ft.
Exterior Wall Framing:	2x4

Foundation Options:
Daylight basement
Crawlspace
(All plans can be built with your choice of foundation and framing. A generic conversion diagram is available. See order form.)

BLUEPRINT PRICE CODE:	B

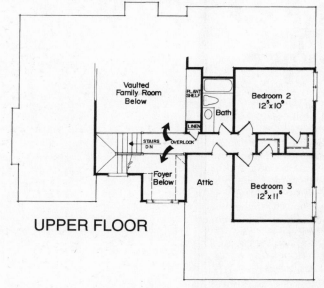

UPPER FLOOR

MAIN FLOOR

Charming Choices

- This charming farmhouse design has a simple and economical structure that can be finished with siding or brick. With four bedrooms, the home is ideal for a large or growing family.
- Comfortably sized formal spaces, open informal areas and lots of windows make the floor plan light and bright. An optional bay window in the living room and fireplace in the family room can add further ambience.
- The breakfast nook's delightful boxed bay provides a sunny site for casual dining. The adjoining kitchen has a windowed sink and easy access to the garage and to the formal dining room.
- All four bedrooms are housed on the upper floor. The master bedroom has a private bath, while the secondary bedrooms share another.

Plan CH-110-B

Bedrooms: 4	Baths: 2½
Living Area:	
Upper floor	860 sq. ft.
Main floor	846 sq. ft.
Total Living Area:	**1,706 sq. ft.**
Basement	834 sq. ft.
Garage	380 sq. ft.
Exterior Wall Framing:	2x4

Foundation Options:

Daylight basement

Standard basement

Crawlspace

(All plans can be built with your choice of foundation and framing. A generic conversion diagram is available. See order form.)

BLUEPRINT PRICE CODE: B

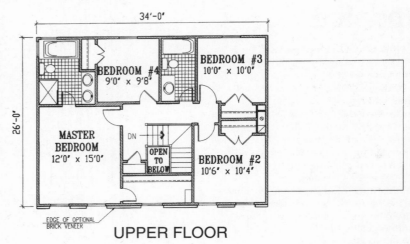

UPPER FLOOR

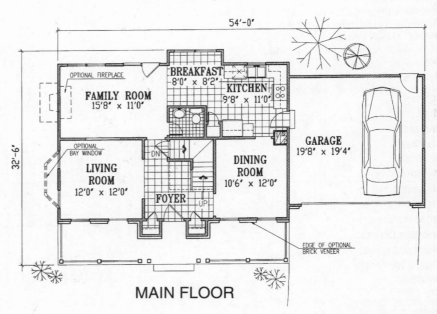

MAIN FLOOR

TO ORDER THIS BLUEPRINT,
CALL TOLL-FREE 1-800-547-5570

Plan CH-110-B

PRICES AND DETAILS
ON PAGES 12-15

Updated Classic

- An interesting blend of exterior styles and a modern floor plan combine to make this home an American favorite.
- A covered front porch ushers guests into the inviting foyer, which leads to a half-bath and and an open-railed staircase.
- To the left of the foyer, the sunken living room features a soaring 17½-ft.-high ceiling and French doors to a patio.
- The formal dining room flows into the kitchen, which incorporates a casual eating area with sliders to the backyard.
- A laundry closet and a pantry are conveniently located at the intersection of the kitchen, the garage entrance and the family room.
- The spacious family room hosts a handsome fireplace, a built-in audio/visual cabinet and a bay window.
- Upstairs, the roomy master suite offers two closets and a private bath. Another full bath serves the remaining bedrooms.

Plan PH-1707

Bedrooms: 3	Baths: 2½
Living Area:	
Upper floor	692 sq. ft.
Main floor	1,015 sq. ft.
Total Living Area:	**1,707 sq. ft.**
Basement	994 sq. ft.
Garage	419 sq. ft.
Exterior Wall Framing:	2x6

Foundation Options:

Daylight basement
Standard basement
Crawlspace
Slab

(All plans can be built with your choice of foundation and framing. A generic conversion diagram is available. See order form.)

BLUEPRINT PRICE CODE: B

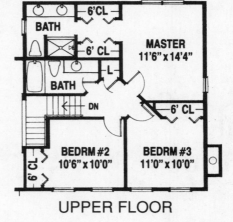

UPPER FLOOR

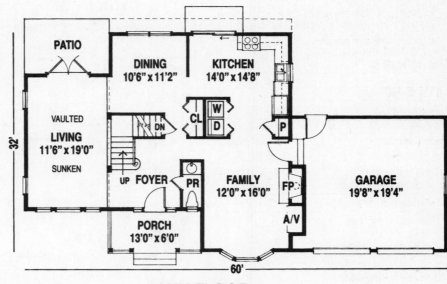

MAIN FLOOR

Compact Two-Story with Spanish Touch

- Living room has vaulted ceiling and wet bar.
- Large study available for home office.
- Master bedroom opens to private balcony, and includes large walk-in closet and private bath.
- Upstairs hallway looks down into living room.

Plan Q-1707-1A

Bedrooms: 3	Baths: 2½
Space:	
Upper floor:	831 sq. ft.
Main floor:	876 sq. ft.
Total living area:	1,707 sq. ft.
Garage:	466 sq. ft.
Exterior Wall Framing:	2x4

Foundation options:
Slab only.
(Foundation & framing conversion diagram available — see order form.)

Blueprint Price Code: B

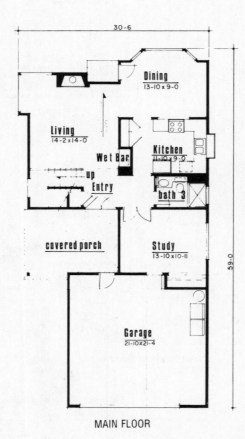

MAIN FLOOR

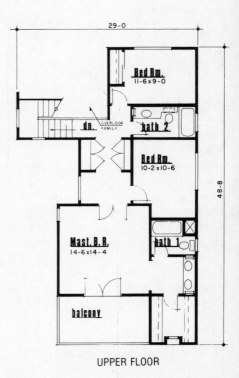

UPPER FLOOR

Photo courtesy of Breland & Farmer Designers, Inc.

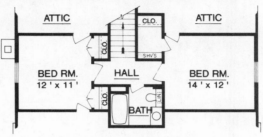

UPPER FLOOR

Cost-Saving Style

- This country-style home has a classic exterior look and an open, space-saving floor plan.
- The U-shaped kitchen flows nicely into the dining room, where an angled hall stretches to the screened-in porch and the living room.
- The deluxe master bedroom is large for a home this size, and includes a separate sink and vanity area that adjoins the main bath.
- A good-sized utility room is convenient to the garage, which features a large storage area.
- The second floor offers two bedrooms, each with extra closet space, and another full bath. Both bedrooms also have access to attic storage space.

Plan E-1626

Bedrooms: 3	Baths: 2
Living Area:	
Upper floor	464 sq. ft.
Main floor	1,136 sq. ft.
Total Living Area:	**1,600 sq. ft.**
Garage	462 sq. ft.
Exterior Wall Framing:	2x6

Foundation Options:
Crawlspace
Slab
(Typical foundation & framing conversion diagram available—see order form.)

BLUEPRINT PRICE CODE: B

**NOTE: The above photographed home may have been modified by the homeowner. Please refer to floor plan and/or drawn elevation shown for actual blueprint details.

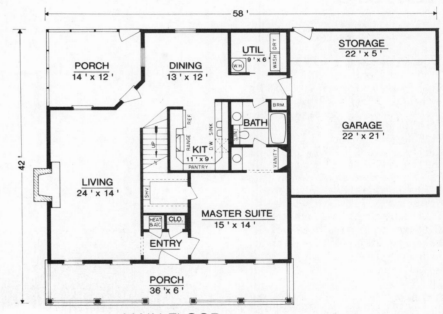

MAIN FLOOR

Indoor/Outdoor Pleasure

- For a scenic lake or mountain lot, this spectacular design takes full advantage of the views.
- A three-sided wraparound deck makes indoor/outdoor living a pleasure.
- The sunken living room—with a 19-ft. cathedral ceiling, a skylight, a beautiful fireplace and glass galore—is the heart of the floor plan.
- Both the formal dining room and the kitchen overlook the living room and the surrounding deck beyond.
- The main-floor master bedroom has a 12-ft. cathedral ceiling and private access to the deck and hall bath.
- Upstairs, two more bedrooms share a skylighted bath and flank a dramatic balcony sitting area that views to the living room below.

Plan AX-98607

Bedrooms: 3	**Baths:** 2
Living Area:	
Upper floor	531 sq. ft.
Main floor	1,098 sq. ft.
Total Living Area:	**1,629 sq. ft.**
Standard basement	894 sq. ft.
Garage	327 sq. ft.
Exterior Wall Framing:	2x4

Foundation Options:

Standard basement
Slab
(All plans can be built with your choice of foundation and framing. A generic conversion diagram is available. See order form.)

BLUEPRINT PRICE CODE:	B

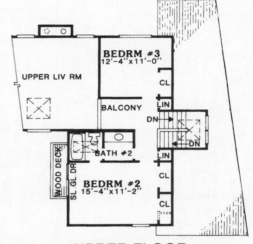

UPPER FLOOR

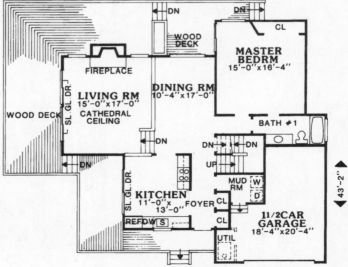

MAIN FLOOR

Instant Impact

- Bold rooflines, interesting angles and unusual window treatments give this stylish home lots of impact.
- Inside, high ceilings and an open floor plan maximize the home's square footage. At only 28 ft. wide, the home also is ideal for a narrow lot.
- A covered deck leads to the main entry, which features a sidelighted door, angled glass walls and a view of the striking open staircase.
- The Great Room is stunning, with its vaulted ceiling, energy-efficient woodstove and access to a large deck.
- A flat ceiling distinguishes the dining area, which shares an angled snack bar/cooktop with the step-saving kitchen. A laundry/mudroom is nearby.
- Upstairs, the master suite offers a sloped ceiling and a clerestory window. A walk-through closet leads to the private bath, which is enhanced by a skylighted, sloped ceiling.
- Linen and storage closets line the hallway leading to the smaller bedrooms, one of which has a sloped ceiling and double closets.

Plans H-1427-3A & -3B

Bedrooms: 3	Baths: 2½
Living Area:	
Upper floor	880 sq. ft.
Main floor	810 sq. ft.
Total Living Area:	**1,690 sq. ft.**
Daylight basement	810 sq. ft.
Garage	409 sq. ft.
Exterior Wall Framing:	2x4
Foundation Options:	**Plan #**
Daylight basement	H-1427-3B
Crawlspace	H-1427-3A
(All plans can be built with your choice of foundation and framing. A generic conversion diagram is available. See order form.)	
BLUEPRINT PRICE CODE:	B

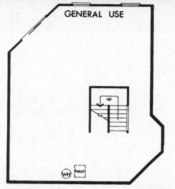

DAYLIGHT BASEMENT

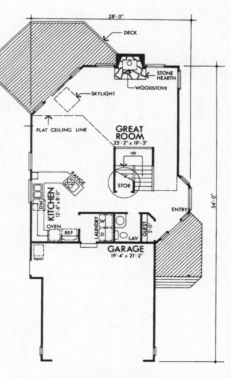

MAIN FLOOR

UPPER FLOOR

STAIRWAY AREA IN CRAWLSPACE VERSION

Open Planning in a Classic Style

Exterior walls are 2x6 construction.
Specify crawlspace or slab foundation.

UPPER LEVEL

PLAN E-1708
WITHOUT BASEMENT

Living area:	1,717 sq. ft.
Porches:	131 sq. ft.
Garage & Storage:	556 sq. ft.
Total:	2,404 sq. ft.

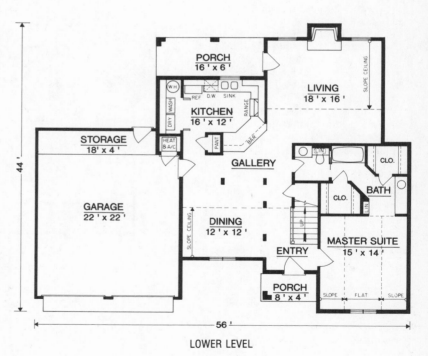

LOWER LEVEL

Blueprint Price Code B
Plan E-1708

**PRICES AND DETAILS
ON PAGES 12-15**

**NOTE:
The above photographed home may have been modified by the homeowner. Please refer to floor plan and/or drawn elevation shown for actual blueprint details.

Traditional Value Appeal

- The high-impact entry of this 1,724 sq. ft. plan, with a vaulted living area and a balcony lit by palladian windows above, demands attention.
- The family/breakfast area has a fireplace and a wet bar.
- The kitchen, between the family/breakfast area and the dining room,

has a view of the backyard deck and easily serves either room.
- Upstairs, the master bedroom has a large walk-in closet, double-bowled vanity and compartmentalized bath.
- The basic shape of the plan is simple to build, which lowers the finished cost.

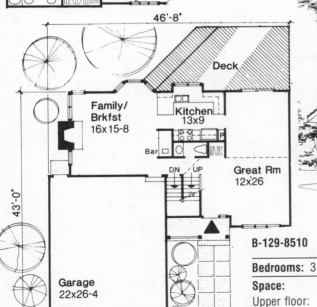

MBr 13-6x15-4 | Br 2 10x8-9 | Br 3 10x12

DN | open to below

UPPER FLOOR

46'-8"

43'-0"

Deck

Family/Brkfst 16x15-8

Kitchen 13x9

Bar

DN | UP

Great Rm 12x26

Garage 22x26-4

MAIN FLOOR

B-129-8510

Bedrooms: 3	Baths: 2½
Space:	
Upper floor:	802 sq. ft.
Main floor:	922 sq. ft.
Total living area:	1,724 sq. ft.
Basement:	922 sq. ft.
Garage:	579 sq. ft.

Exterior Wall Framing: 2x4

Foundation options:
Standard Basement.
(Foundation & framing conversion diagram available — see order form.)

Blueprint Price Code: B

Affordable Victorian

- This compact Victorian design incorporates four bedrooms and three full baths into an attractive, affordable home that's only 30 ft. wide.
- The upstairs master suite includes a deluxe bath and a bayed sitting area.
- The roomy parlor includes a fireplace, and the formal dining room has a beautiful bay window.
- The downstairs bedroom, with its adjoining full bath, makes a great office or guest bedroom.
- Upstairs, the master suite features an adjoining sitting area with a cathedral ceiling. The luxurious master bath includes a dual-sink vanity and whirlpool tub with a shower. Two more large bedrooms and another full bath complete the upper floor.
- An attached two-car garage off the kitchen is available upon request.

Plan C-8347-A

Bedrooms: 3+	Baths: 3
Living Area:	
Upper floor	783 sq. ft.
Main floor	954 sq. ft.
Total Living Area:	**1,737 sq. ft.**
Exterior Wall Framing:	2x4

Foundation Options:

Crawlspace

Slab

(All plans can be built with your choice of foundation and framing. A generic conversion diagram is available. See order form.)

BLUEPRINT PRICE CODE:	**B**

UPPER FLOOR

MAIN FLOOR

Plan C-8347-A

PRICES AND DETAILS ON PAGES 12-15

Rustic Home Offers Comfort, Economy

- Rustic and compact, this home offers economy of construction and good looks.
- The homey front porch, multi-paned windows, shutters and horizontal siding combine to create a rustic exterior.
- An L-shaped kitchen is open to the dining room and also to the living room to create a Great Room feel to the floor plan.
- The living room includes a raised-hearth fireplace.
- The main-floor master suite features a large walk-in closet and a double vanity in the master bath.
- An open two-story-high foyer leads to the second floor, which includes two bedrooms with walk-in closets and a full bath with two linen closets.

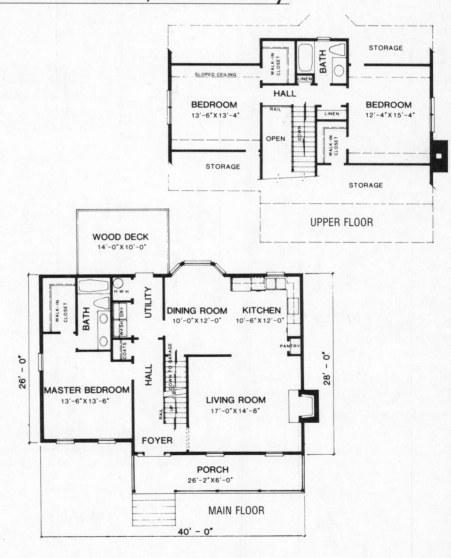

Plan C-8339

Plan C-8339	
Bedrooms: 3	**Baths:** 2
Space:	
Upper floor	660 sq. ft.
Main floor	1,100 sq. ft.
Total Living Area	**1,760 sq. ft.**
Basement	approx. 1,100 sq. ft.
Garage	Included in basement
Exterior Wall Framing	2x4
Foundation options:	
Daylight Basement (Foundation & framing conversion diagram available—see order form.)	
Blueprint Price Code	B

Clean, Stylish Lines

- The sweeping roofline and arched windows give this home plenty of "presence", even though it is fairly modest in size.
- Besides being stylish, the plan is also sturdy and energy-efficient, with 2x6 walls, R-19 perimeter insulation and R-38 in the ceilings.
- The sheltered entry leads to an effective foyer which in turn leads visitors to the dining area or living room. These two spaces flow together to create a huge space for entertaining.
- The roomy kitchen includes abundant cabinet and counter space. A utility room is in the garage entry area.
- A large downstairs bedroom adjoins a full bath and includes a large walk-in closet. This would make a great guest or in-law suite.
- Upstairs, another large bedroom features a private bath and walk-in closet.
- A versatile loft overlooks the living room below, and provides room for children to play or for adults to keep a library, sewing room, studio or study.

UPPER FLOOR

BASEMENT

Plans H-1448-1 & -1A

Bedrooms: 2-3		**Baths:** 2
Space:		
Upper floor		487 sq. ft.
Main floor		1,278 sq. ft.
Total Living Area		**1,765 sq. ft.**
Basement		1,278 sq. ft.
Garage		409 sq. ft.
Exterior Wall Framing		2x6
Foundation options:		Plan #
Standard Basement		H-1448-1
Crawlspace		H-1448-1A
(Foundation & framing conversion diagram available—see order form.)		
Blueprint Price Code		**B**

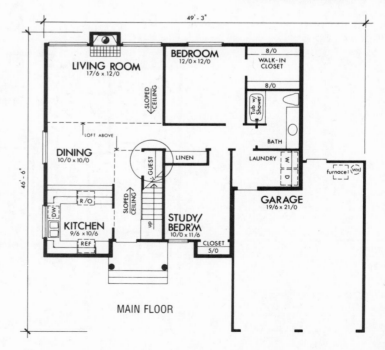

MAIN FLOOR

Compact and Luxurious

- The best from the past and the present is bundled up in this compact design, reminiscent of a New England saltbox.
- The cozy kitchen has a center island with a breakfast counter and a built-in range and oven. The corner sink saves on counter space.
- A decorative railing separates the formal dining room from the sunken living room.
- The living room features a vaulted ceiling, built-in shelves, a central fireplace and access to a large rear deck.
- The upper-floor master suite boasts a spa bath, a separate shower and a walk-in closet.

Plan H-1453-1A

Bedrooms: 3	Baths: 2

Living Area:	
Upper floor	386 sq. ft.
Main floor	1,385 sq. ft.
Total Living Area:	**1,771 sq. ft.**
Garage	409 sq. ft.
Exterior Wall Framing:	2x6

Foundation Options:

Crawlspace
(Typical foundation & framing conversion diagram available—see order form.)

BLUEPRINT PRICE CODE:	**B**

UPPER FLOOR

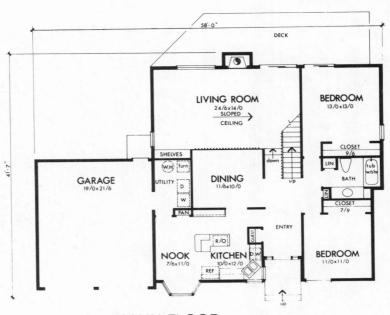

MAIN FLOOR

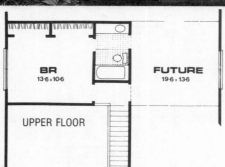

BR
13·6 x 10·6

FUTURE
19·6 x 13·6

UPPER FLOOR

Expandable Traditional

- This homey traditional will be at home in any neighborhood, rural or urban.
- A gracious porch leads into the large living room which features a cozy fireplace.
- A sunny breakfast nook provides space for family and guest dining.

- The galley-type kitchen opens onto a back porch.
- The master suite is generously sized and exhibits a raised ceiling; a private bath and large closet are also part of the master suite.
- A second bedroom, another bath and convenient utility areas complete the first floor.
- Upstairs, you'll find a third bath and third bedroom, plus a large space that could be finished in the future for any number of purposes.

PORCH

KIT
10 x 8

BR
11·6 x 10·3

MBR
16·6 x 13
RAISED CEILING

BKFST
13 x 11

UTIL

w
d

LIVING
15·6 x 15

GARAGE
19·3 x 19·3

50·4

PORCH
20 x 6

MAIN FLOOR

40

Plan J-8636

Bedrooms: 3	Baths: 3
Space:	
Upper floor:	270 sq. ft.
Main floor:	1,253 sq. ft.
Bonus area:	270 sq. ft.
Total living area:	**1,793 sq. ft.**
Basement:	1,287 sq. ft.
Garage:	390 sq. ft.
Porches:	155 sq. ft.
Exterior Wall Framing:	**2x4**

Foundation options:
Standard basement.
Crawlspace.
Slab.
(Foundation & framing conversion diagram available — see order form.)

Blueprint Price Code:	B

Country Styling for Up-to-Date Living

- Nearly surrounded by a covered wood porch, this traditional 1,860 square-foot farm-styled home is modernized for today's active, up-to-date family.
- Inside, the efficient floor plan promotes easy mobility with a minimum of cross-traffic.
- The spacious living and dining area is warmed by a fireplace with a stone hearth; the U-shaped country kitchen is centrally located between these areas and the nook and family room with wood stove on the other side.
- Sliding glass doors lead out to both the rear patio and the deck that adjoins the dining and living rooms.
- The large master bedroom with corner window, dressing area and private bath and two other bedrooms with a second shared bath are found on the upper level.

Plans P-7677-2A & -2D	
Bedrooms: 3	Baths: 2 ½
Space:	
Upper floor	825 sq. ft.
Main floor	1,035 sq. ft.
Total Living Area	**1,860 sq. ft.**
Basement	1,014 sq. ft.
Garage	466 sq. ft.
Exterior Wall Framing	2x6
Foundation options:	Plan #
Daylight Basement	P-7677-2D
Crawlspace	P-7677-2A
(Foundation & framing conversion diagram available—see order form.)	
Blueprint Price Code	B

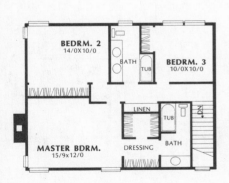

PLAN P-7677-2D
WITH DAYLIGHT BASEMENT

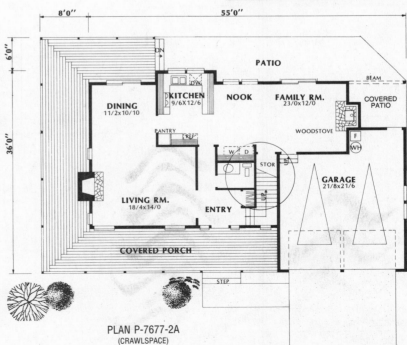

PLAN P-7677-2A
(CRAWLSPACE)

Cost-Efficient Cottage with Luxury Features

- This country cottage is easy to build, economical and attractive.
- The basic rectangular shape simplifies construction, and the steeply pitched roof accommodates upstairs bedrooms in space that would often otherwise be simply attic overhead.
- A huge living room with fireplace dominates the main floor.
- The dining room, kitchen, utility area and half bath make an efficient and livable area for casual family life.
- The main-floor master suite includes a spacious private bath with separate tub and shower, and a large closet.
- Upstairs, two bedrooms share another full bath.

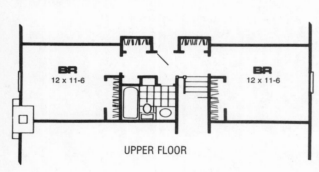

UPPER FLOOR

Plan J-86131

Bedrooms: 3	Baths: 2½

Space:

Upper floor:	500 sq. ft.
Main floor:	1,369 sq. ft.
Total living area:	**1,869 sq. ft.**
Basement:	1,369 sq. ft.
Carport:	416 sq. ft.
Storage:	124 sq. ft.
Porch:	258 sq. ft.

Exterior Wall Framing:	2x4

Foundation options:
Standard basement.
Crawlspace.
Slab.
(Foundation & framing conversion diagram available — see order form.)

Blueprint Price Code:	B

MAIN FLOOR

Photo by Strode Photography

Nicely Sized and Styled

- Eye-catching entry columns and varying rooflines accent this versatile two-story.
- The vaulted entry and living room are open to the upper level. Decorative columns, a lovely corner window and a front window seat are found in the living room, which is open to the hall and the stairway.
- The roomy kitchen and breakfast area at the rear of the home offers a pantry and a bayed window that overlooks a rear patio. The kitchen also has easy access to the formal dining room and a handy pass-through to the casual family room.
- Sliding glass doors in the family room open to the patio; an optional fireplace may also be added.
- A nice-sized laundry room is convenient to the garage entrance, and a powder room is centrally located.
- All four bedrooms are found on the upper level, where a balcony overlooks the living room below. The master suite includes built-in shelves and a luxurious private bath.

Plan AG-1801

Bedrooms: 4	Baths: 2½
Living Area:	
Upper floor	890 sq. ft.
Main floor	980 sq. ft.
Total Living Area:	**1,870 sq. ft.**
Standard basement	980 sq. ft.
Garage	480 sq. ft.
Exterior Wall Framing:	2x6

Foundation Options:

Standard basement

(All plans can be built with your choice of foundation and framing. A generic conversion diagram is available. See order form.)

BLUEPRINT PRICE CODE:	B

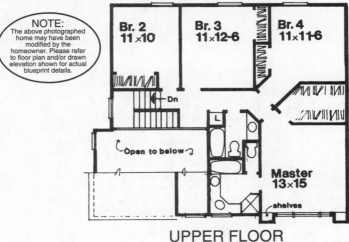

NOTE:
The above photographed home may have been modified by the homeowner. Please refer to floor plan and/or drawn elevation shown for actual blueprint details.

Br. 2 11×10
Br. 3 11×12-6
Br. 4 11×11-6
Dn
Open to below
Master 13×15
shelves

UPPER FLOOR

45'-8

Patio
Dine 11×11-5
Kit/Brk 11×13
Family 13-6×15-5
Pass thru
Optional Fireplace
Dn
Up
Living 14×14 vaulted
Window seat
util.
d w
Garage 20×24
42'-0

MAIN FLOOR

Photo by Mark Englund/HomeStyles

Exciting, Economical Design

Exciting but economical, this 1,895 sq. ft., three-bedroom house is arranged carefully for maximum use and enjoyment on two floors, and is only 42 feet wide to minimize lot size requirements. The multi-paned bay windows of the living room and an upstairs bedroom add contrast to the hip rooflines and lead you to the sheltered front entry porch.

The open, vaulted foyer is brightened by a skylight as it sorts traffic to the downstairs living areas or to the upper bedroom level. A few steps to the right puts you in the vaulted living room and the adjoining dining area. Sliding doors in the dining area and the nook, and a pass-through window in the U-shaped kitchen, make the patio a perfect place for outdoor activities and meals.

A large fireplace warms the spacious family room, which has a corner wet bar for efficient entertaining. A utility room leading to the garage and a powder room complete the 1,020 sq. ft. main floor.

An open stairway in the foyer leads to the 875 sq. ft. upper level. The master bedroom has a large walk-in wardrobe, twin vanity, shower and bathroom. The front bedroom has a seat in the bay window and the third bedroom has a built-in seat overlooking the vaulted living room. A full bath with twin vanity serves these bedrooms.

The daylight basement version of the plan adds 925 sq. ft. of living space.

PLAN P-7681-3D
BASEMENT LEVEL: 925 sq. ft.

Main floor:	1,020 sq. ft.
Upper floor:	875 sq. ft.
Total living area:	1,895 sq. ft.
(Not counting basement or garage)	

MAIN LEVEL

PLAN P-7681-3A
WITHOUT BASEMENT
(CRAWLSPACE FOUNDATION)

PLAN P-7681-3D
WITH DAYLIGHT BASEMENT

UPPER LEVEL

Blueprint Price Code B

Plans P-7681-3A & 3D

TO ORDER THIS BLUEPRINT, CALL TOLL-FREE 1-800-547-5570

PRICES AND DETAILS ON PAGES 12-15

Master Suite Is Hard to Resist

- A covered front entry, topped by a dormer with a half-round window, gives this three-bedroom home an updated traditional look.
- Inside, volume spaces are created by high ceilings and lots of windows.
- The formal dining room is distinguished by a tray ceiling and a large picture window overlooking the front porch.
- The vaulted Great Room features floor-to-ceiling windows facing the backyard and a fireplace that can be enjoyed from the adjoining kitchen and breakfast area. The kitchen, which has a flat ceiling, includes a corner sink, an island cooktop and a large pantry. The vaulted breakfast nook is filled with glass and features a built-in desk.
- The master suite is hard to resist, with its inviting window seat and vaulted ceiling. The luxurious bath is also vaulted and boasts a garden tub in addition to a shower. A walk-in closet is opposite a clever vanity with a sit-down makeup area between the two sinks.
- The two bedrooms upstairs share another full bath.

Plan B-89061

Bedrooms: 3	Baths: 2½
Living Area:	
Upper floor	436 sq. ft.
Main floor	1,490 sq. ft.
Total Living Area:	**1,926 sq. ft.**
Standard basement	1,490 sq. ft.
Garage	400 sq. ft.
Exterior Wall Framing:	2x4

Foundation Options:

Standard basement
(All plans can be built with your choice of foundation and framing. A generic conversion diagram is available. See order form.)

BLUEPRINT PRICE CODE: B

NOTE: The above photographed home may have been modified by the homeowner. Please refer to floor plan and/or drawn elevation shown for actual blueprint details.

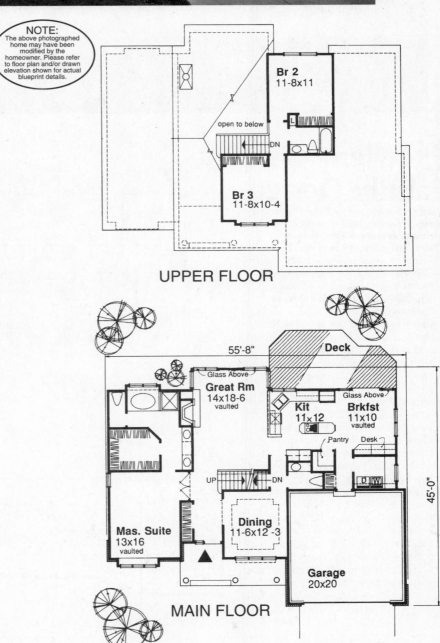

UPPER FLOOR

MAIN FLOOR

Excellent Family Design

- Long sloping rooflines and bold design features make this home attractive for any neighborhood.
- Inside, a vaulted entry takes visitors into an impressive vaulted Great Room with a wood stove and window-wall facing the house-spanning rear deck.
- Clerestory windows flanking the stove area and large windows front and rear flood the Great Room with natural light.
- The magnificent kitchen includes a stylish island and opens to the informal dining area which in turn flows into the Great Room.
- Two bedrooms on the main floor share a full bath, and bedroom #2 boasts easy access to the rear deck which spans the width of the house.
- The upstairs comprises an "adult retreat," with a roomy master suite, luxurious bath with double sinks, and a large walk-in closet.
- A daylight basement version adds another 1,410 sq. ft. of space for entertaining and recreation, plus a fourth bedroom and a large shop/storage area.

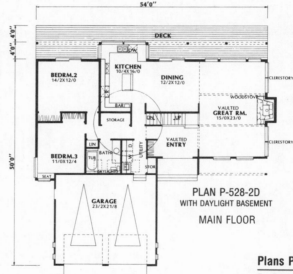

PLAN P-528-2D
WITH DAYLIGHT BASEMENT
MAIN FLOOR

UPPER FLOOR

PLAN P-528-2A
WITHOUT BASEMENT
(CRAWLSPACE FOUNDATION)

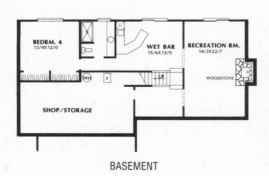

BASEMENT

Plans P-528-2A & -2D

Bedrooms: 3-4	Baths: 2-3

Space:

Upper floor:	498 sq. ft.
Main floor:	1,456 sq. ft.
Total living area:	**1,954 sq. ft.**
Basement:	1,410 sq. ft.
Garage:	502 sq. ft.

Exterior Wall Framing:	2x6

Foundation options:
Daylight basement (Plan P-528-2D).
Crawlspace (Plan P-528-2A).
(Foundation & framing conversion diagram available — see order form.)

Blueprint Price Code:

Without basement:	B
With basement:	E

Neatly Arranged

- Four bedrooms and good-sized living areas are found in this well-planned compact home.
- Off the foyer and open to the upper floor, the skylighted living room boasts a 16-ft.-high cathedral ceiling. The living room flows into the dining room, for plenty of entertainment space.
- The expansive family room features a large masonry fireplace and easy outdoor access through sliding glass doors. A wide bay window enhances the inviting country kitchen. The nearby laundry room provides lots of extra storage space.
- Also on the main floor, the secluded master suite offers a dressing area and a skylighted bath.
- Three additional bedrooms and a second full bath share the upper floor.

Plan AX-8817-A

Bedrooms: 4	Baths: 2½
Living Area:	
Upper floor	600 sq. ft.
Main floor	1,110 sq. ft.
Total Living Area:	**1,710 sq. ft.**
Standard basement	1,110 sq. ft.
One-car garage	240 sq. ft.
Optional two-car garage	413 sq. ft.
Exterior Wall Framing:	2x4

Foundation Options:

Standard basement
Slab

(All plans can be built with your choice of foundation and framing. A generic conversion diagram is available. See order form.)

BLUEPRINT PRICE CODE: B

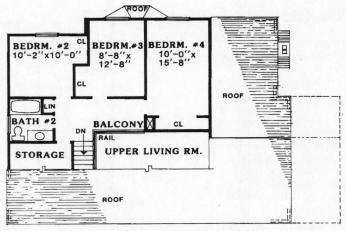

UPPER FLOOR

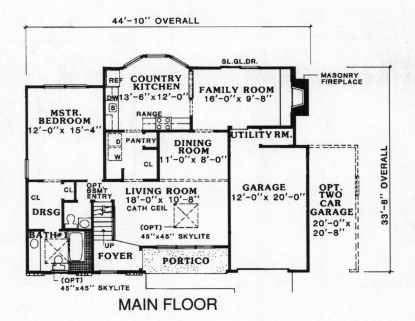

MAIN FLOOR

Family Farmhouse

- There's more to this house than its charming front porch, steeply pitched roof and dormer windows.
- A feeling of spaciousness is emphasized by the open floor plan, with the living room adjoining the kitchen and bayed breakfast area. A snack bar allows easy service to the living room.
- The back door leads from the carport to the utility room, which is convenient to the kitchen and half-bath.
- The secluded main-floor master bedroom offers a large walk-in closet and a private bathroom.
- Upstairs, two bedrooms share another full bath. One includes dormer windows and the other a window seat. A door at the top of the stairs provides access to attic space that could be turned into an extra bedroom.

Plan J-86133

Bedrooms: 3	Baths: 2½
Living Area:	
Upper floor	559 sq. ft.
Main floor	1,152 sq. ft.
Total Living Area:	**1,711 sq. ft.**
Standard basement	1,152 sq. ft.
Carport	387 sq. ft.
Storage	85 sq. ft.
Exterior Wall Framing:	2x4

Foundation Options:

Standard basement
Crawlspace
Slab
(All plans can be built with your choice of foundation and framing. A generic conversion diagram is available. See order form.)

BLUEPRINT PRICE CODE: B

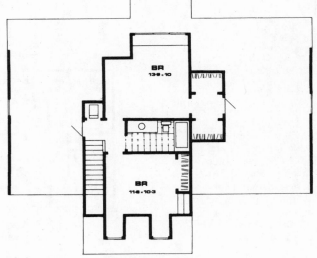

UPPER FLOOR

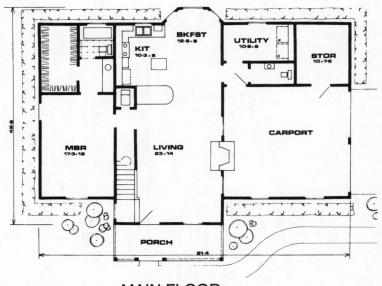

MAIN FLOOR

Plan J-86133

PRICES AND DETAILS ON PAGES 12-15

Panoramic Prow View

- This glass-filled prow gable design is almost as spectacular as the panoramic view from inside.
- French doors open from the front deck to the dining room. A stunning window wall illuminates the adjoining living room, which flaunts a 20-ft.-high cathedral ceiling.

- The open, corner kitchen is perfectly angled to service the dining room and the family room, while offering views of the front and rear decks.
- A handy utility/laundry room opens to the rear deck. Two bedrooms share a full bath, to complete the main floor.
- A dramatic, open-railed stairway leads up to the secluded master bedroom, which boasts a dressing room and a private bath with a dual-sink vanity and a separate tub and shower.

Plan NW-196	
Bedrooms: 3	**Baths: 2**
Living Area:	
Upper floor	394 sq. ft.
Main floor	1,317 sq. ft.
Total Living Area:	**1,711 sq. ft.**
Exterior Wall Framing:	2x6
Foundation Options:	

Crawlspace
(All plans can be built with your choice of foundation and framing. A generic conversion diagram is available. See order form.)

BLUEPRINT PRICE CODE:	**B**

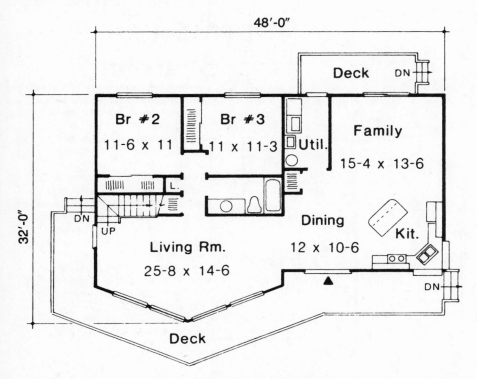

MAIN FLOOR

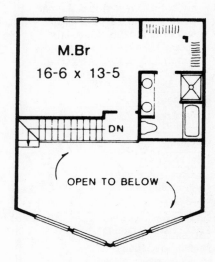

UPPER FLOOR

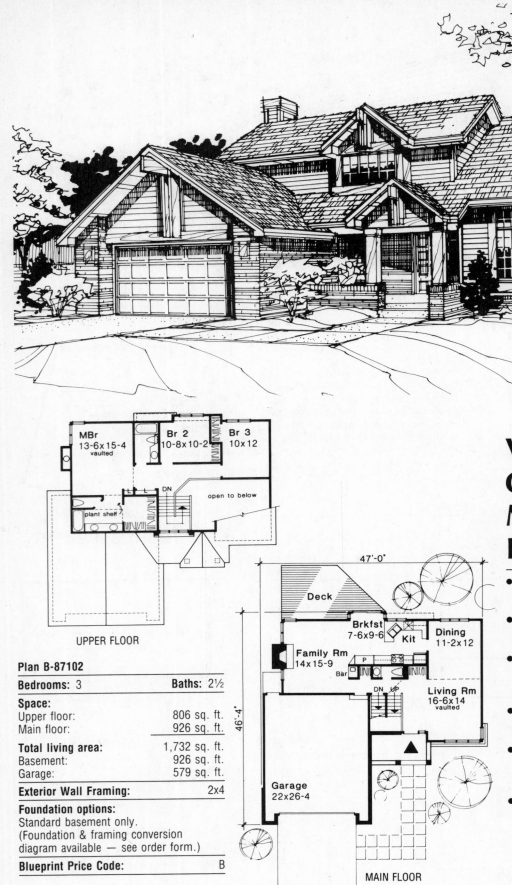

UPPER FLOOR

MBr
13-6x15-4
vaulted

Br 2
10-8x10-2

Br 3
10x12

DN

open to below

plant shelf

Plan B-87102

Bedrooms: 3	Baths: 2½

Space:

Upper floor:	806 sq. ft.
Main floor:	926 sq. ft.

Total living area:	**1,732 sq. ft.**
Basement:	926 sq. ft.
Garage:	579 sq. ft.

Exterior Wall Framing:	2x4

Foundation options:
Standard basement only.
(Foundation & framing conversion
diagram available — see order form.)

Blueprint Price Code:	B

47'-0"

Deck

Brkfst
7-6x9-6

Kit

Dining
11-2x12

Family Rm
14x15-9

Bar

P

46'-4"

DN UP

Living Rm
16-6x14
vaulted

Garage
22x26-4

MAIN FLOOR

Vaulted Ceiling in Master Bedroom

- Here's a plan that provides good family living space on a small foundation.
- A protected entry leads into a vaulted living room with an adjoining dining area.
- The kitchen/breakfast area and family room combination is large and includes a pantry, bar, fireplace and easy access to the outdoors.
- The master bedroom upstairs includes a private bath and large walk-in closet.
- Two secondary bedrooms share another full bath and open onto a balcony hallway overlooking the living room below.
- The deep garage allows storage space in front of the vehicles.

TO ORDER THIS BLUEPRINT,
CALL TOLL-FREE 1-800-547-5570

Plan B-87102

PRICES AND DETAILS
ON PAGES 12-15

Dynamic Design

- This dynamic five-sided design is perfect for scenic sites. The front (or street) side of the home is shielded by a two-car garage, while the back of the home hosts a glass-filled living area surrounded by a spectacular deck.
- The unique shape of the home allows for an unusually open and spacious interior design.
- The living/dining room is further expanded by a 20-ft.-high vaulted ceiling. The centrally located fireplace provides a focal point while distributing heat efficiently.
- The space-saving galley-style kitchen is connected to the living/dining area by a snack bar.
- A large main-floor bedroom has two closets and easy access to a full bath.
- The upper floor is highlighted by a breathtaking balcony overlook. Also, two bedrooms share a nice-sized bath.
- The optional daylight basement includes a huge recreation room.

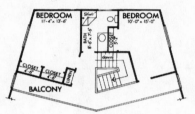

UPPER FLOOR

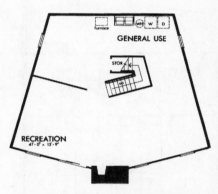

DAYLIGHT BASEMENT

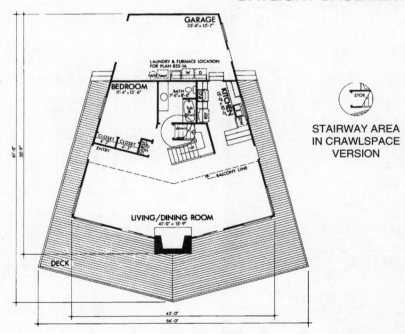

STAIRWAY AREA
IN CRAWLSPACE
VERSION

MAIN FLOOR

Plans H-855-1 & -1A

Bedrooms: 3	Baths: 2
Living Area:	
Upper floor	625 sq. ft.
Main floor	1,108 sq. ft.
Daylight basement	1,108 sq. ft.
Total Living Area:	**1,733/2,841 sq. ft.**
Garage	346 sq. ft.
Exterior Wall Framing:	**2x6**
Foundation Options:	**Plan #**
Daylight basement	H-855-1
Crawlspace	H-855-1A

(All plans can be built with your choice of foundation and framing. A generic conversion diagram is available. See order form.)

BLUEPRINT PRICE CODE:	**B/D**

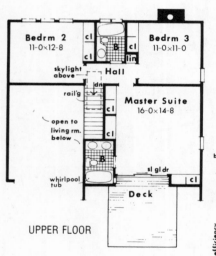

Bedrm 2 11-0×12-8
Bedrm 3 11-0×11-0
cl cl cl lin
B
skylight above
Hall
rail'g
dn
Master Suite 16-0×14-8
cl
open to living rm. below
cl
B
whirlpool tub
sl gl dr
cl
Deck

UPPER FLOOR

Plan K-649-P

Bedrooms: 3-4	Baths: 3

Space:

Upper floor:	724 sq. ft.
Main floor:	1,013 sq. ft.

Total living area:	**1,737 sq. ft.**
Basement:	1,013 sq. ft.
Garage:	400 sq. ft.

Exterior Wall Framing: 2x4
(with 2x6 option included)

Foundation options:
Standard basement.
Slab.
(Foundation & framing conversion diagram available — see order form.)

Blueprint Price Code: B

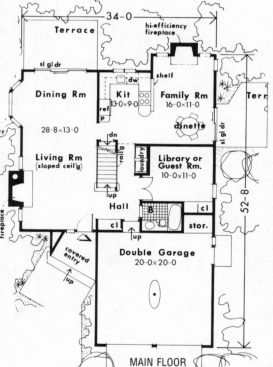

34-0

Terrace
hi-efficiency fireplace
shelf
sl gl dr
dw
Dining Rm 28-8×13-0
Kit 13-0×9-0
ref p
Family Rm 16-0×11-0
dinette
bay
Living Rm (sloped ceil'g)
dn
rail'g
laundry
Library or Guest Rm. 10-0×11-0
sl gl dr
up
hi-efficiency fireplace
Hall
B
cl
stor.
cl
up
covered entry
up
52-8
Terr.
Double Garage 20-0×20-0

MAIN FLOOR

Contemporary Features Unusual Roof Deck

- Upstairs master suite includes a private deck, sunken into a cavity in the garage roof.
- Balance of the plan is also designed to be open and airy.
- The living room has a sloped ceiling and an impressive fireplace, and flows into the dining area.
- The kitchen, family room and dinette area function well together for family dining and other activities.
- A library or guest bedroom with a full bath also offers the option of becoming a home office.

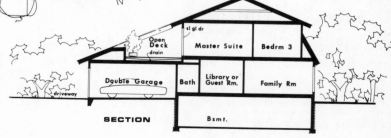

sl gl dr
Open Deck drain
Master Suite
Bedrm 3
Double Garage
driveway
Bath
Library or Guest Rm.
Family Rm
SECTION
Bsmt.

TO ORDER THIS BLUEPRINT, CALL TOLL-FREE 1-800-547-5570

Plan K-649-P

PRICES AND DETAILS ON PAGES 12-15

Class with Comfort

- Twin gables, great window treatments and the rich look of brick lend a sophisticated air to this design.
- Inside, the floor plan is comfortable and unpretentious. The foyer is open to the formal spaces, which flow freely into the casual living areas.
- The kitchen, breakfast nook and family room combine to create a highly livable area with no wasted space.
- The kitchen's angled serving bar accommodates those in the family room and in the nook. The bay-windowed nook has a convenient, space-saving laundry closet. The family room's fireplace warms the entire area.
- The upper floor is highlighted by an irresistible master suite featuring a 9½-ft. tray ceiling, his-and-hers walk-in closets and a 13½-ft.-high vaulted bath with a garden tub.

Plan FB-1744-L

Bedrooms: 4	Baths: 2½
Living Area:	
Upper floor	860 sq. ft.
Main floor	884 sq. ft.
Total Living Area:	**1,744 sq. ft.**
Daylight basement	884 sq. ft.
Garage	456 sq. ft.
Exterior Wall Framing:	2x4

Foundation Options:

Daylight basement
Crawlspace
Slab

(All plans can be built with your choice of foundation and framing. A generic conversion diagram is available. See order form.)

BLUEPRINT PRICE CODE:	**B**

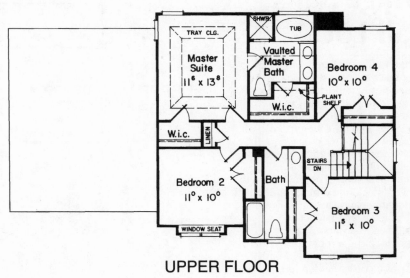

UPPER FLOOR

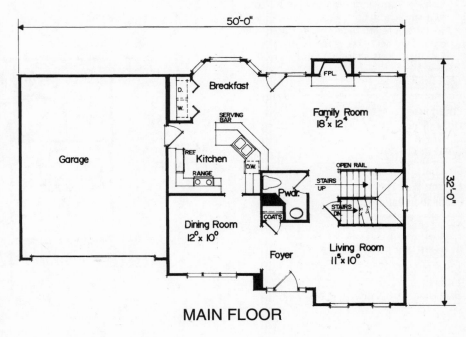

MAIN FLOOR

Cottage Suits Small Lot

- Designed to fit on a sloping or small lot, this compact country-style cottage has the amenities of a much larger home.
- The large front porch opens to the home's surprising two-story-high foyer, which views into the living room.
- The spacious living room is warmed by a handsome fireplace that is centered between built-in bookshelves.
- Enhanced by a sunny bay that opens to a backyard deck, the dining room offers a comfortable eating area that is easily served by the island kitchen.
- The secluded main-floor master bedroom includes a roomy walk-in closet. The spectacular master bath showcases a corner garden tub, a designer shower, a built-in bench and a dual-sink vanity.
- Upstairs, a railed balcony overlooks the foyer. Two secondary bedrooms with walk-in closets share a central bath.

Plan C-8870

Bedrooms: 3	Baths: 2
Living Area:	
Upper floor	664 sq. ft.
Main floor	1,100 sq. ft.
Total Living Area:	**1,764 sq. ft.**
Daylight basement/garage	1,100 sq. ft.
Exterior Wall Framing:	2x4

Foundation Options:

Daylight basement

(All plans can be built with your choice of foundation and framing. A generic conversion diagram is available. See order form.)

BLUEPRINT PRICE CODE: B

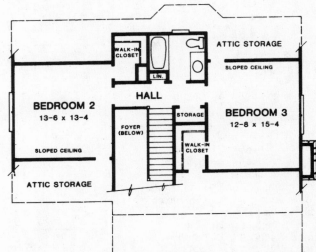

UPPER FLOOR

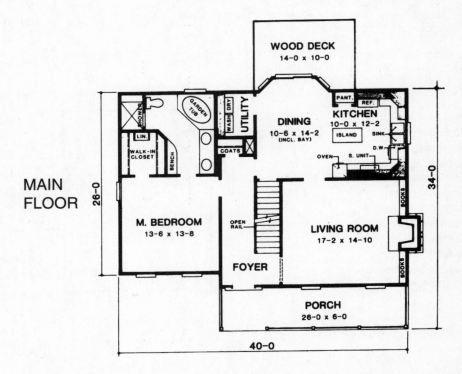

MAIN FLOOR

Plan C-8870

Deck and Spa!

- Designed for relaxation as well as for active indoor/outdoor living, this popular home offers a gigantic deck and an irresistible spa room.
- A covered porch welcomes guests into the entry hall, which flows past the central, open-railed stairway to the spectacular Great Room.
- Sliding glass doors on each side of the Great Room extend the living space to the huge V-shaped deck. The 22-ft. sloped ceiling and a woodstove add to the stunning effect.
- The master suite features a cozy window seat, a walk-in closet and private access to a full bath.
- The passive-solar spa room can be reached from the master suite as well as the backyard deck.
- The upper floor hosts two additional bedrooms, a full bath and a balcony hall that overlooks the Great Room.

REAR VIEW

Plans H-952-1A & -1B

Bedrooms: 3+	Baths: 2-3
Living Area:	
Upper floor	470 sq. ft.
Main floor	1,207 sq. ft.
Passive spa room	102 sq. ft.
Daylight basement	1,105 sq. ft.
Total Living Area:	**1,779/2,884 sq. ft.**
Garage	496 sq. ft.
Exterior Wall Framing:	2x6
Foundation Options:	**Plan #**
Daylight basement	H-952-1B
Crawlspace	H-952-1A

(All plans can be built with your choice of foundation and framing. A generic conversion diagram is available. See order form.)

BLUEPRINT PRICE CODE:	**B/D**

UPPER FLOOR

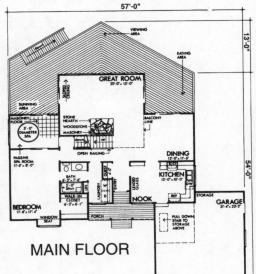

MAIN FLOOR

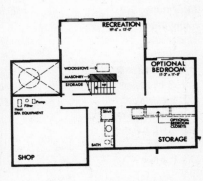

DAYLIGHT BASEMENT

Casual Country Living

- With its covered wraparound porch, this gracious design is ideal for warm summer days or starry evenings.
- The spacious living room boasts a handsome brick-hearth fireplace and built-in book and gun storage. A French door accesses the backyard.
- The open kitchen design provides plenty of space for food storage and preparation with its pantry and oversized central island.
- Two mirror-imaged baths service the three bedrooms on the upper floor. Each secondary bedroom features a window seat and two closets. The master bedroom has a large walk-in closet and a private bath.
- A versatile hobby or sewing room is also included.
- An optional carport off the dining room is available upon request. Please specify when ordering.

Plan J-8895

Bedrooms: 3	Baths: 2½
Living Area:	
Upper floor	860 sq. ft.
Main floor	919 sq. ft.
Total Living Area:	**1,779 sq. ft.**
Standard basement	919 sq. ft.
Optional carport	462 sq. ft.
Exterior Wall Framing:	2x4

Foundation Options:

Standard basement

Crawlspace

Slab

(All plans can be built with your choice of foundation and framing. A generic conversion diagram is available. See order form.)

BLUEPRINT PRICE CODE:	B

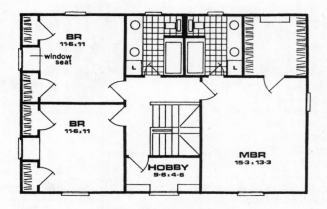

UPPER FLOOR

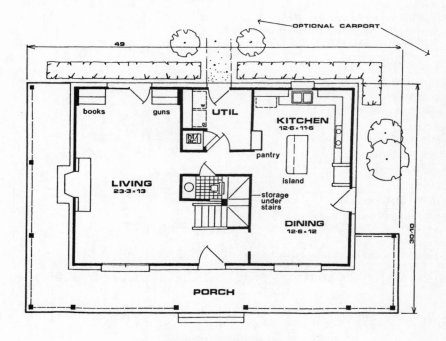

MAIN FLOOR

Attention to Tradition

- This unique design combines contemporary exterior styling with traditional elements.
- The covered front porch flows into a two-story-high foyer, highlighted by a window above.
- Decorative columns and open railings define the adjoining living room, also accented with a lovely corner window, a front-facing window seat and a vaulted ceiling open to the upper floor.
- Conveniently located on the main floor yet out of sight is an oversized laundry room near the garage entrance.
- The sunny, bayed eat-in kitchen is nestled between the formal dining room and the informal family room. A handy serving counter extends from the kitchen into the family room, which also offers a two-story volume ceiling, an optional fireplace and patio access.
- Three nice-sized bedrooms and two full baths share the upper floor.

Plan AG-1605

Bedrooms: 3	Baths: 2½
Living Area:	
Upper floor	821 sq. ft.
Main floor	980 sq. ft.
Total Living Area:	**1,801 sq. ft.**
Standard basement	980 sq. ft.
Garage	480 sq. ft.
Exterior Wall Framing:	2x4

Foundation Options:

Standard basement

(All plans can be built with your choice of foundation and framing. A generic conversion diagram is available. See order form.)

BLUEPRINT PRICE CODE:	**B**

UPPER FLOOR

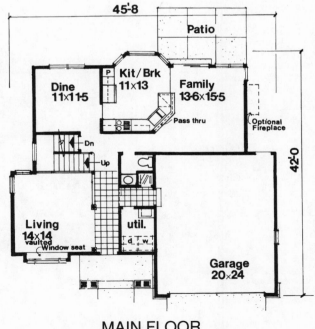

MAIN FLOOR

Something for Everyone

- This space-efficient traditional home has a clever and unique floor plan with something special for everyone.
- Past the elegant double-columned brick porch, the inviting entry flows into the spacious living room.
- Warmed by a corner fireplace, the living room is brightened by a large front window. The adjoining formal dining room is close to the kitchen.
- The modern kitchen is open to the bay-windowed morning room, which has sliding glass doors to a backyard patio. A laundry closet is nearby.
- Upstairs, the master bedroom includes a walk-in closet and a private bath with a garden tub and a dual-sink vanity.
- The second bedroom features a sunny bay window, while the third bedroom boasts a round-top window, a 10-ft. sloped ceiling and a walk-in closet.

Plan DD-1782

Bedrooms: 3+	Baths: 2½
Living Area:	
Upper floor	1,080 sq. ft.
Main floor	785 sq. ft.
Total Living Area:	**1,865 sq. ft.**
Standard basement	785 sq. ft.
Garage	409 sq. ft.
Exterior Wall Framing:	2x4

Foundation Options:

Standard basement

Crawlspace

Slab

(All plans can be built with your choice of foundation and framing. A generic conversion diagram is available. See order form.)

BLUEPRINT PRICE CODE: B

UPPER FLOOR

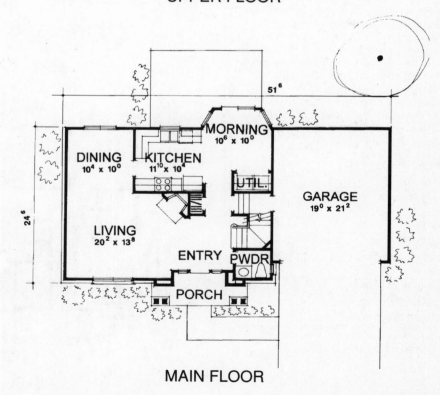

MAIN FLOOR

Plan DD-1782

PRICES AND DETAILS ON PAGES 12-15

Octagonal Dining Bay

- Classic traditional styling is recreated with a covered front porch and triple dormers with half-round windows.
- Off the entry porch, double doors reveal the reception area, with a walk-in closet and a half-bath.

- The living room features a striking fireplace and leads to the dining room, with its octagonal bay.
- The island kitchen overlooks the dinette and the family room, which features a second fireplace and sliding glass doors to a rear deck.
- Upstairs, the master suite boasts a walk-in closet and a whirlpool bath. A skylighted hallway connects three more bedrooms and another full bath.

Plan K-680-R

Bedrooms: 4	**Baths:** 2½
Living Area:	
Upper floor	853 sq. ft.
Main floor	1,047 sq. ft.
Total Living Area:	**1,900 sq. ft.**
Standard basement	1,015 sq. ft.
Garage and storage	472 sq. ft.
Exterior Wall Framing:	2x4 or 2x6

Foundation Options:
Standard basement
Slab
(All plans can be built with your choice of foundation and framing. A generic conversion diagram is available. See order form.)

BLUEPRINT PRICE CODE:	**B**

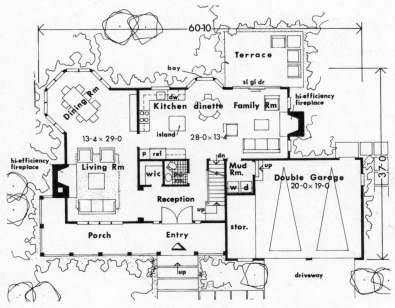

MAIN FLOOR

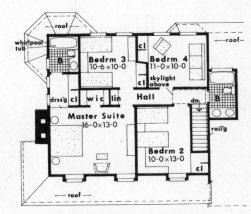

UPPER FLOOR

VIEW INTO LIVING ROOM AND DINING ROOM

Two-Story Great Room

- An expansive two-story-high Great Room, with an oversized hearth and high transom windows, is the highlight of this updated traditional design.
- The cozy front porch and bright, open foyer welcome visitors.
- A 16-ft. vaulted ceiling in the Great Room creates an open expanse as it merges with the nice-sized dining room. Sliding glass doors open to the backyard from the dining area, and the adjoining island kitchen boasts a pantry and windows above the sink.
- The main-floor master suite is in a separate wing for privacy and features a whirlpool tub and a separate shower.
- Upstairs, a balcony joins two bedrooms and a hall bath. The balcony overlooks the Great Room and the foyer.

Plan PI-92-510

Bedrooms: 3	Baths: 2½
Living Area:	
Upper floor	574 sq. ft.
Main floor	1,298 sq. ft.
Total Living Area:	**1,872 sq. ft.**
Daylight basement	1,298 sq. ft.
Garage	660 sq. ft.
Exterior Wall Framing:	2x6

Foundation Options:

Daylight basement
(All plans can be built with your choice of foundation and framing. A generic conversion diagram is available. See order form.)

BLUEPRINT PRICE CODE:	B

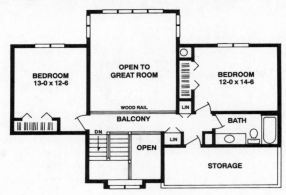

UPPER FLOOR

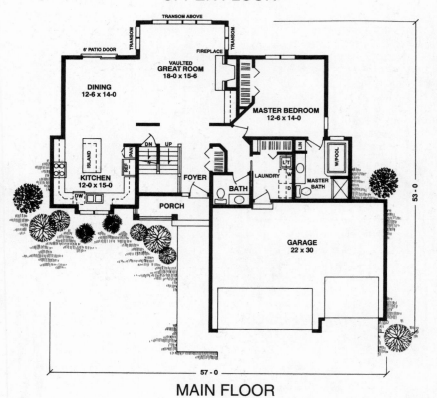

MAIN FLOOR

Plan PI-92-510

Customize Your Floor Plan!

- An optional bonus room and a choice between a loft or a bedroom allow you to customize the floor plan of this striking two-story traditional.

- The 18-ft. vaulted foyer leads guests past a handy powder room and directly into the living areas. Straight ahead is an 18-ft. vaulted family room with a handsome centered fireplace. To the right of the foyer is the formal dining room. The spaces are pleasantly set off by a beautiful open-railed staircase.

- The sunny breakfast room is open to the island kitchen. A pantry closet, a lot of counter space and direct access to the laundry room and the garage add to the kitchen's efficiency.

- The main-floor master suite is a treasure, with its 11-ft. tray ceiling and vaulted, amenity-filled master bath.

- Upstairs, two bedrooms, a full bath and an optional loft and bonus room provide plenty of opportunity for expansion and customization.

Plan FB-1874

Bedrooms: 3+	Baths: 2½
Living Area:	
Upper floor	554 sq. ft.
Main floor	1,320 sq. ft.
Total Living Area:	**1,874 sq. ft.**
Daylight basement	1,320 sq. ft.
Garage	240 sq. ft.
Storage	38 sq. ft.
Bonus room	155 sq. ft.
Exterior Wall Framing:	2x4
Foundation Options:	

Daylight basement

(All plans can be built with your choice of foundation and framing. A generic conversion diagram is available. See order form.)

BLUEPRINT PRICE CODE:	C

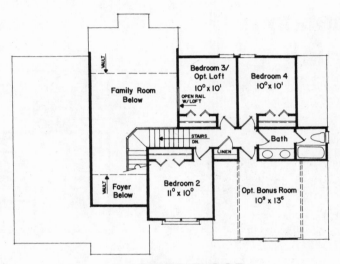

UPPER FLOOR

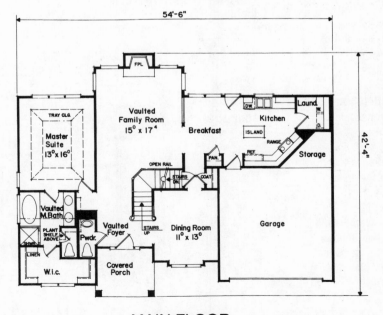

MAIN FLOOR

Exemplary Colonial

- Inside this traditionally designed home is an exciting floor plan for today's lifestyles.
- The classic center-hall arrangement of this Colonial allows easy access to each of the living areas.
- Plenty of views are possible from the formal rooms at the front of the home, as well as from the informal areas at the rear.
- The spacious kitchen offers lots of counter space, a handy work island, a laundry closet and a sunny bayed breakfast nook.
- The adjoining family room shows off a fireplace and elegant double doors to the rear. An optional set of double doors opens to the living room.
- The beautiful master suite on the upper level boasts a 10-ft., 10-in. vaulted ceiling, two closets, dual sinks, a garden tub and a separate shower.

Plan CH-100-A

Bedrooms: 4	Baths: 2½
Living Area:	
Upper floor	923 sq. ft.
Main floor	965 sq. ft.
Total Living Area:	**1,888 sq. ft.**
Basement	952 sq. ft.
Garage	462 sq. ft.
Exterior Wall Framing:	2x4

Foundation Options:
Daylight basement
Standard basement
Crawlspace
(All plans can be built with your choice of foundation and framing. A generic conversion diagram is available. See order form.)

BLUEPRINT PRICE CODE: B

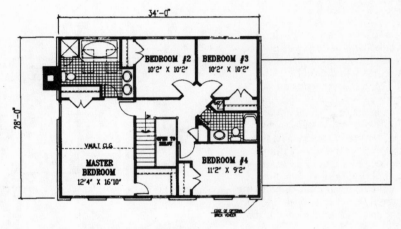

UPPER FLOOR

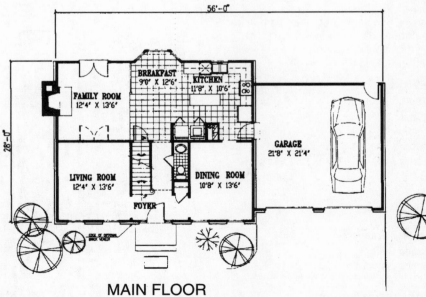

MAIN FLOOR

CH-210-B

Alternate Exteriors

- Timeless exterior detailing and a functional, cost-effective interior are found in this traditional home.
- The kitchen, bayed breakfast room and vaulted family room with skylights and fireplace flow together to form the heart of the home.
- Lots of light filters into the front-facing formal living room.
- Upstairs, the master suite boasts a vaulted ceiling, large walk-in closet and private luxury bath.
- For the flavor of a full, covered front porch, Plan CH-210-B should be your choice.

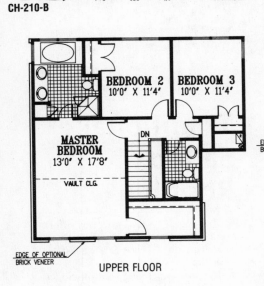

UPPER FLOOR

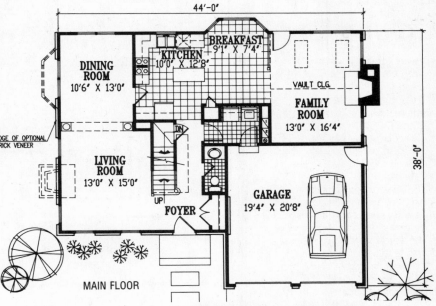

MAIN FLOOR

Plan CH-210-A & -B	
Bedrooms: 3	**Baths:** 2½
Space:	
Upper floor	823 sq. ft.
Main floor	1,079 sq. ft.
Total Living Area	**1,902 sq. ft.**
Basement	978 sq. ft.
Garage	400 sq. ft.
Exterior Wall Framing	2x4
Foundation options:	
Standard Basement	
Daylight Basement	
Crawlspace	
(Foundation & framing conversion diagram available—see order form.)	
Blueprint Price Code	**B**

CH-210-A

Plan M-2214

Bedrooms: 4	Baths: 2½

Space:

Upper floor:	940 sq. ft.
Main floor:	964 sq. ft.

Total living area:	**1,904 sq. ft.**
Basement:	approx. 964 sq. ft.
Garage:	440 sq. ft.

Exterior Wall Framing: 2x4

Foundation options:
Standard basement only.
(Foundation & framing conversion
diagram available — see order form.)

Blueprint Price Code: B

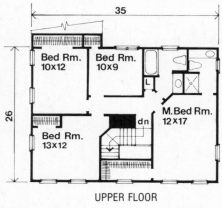

UPPER FLOOR

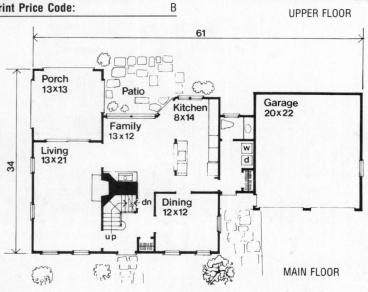

MAIN FLOOR

Traditional Saltbox Roofline

- This classic saltbox exterior offers an open, flexible interior, with well-planned space for the large, busy family.
- The spacious living room includes an impressive fireplace and sliding doors to a screened porch at the rear of the home.
- The large, open-design kitchen blends in with the family room to create a delightful space for food preparation and family life.
- A formal dining room is found at the right as you enter the foyer.
- Upstairs, a deluxe master suite includes a private bath and large closet.
- Three secondary bedrooms share a second upstairs bath.
- Note the convenient washer/dryer area and half-bath off the kitchen.

Plan M-2214

PRICES AND DETAILS
ON PAGES 12-15

Spacious and Open

- A brilliant wall of windows invites guests into the two-story-high foyer of this striking traditional home.
- At the center of this open floor plan, the sunken family room boasts a 21-ft. vaulted ceiling and a striking fireplace with flanking windows.
- The cozy dinette merges with the family room and the island kitchen, creating a spacious, open atmosphere. A pantry closet, a laundry room, a half-bath and garage access are all nearby.
- The formal living and dining rooms are found at the front of the home. The living room boasts a 10½-ft. cathedral ceiling and a lovely window arrangement.
- The main-floor master bedroom has a 10-ft., 10-in. tray ceiling, a walk-in closet and a lush bath designed for two.
- Upstairs, two bedrooms share another full bath and a balcony landing that overlooks the family room and foyer.

Plan A-2207-DS

Bedrooms: 3	Baths: 2½
Living Area:	
Upper floor	518 sq. ft.
Main floor	1,389 sq. ft.
Total Living Area:	**1,907 sq. ft.**
Standard basement	1,389 sq. ft.
Garage	484 sq. ft.
Exterior Wall Framing:	2x6

Foundation Options:

Standard basement

(All plans can be built with your choice of foundation and framing. A generic conversion diagram is available. See order form.)

BLUEPRINT PRICE CODE: B

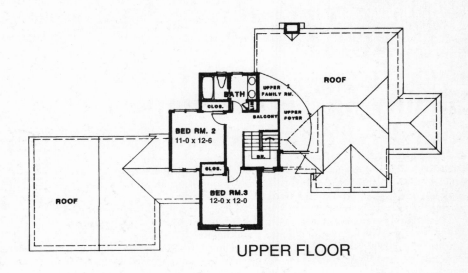

UPPER FLOOR

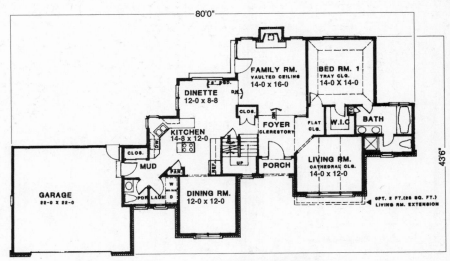

MAIN FLOOR

Quality Space in Compact Four-Bedroom Design

- This well-planned design makes good use of a small lot by putting 1,909 sq. ft. of space on a foundation less than 1,000 sq. ft. in size.
- A large family room/breakfast/kitchen area is great for family dining and other activities.
- Roomy, vaulted living room

includes an impressive fireplace, a feature not often found in homes of this modest size.
- Upstairs, you'll find four bedrooms and a balcony overlooking the living room below.
- The master bedroom includes a private bath and large walk-in closet.

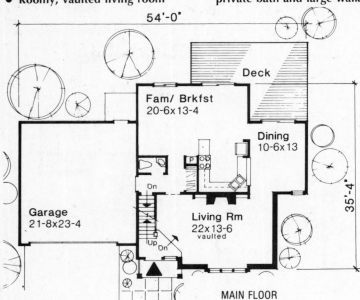

MAIN FLOOR

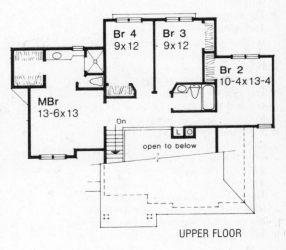

UPPER FLOOR

Plan B-117-8506

Bedrooms: 4	Baths: 2½

Space:

Upper floor:	915 sq. ft.
Main floor:	994 sq. ft.
Total living area:	**1,909 sq. ft.**
Basement:	994 sq. ft.
Garage:	505 sq. ft.

Exterior Wall Framing:	2x4

Foundation options:
Standard basement only.
(Foundation & framing conversion diagram available — see order form.)

Blueprint Price Code:	B

TO ORDER THIS BLUEPRINT,
CALL TOLL-FREE 1-800-547-5570

Plan B-117-8506

PRICES AND DETAILS
ON PAGES 12-15

Solar Design that Shines

- A passive-solar sun room, an energy-efficient woodstove and a panorama of windows make this design really shine.
- The open living/dining room features a 16-ft.-high vaulted ceiling, glass-filled walls and access to the dramatic decking. A balcony above gives the huge living/dining area definition while offering spectacular views.
- The streamlined kitchen has a convenient serving bar that connects it to the living/dining area.
- The main-floor bedroom features dual closets and easy access to a full bath. The laundry room, located just off the garage, doubles as a mudroom and includes a handy coat closet.
- The balcony hallway upstairs is bathed in natural light. The two nice-sized bedrooms are separated by a second full bath.

Plans H-855-3A & -3B

Bedrooms: 3	Baths: 2-3
Living Area:	
Upper floor	586 sq. ft.
Main floor	1,192 sq. ft.
Sun room	132 sq. ft.
Daylight basement	1,192 sq. ft.
Total Living Area:	**1,910/3,102 sq. ft.**
Garage	520 sq. ft.
Exterior Wall Framing:	2x6
Foundation Options:	**Plan #**
Daylight basement	H-855-3B
Crawlspace	H-855-3A

(All plans can be built with your choice of foundation and framing. A generic conversion diagram is available. See order form.)

BLUEPRINT PRICE CODE:	**B/E**

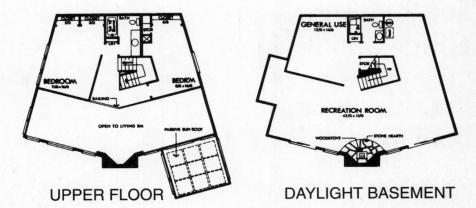

UPPER FLOOR

DAYLIGHT BASEMENT

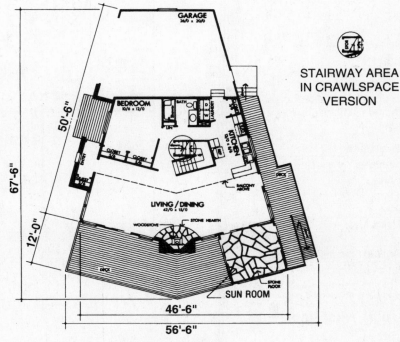

STAIRWAY AREA IN CRAWLSPACE VERSION

MAIN FLOOR

Southwestern Grace and Style

- This exciting home, perfect for narrow lots, is highlighted by a clay tile roof, a stucco exterior and a built-in planter.
- The tiled foyer leads into the 17½-ft. vaulted living room, which opens into the dining room to create an air of spaciousness.
- The L-shaped kitchen features a garden sink and plenty of work space.
- A breathtaking 11½-ft. cathedral ceiling accents the expansive family room, which offers a fireplace and sliding glass doors to a covered patio.
- The stunning master suite has its own doors to the covered patio, plus a huge walk-in closet and a private bath with a whirlpool tub.
- The study or guest room has convenient access to a hall bath.
- Two upper-floor bedrooms share a full bath and a balcony overlooking the living room.

Plan Q-1915-1A

Bedrooms: 3+	Baths: 3
Living Area:	
Upper floor	515 sq. ft.
Main floor	1,400 sq. ft.
Total Living Area:	**1,915 sq. ft.**
Garage	390 sq. ft.
Exterior Wall Framing:	2x4

Foundation Options:

Slab

(All plans can be built with your choice of foundation and framing. A generic conversion diagram is available. See order form.)

BLUEPRINT PRICE CODE: **B**

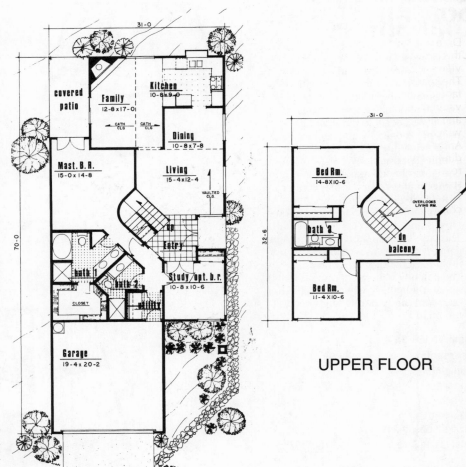

MAIN FLOOR

UPPER FLOOR

Plan Q-1915-1A

PRICES AND DETAILS ON PAGES 12-15

Soaring Design

- Dramatic windows soar to the peak of this prowed chalet, offering unlimited views of outdoor scenery.
- The spacious living room flaunts a fabulous fireplace, a soaring 26-ft. vaulted ceiling, a striking window wall and sliding glass doors to a wonderful wraparound deck.
- An oversized window brightens a dining area on the left side of the living room. The sunny, L-shaped kitchen is spacious and easily accessible.
- The secluded main-floor bedroom has convenient access to a full bath, a linen

closet, a good-sized laundry room and the rear entrance.
- A central, open-railed staircase leads to the upper floor, which contains two more bedrooms and a full bath.
- A skylighted balcony is the high point of this design, offering a railed overlook into the living room below and sweeping outdoor vistas through the wall of windows.
- The optional daylight basement provides another fireplace in a versatile recreation room. The extra-long, tuck-under garage includes plenty of room for hobbies, while the service room offers additional storage space.

Plans H-930-1 & -1A	
Bedrooms: 3	**Baths:** 2
Living Area:	
Upper floor	710 sq. ft.
Main floor	1,210 sq. ft.
Daylight basement	605 sq. ft.
Total Living Area:	**1,920/2,525 sq. ft.**
Tuck-under garage/shop	605 sq. ft.
Exterior Wall Framing:	2x6
Foundation Options:	**Plan #**
Daylight basement	H-930-1
Crawlspace	H-930-1A

(All plans can be built with your choice of foundation and framing. A generic conversion diagram is available. See order form.)

BLUEPRINT PRICE CODE:	**B/D**

DAYLIGHT BASEMENT

STAIRWAY AREA IN CRAWLSPACE VERSION

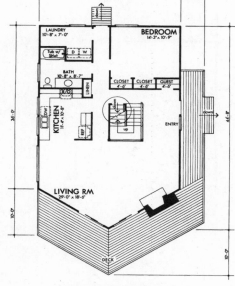

MAIN FLOOR

UPPER FLOOR

Farmhouse for Today

- An inviting covered porch and decorative dormer windows lend traditional warmth and charm to this attractive design.
- The up-to-date interior includes ample space for entertaining as well as for daily family activities.
- The elegant foyer is flanked on one side by the formal, sunken living room and on the other by a sunken family room with a fireplace and an entertainment center. Each room features an 8½-ft. tray ceiling and views of the porch.
- The dining room flows from the living room to increase the entertaining space.
- The kitchen/nook/laundry area forms a large expanse for casual family living and domestic chores.
- Upstairs, the grand master suite includes a large closet and a private bath with a garden tub, a designer shower and a private deck.
- A second full bath serves the two secondary bedrooms.

Plan U-87-203

Bedrooms: 3	Baths: 2½
Living Area:	
Upper floor	857 sq. ft.
Main floor	1,064 sq. ft.
Total Living Area:	**1,921 sq. ft.**
Standard basement	1,064 sq. ft.
Garage	552 sq. ft.
Exterior Wall Framing:	2x4 or 2x6

Foundation Options:

Standard basement
Crawlspace
Slab

(All plans can be built with your choice of foundation and framing. A generic conversion diagram is available. See order form.)

BLUEPRINT PRICE CODE:	**B**

UPPER FLOOR

MAIN FLOOR

TO ORDER THIS BLUEPRINT, CALL TOLL-FREE 1-800-547-5570

Plan U-87-203

PRICES AND DETAILS ON PAGES 12-15

Decked-Out Chalet

- This gorgeous chalet is partially surrounded by a large and roomy deck that is great for indoor/outdoor living.
- The living and dining area shows off a fireplace with a raised hearth, plus large windows to take in the outdoor views. The area is further expanded by a 17½-ft.-high vaulted ceiling in the dining room and sliding glass doors that lead to the deck.
- The kitchen offers a breakfast bar that separates it from the dining area. A convenient laundry room is nearby.
- The main-floor master bedroom is just steps away from a linen closet and a hall bath. Two upstairs bedrooms share a second full bath.
- The highlight of the upper floor is a balcony room with a 12½-ft.-high vaulted ceiling, exposed beams and tall windows. A decorative railing provides an overlook into the dining area below.

Plans H-919-1 & -1A

Bedrooms: 3	Baths: 2
Living Area:	
Upper floor	869 sq. ft.
Main floor	1,064 sq. ft.
Daylight basement	475 sq. ft.
Total Living Area:	**1,933/2,408 sq. ft.**
Tuck-under garage	501 sq. ft.
Exterior Wall Framing:	2x6
Foundation Options:	**Plan #**
Daylight basement	H-919-1
Crawlspace	H-919-1A

(All plans can be built with your choice of foundation and framing. A generic conversion diagram is available. See order form.)

BLUEPRINT PRICE CODE:	**B/C**

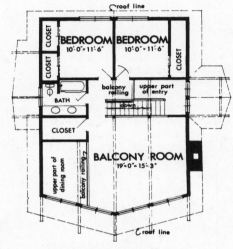

UPPER FLOOR

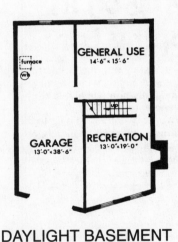

DAYLIGHT BASEMENT

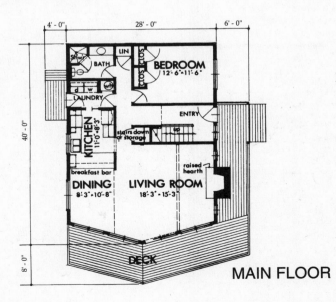

MAIN FLOOR

Living on a Sloping Lot

- The interesting roofline, attractive front deck and dramatic windows of this stylish family home give it lasting contemporary appeal.
- The two-story entry opens up to the spacious living room, which boasts floor-to-ceiling windows and an 11½-ft. vaulted ceiling with exposed beams.

- The adjoining dining area provides access to a wraparound railed deck.
- The updated kitchen offers a walk-in pantry, an eating bar and a breakfast nook with sliding glass doors to a second railed deck.
- A fireplace and access to a rear patio highlight the attached family room.
- Upstairs, a washer and dryer in the hall bath are convenient to all three bedrooms, making laundry a breeze.
- The master bedroom has an 11½-ft. vaulted ceiling and a private bath.

Plan P-7737-4D	
Bedrooms: 3	**Baths:** 2½
Living Area:	
Upper floor	802 sq. ft.
Main floor	1,158 sq. ft.
Total Living Area:	**1,960 sq. ft.**
Tuck-under garage	736 sq. ft.
Exterior Wall Framing:	2x6
Foundation Options:	
Crawlspace	

(All plans can be built with your choice of foundation and framing. A generic conversion diagram is available. See order form.)

BLUEPRINT PRICE CODE: B

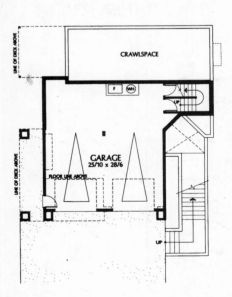

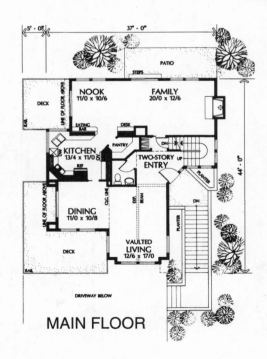

MAIN FLOOR

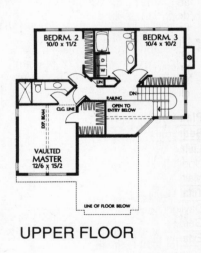

UPPER FLOOR

Plan P-7737-4D

PRICES AND DETAILS ON PAGES 12-15

Farmhouse with Style

- A covered porch, dormer windows and a rear deck give this farmhouse the style and function demanded by today's homeowners.
- Inside, the 16-ft.-high vaulted foyer leads directly to the living room and flaunts a beautiful open-railed staircase.
- The living room flows into the formal dining room, which has a French door opening to the front porch.
- A pocket door reveals the informal areas, where the kitchen offers a snack bar to the sunny nook, and the adjoining family room accesses a rear deck. The space is enhanced by a warm fireplace.
- Upstairs, an arched opening adorns the entrance to the master bedroom's private bath. Three more bedrooms share another full bath, and a laundry closet is handy to all the bedrooms.

Plan CDG-2002

Bedrooms: 4	Baths: 2½
Living Area:	
Upper floor	1,077 sq. ft.
Main floor	888 sq. ft.
Total Living Area:	**1,965 sq. ft.**
Daylight basement	682 sq. ft.
Garage	441 sq. ft.
Exterior Wall Framing:	2x6

Foundation Options:

Daylight basement

Crawlspace

(All plans can be built with your choice of foundation and framing. A generic conversion diagram is available. See order form.)

BLUEPRINT PRICE CODE:	B

UPPER FLOOR

DAYLIGHT BASEMENT

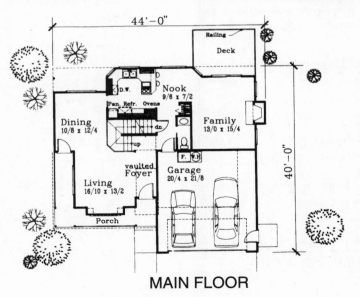

MAIN FLOOR

Light-Filled Interior

- A stylish contemporary exterior and an open, light-filled interior define this two-level home.
- The covered entry leads to a central gallery. The huge living room and dining room combine to generate a spacious ambience that is enhanced by a 15½-ft. cathedral ceiling and a warm fireplace with tall flanking windows.
- Oriented to the rear and overlooking a terrace and backyard landscaping are the informal spaces. The family room, the sunny semi-circular dinette and the modern kitchen share a snack bar.
- The main-floor master suite boasts a 13-ft. sloped ceiling, a private terrace, a dressing area and a personal bath with a whirlpool tub.
- Two to three extra bedrooms with 11-ft. ceilings share a skylighted bath on the upper floor.

Plan K-683-D

Bedrooms: 3+	Baths: 2½+
Living Area:	
Upper floor	491 sq. ft.
Main floor	1,475 sq. ft.
Total Living Area:	**1,966 sq. ft.**
Standard basement	1,425 sq. ft.
Garage and storage	487 sq. ft.
Exterior Wall Framing:	2x4 or 2x6

Foundation Options:

Standard basement

Slab

(All plans can be built with your choice of foundation and framing. A generic conversion diagram is available. See order form.)

BLUEPRINT PRICE CODE: **B**

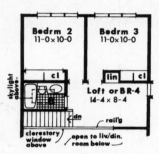

UPPER FLOOR

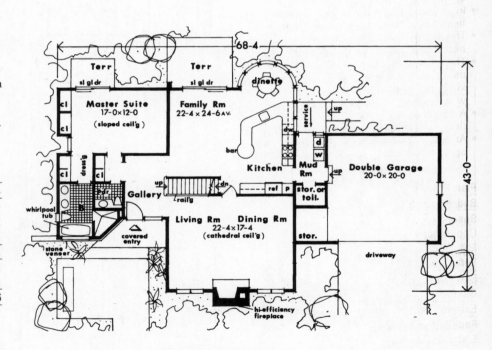

MAIN FLOOR

TO ORDER THIS BLUEPRINT, CALL TOLL-FREE 1-800-547-5570

Plan K-683-D

PRICES AND DETAILS ON PAGES 12-15

Attractive, Open Interior

- Multiple rooflines and an articulate facade generate an attractive curb appeal.
- Inside, sloped ceilings and jutting bays heighten the open, airy atmosphere.
- The formal living and dining rooms are highlighted by an angled fireplace.
- The informal living areas at the rear of the home include a modern, open kitchen flanked by a cozy family room with fireplace and a bright dinette.
- A den or fourth bedroom and a main-floor laundry room complete this level.
- An angled stairway leads to the three additional bedrooms on the upper level.

Plan K-684-D

Bedrooms: 3-4	Baths: 3
Space:	
Upper floor	702 sq. ft.
Main floor	1,273 sq. ft.
Total Living Area	**1,975 sq. ft.**
Basement	1,225 sq. ft.
Garage	440 sq. ft.
Exterior Wall Framing	2x4 or 2x6

Foundation options:
Standard Basement
Slab
(Foundation & framing conversion diagram available—see order form.)

Blueprint Price Code	B

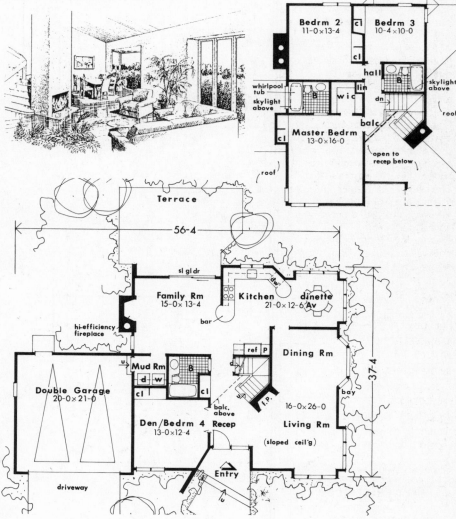

Old Homestead

Almost everyone has a soft place in his heart for a certain home in his childhood. A home like this one, with understated farmhouse styling and wrap-around porch, may be the image of "Home" that your children remember.

Two versions of the first floor plan provide a choice between a country kitchen and a more formal dining room.

All versions feature 2x6 exterior wall framing.

Upper floor:	626 sq. ft.
Main floor:	1,359 sq. ft.
Total living area:	1,985 sq. ft.

(Not counting basement or garage)
(Non-basement versions designed with crawlspace)

Garage:	528 sq. ft.

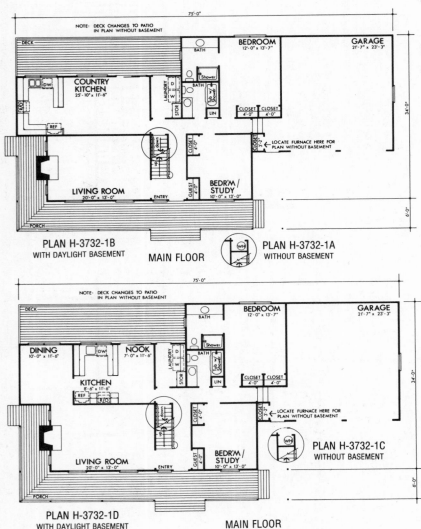

NOTE: DECK CHANGES TO PATIO IN PLAN WITHOUT BASEMENT

75'-0"

DECK

COUNTRY KITCHEN 25'-10" x 11'-6"

BEDROOM 12'-0" x 13'-7"

GARAGE 21'-7" x 23'-3"

BATH

LAUNDRY

STOR

LIN

CLOSET 4'-0" CLOSET 4'-0"

REF

LOCATE FURNACE HERE FOR PLAN WITHOUT BASEMENT

LIVING ROOM 20'-0" x 13'-0"

CLOSET 4'-0"

GUEST 4'-0"

BEDR'M / STUDY 10'-0" x 13'-0"

ENTRY

PORCH

34'-0"

6'-0"

PLAN H-3732-1B WITH DAYLIGHT BASEMENT

MAIN FLOOR

PLAN H-3732-1A WITHOUT BASEMENT

NOTE: DECK CHANGES TO PATIO IN PLAN WITHOUT BASEMENT

75'-0"

DECK

DINING 10'-0" x 11'-6"

NOOK 7'-0" x 11'-6"

KITCHEN 8'-6" x 11'-6"

BEDROOM 12'-0" x 13'-7"

GARAGE 21'-7" x 23'-3"

BATH

LAUNDRY

STOR

LIN

CLOSET 4'-0" CLOSET 4'-0"

REF

LOCATE FURNACE HERE FOR PLAN WITHOUT BASEMENT

LIVING ROOM 20'-0" x 13'-0"

CLOSET 4'-0"

GUEST 4'-0"

BEDR'M / STUDY 10'-0" x 13'-0"

ENTRY

PORCH

34'-0"

6'-0"

PLAN H-3732-1C WITHOUT BASEMENT

PLAN H-3732-1D WITH DAYLIGHT BASEMENT

MAIN FLOOR

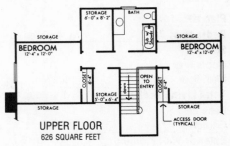

STORAGE 6'-0" x 8'-2"

BATH

STORAGE

STORAGE

BEDROOM 12'-4" x 12'-0"

BEDROOM 12'-4" x 12'-0"

CLOSET

STORAGE 5'-0" x 6'-4"

OPEN TO ENTRY

CLOSET

STORAGE

STORAGE

ACCESS DOOR (TYPICAL)

UPPER FLOOR 626 SQUARE FEET

Blueprint Price Code B

Plans H-3732-1A, -1B, -1C & -1D

PRICES AND DETAILS ON PAGES 12-15

Classic Economy

- The basic rectangular shape of this two-story makes it economical to build. All four bedrooms are located on the upper level.
- The main-floor central hallway is decorated by an open stairway; it is flanked by a dining room and a formal living room with an attractive fireplace that can be seen from the foyer. Sliding glass doors at the rear overlook the back porch.
- A brilliant family room, bayed dinette and kitchen combine at the rear for an open, yet intimate, atmosphere. A wood-beam ceiling adds a homey touch.
- Main-floor laundry facilities, a half-bath and a handy service porch are located near the garage access.

Plan HFL-1070-RQ

Bedrooms: 4	Baths: 2 ½
Space:	
Upper floor	1,013 sq. ft.
Main floor	983 sq. ft.
Total Living Area	**1,996 sq. ft.**
Basement	889 sq. ft.
Garage	403 sq. ft.
Exterior Wall Framing	**2x6**

Foundation options:
Standard Basement
Slab
(Foundation & framing conversion diagram available—see order form.)

Blueprint Price Code	**B**

VIEW OF KITCHEN AND DINETTE FROM FAMILY ROOM.

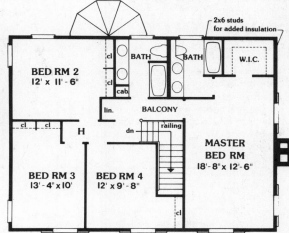

UPPER FLOOR

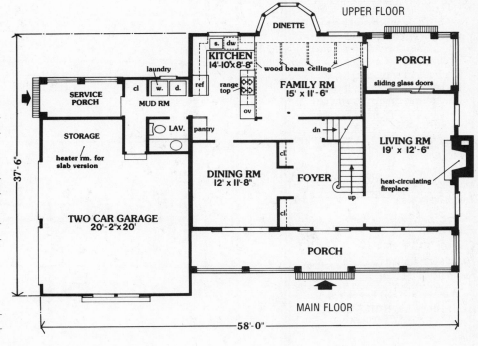

MAIN FLOOR

Relax on the Front Porch

- With its wraparound covered porch, this quaint two-story home makes summer evenings a breeze.
- Inside, a beautiful open stairway welcomes guests into the vaulted foyer, which connects the formal areas. The front-facing living and dining rooms have views of the covered front porch.
- French doors open from the living room to the family room, where a fireplace and corner windows warm and brighten this spacious activity area.
- The breakfast nook, set off by a half-wall, hosts a handy work desk and opens to the back porch.
- The country kitchen offers an oversized island, a pantry closet and illuminating windows flanking the corner sink.
- The upper-floor master suite boasts two walk-in closets and a private bath with a tub and a separate shower. Two more bedrooms, another full bath and a laundry room are also included.

Plan AGH-1997

Bedrooms: 3	Baths: 2½
Living Area:	
Upper floor	933 sq. ft.
Main floor	1,064 sq. ft.
Total Living Area:	**1,997 sq. ft.**
Standard basement	1,064 sq. ft.
Garage	662 sq. ft.
Exterior Wall Framing:	2x6

Foundation Options:

Standard basement

(All plans can be built with your choice of foundation and framing. A generic conversion diagram is available. See order form.)

BLUEPRINT PRICE CODE:	B

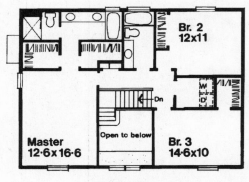

UPPER FLOOR

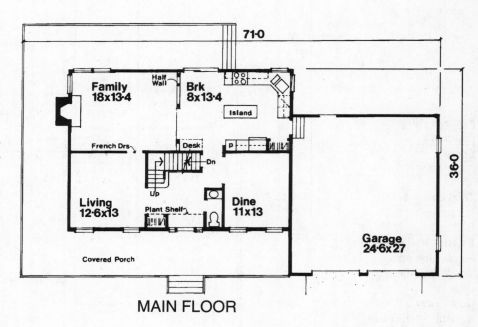

MAIN FLOOR

Plan AGH-1997

PRICES AND DETAILS ON PAGES 12-15

Bridge to Yesteryear

- Decorative gables, detailed brickwork and a distinguished wraparound porch give this country home its timeless look.
- Off the inviting two-story high foyer, the formal dining room features a bright boxed-out window.
- Flanked by two levels of windows, the handsome fireplace is the focal point of the two-story-high family room. A French door opens to the backyard.
- The updated kitchen offers a pantry and windows above the sink. The adjoining breakfast room enjoys French doors to the covered wraparound porch.
- The master suite boasts an elegant tray ceiling and a roomy walk-in closet. The vaulted master bath has a 14-ft. ceiling, a garden tub, a separate shower and a dual-sink vanity.
- Upstairs, a railed bridge overlooking the foyer and the family room leads to two additional bedrooms, which share a full bath. A bonus room above the garage would make a great playroom.

Plan FB-5349-CARO

Bedrooms: 3+	Baths: 2½
Living Area:	
Upper floor	433 sq. ft.
Main floor	1,182 sq. ft.
Bonus room	410 sq. ft.
Total Living Area:	**2,025 sq. ft.**
Daylight basement	1,182 sq. ft.
Garage	400 sq. ft.
Exterior Wall Framing:	2x4

Foundation Options:

Daylight basement

(All plans can be built with your choice of foundation and framing. A generic conversion diagram is available. See order form.)

BLUEPRINT PRICE CODE:	C

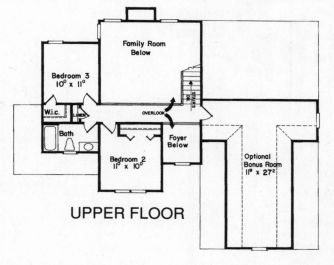

UPPER FLOOR

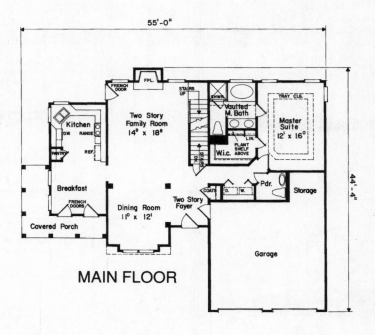

MAIN FLOOR

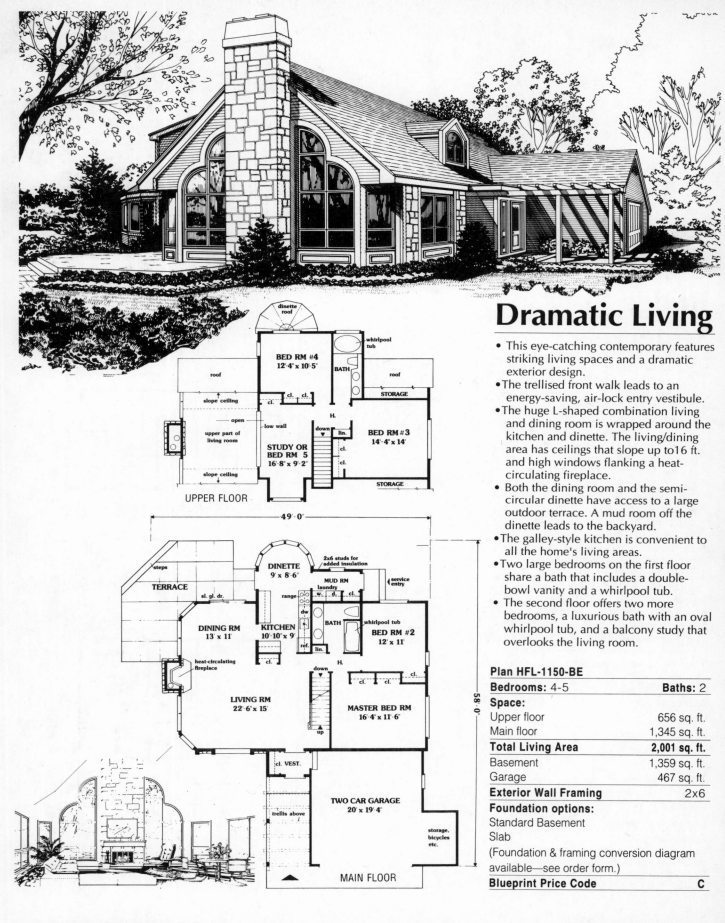

Dramatic Living

- This eye-catching contemporary features striking living spaces and a dramatic exterior design.
- The trellised front walk leads to an energy-saving, air-lock entry vestibule.
- The huge L-shaped combination living and dining room is wrapped around the kitchen and dinette. The living/dining area has ceilings that slope up to 16 ft. and high windows flanking a heat-circulating fireplace.
- Both the dining room and the semi-circular dinette have access to a large outdoor terrace. A mud room off the dinette leads to the backyard.
- The galley-style kitchen is convenient to all the home's living areas.
- Two large bedrooms on the first floor share a bath that includes a double-bowl vanity and a whirlpool tub.
- The second floor offers two more bedrooms, a luxurious bath with an oval whirlpool tub, and a balcony study that overlooks the living room.

Plan HFL-1150-BE

Bedrooms: 4-5	Baths: 2
Space:	
Upper floor	656 sq. ft.
Main floor	1,345 sq. ft.
Total Living Area	**2,001 sq. ft.**
Basement	1,359 sq. ft.
Garage	467 sq. ft.
Exterior Wall Framing	2x6

Foundation options:
Standard Basement
Slab
(Foundation & framing conversion diagram available—see order form.)

Blueprint Price Code	C

UPPER FLOOR

- BED RM #4 12'-4" x 10'-5"
- BATH
- roof
- STORAGE
- roof
- slope ceiling
- open
- low wall
- upper part of living room
- down
- lin.
- BED RM #3 14'-4" x 14'
- STUDY OR BED RM 5 16'-8" x 9'-2"
- cl.
- cl.
- slope ceiling
- STORAGE
- whirlpool tub
- dinette roof

MAIN FLOOR

— 49'-0" —

58'-0"

- steps
- TERRACE
- DINETTE 9' x 8'-6"
- 2x6 studs for added insulation
- MUD RM laundry
- service entry
- sl. gl. dr.
- range
- w.
- d.
- cl.
- DINING RM 13' x 11'
- KITCHEN 10'-10" x 9'
- dw
- s.
- BATH
- whirlpool tub
- BED RM #2 12' x 11'
- ref.
- lin.
- cl.
- H.
- heat-circulating fireplace
- LIVING RM 22'-6" x 15'
- down
- up
- cl.
- cl.
- MASTER BED RM 16'-4" x 11'-6"
- cl. VEST.
- trellis above
- TWO CAR GARAGE 20' x 19'-4"
- storage, bicycles etc.

Plan HFL-1150-BE

PRICES AND DETAILS ON PAGES 12-15

Updated Colonial

- This home offers Colonial styling on the outside, with an updated, ultra-modern floor plan inside.
- Guests are welcomed into a formal gallery that leads to all of the main-floor living areas. The large living room and the formal dining room flank the gallery. Optional folding doors open the living room to the family room.
- The family room features an inviting fireplace as its hub and sliding-door access to a backyard terrace.
- The kitchen is located for easy service to the formal dining room as well as the bayed dinette. A mudroom/laundry room and a powder room are nearby.
- Upstairs, the master suite boasts a private bath and a wall of closets. Three unique secondary bedrooms share a hall bath, which has a dual-sink vanity.

Plan K-274-M

Bedrooms: 4	Baths: 2½
Living Area:	
Upper floor	990 sq. ft.
Main floor	1,025 sq. ft.
Total Living Area:	**2,015 sq. ft.**
Standard basement	983 sq. ft.
Garage and storage	520 sq. ft.
Exterior Wall Framing:	2x4 or 2x6

Foundation Options:

Standard basement
Slab
(All plans can be built with your choice of foundation and framing. A generic conversion diagram is available. See order form.)

BLUEPRINT PRICE CODE:	C

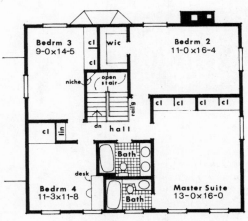

UPPER FLOOR

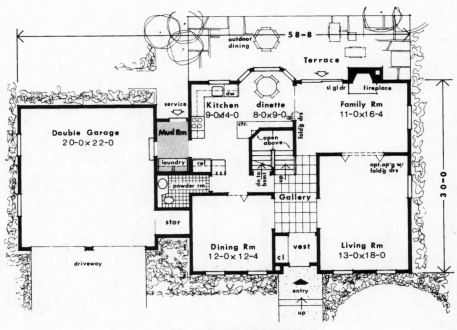

MAIN FLOOR

Stylish Brick and Windows

- This home features rich-looking brick, stylish windows and a space-saving L-shaped design.
- The foyer flows toward the living room, which boasts a 16-ft. cathedral ceiling and a fireplace flanked by sliding glass doors that open to an optional deck.
- The gourmet kitchen offers a built-in desk, a snack bar to the breakfast area and easy service to the dining room. A handy laundry/mudroom opens to the garage and the side yard.
- An optional glass-enclosed greenhouse is ideally located off the deck and the breakfast area.
- A secluded main-floor master suite includes private access to the deck and a bath with an 11-ft. cathedral ceiling, a garden tub and a separate shower.
- A tall window brightens the stairway to the upper floor, where a balcony hall leads to two bedrooms that share another full bath.

Plan AX-97144

Bedrooms: 3	**Baths:** 2½
Living Area:	
Upper floor	529 sq. ft.
Main floor	1,491 sq. ft.
Total Living Area:	**2,020 sq. ft.**
Standard basement	1,412 sq. ft.
Garage	440 sq. ft.
Exterior Wall Framing:	2x4

Foundation Options:
Standard basement
Crawlspace
Slab
(All plans can be built with your choice of foundation and framing. A generic conversion diagram is available. See order form.)

BLUEPRINT PRICE CODE:	C

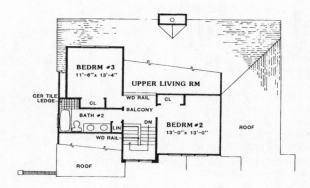

UPPER FLOOR

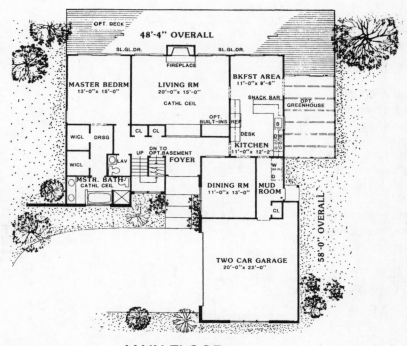

MAIN FLOOR

TO ORDER THIS BLUEPRINT, CALL TOLL-FREE 1-800-547-5570

Plan AX-97144

PRICES AND DETAILS ON PAGES 12-15

Farmhouse with Modern Touch

- This classic center-hall design features an All-American Farmhouse exterior wrapped around a super-modern interior.
- A large family room features a built-in entertainment center and adjoins a convenient dinette for quick family meals.
- The spacious living and dining rooms adjoin to provide abundant space for large gatherings.

- An inviting porch leads into a roomy foyer which highlights a curved staircase.
- The second floor features a deluxe master suite and three secondary bedrooms.

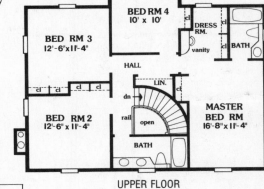

VIEW INTO LIVING ROOM FROM FOYER.

Upper Floor

BED RM 4
10' x 10'

DRESS RM.

BATH

BED RM 3
12'-6" x 11'-4"

vanity

HALL

LIN.

BED RM 2
12'-6" x 11'-4"

dn

rail

open

MASTER BED RM
16'-8" x 11'-4"

BATH

UPPER FLOOR

Main Floor

60'-0"

35'-6"

TERRACE

sliding glass doors

s.

dw

range

sliding glass doors

service entry

MUD RM

cl

KITCHEN
10'-8" x 10'

ref.

DINING RM
12'-6" x 11'-6"

LAV.

DINETTE
8'-8" x 8'-8"

LAUNDRY

d. w.

TWO CAR GARAGE
21'-4" x 19'-8"

heat-circulating fireplace

dn

railing

open

FAMILY RM
16' x 12'-2"(avg.)

entertainment center

LIVING RM
19'-8" x 12'-6"

FOYER

cl

up

high ceiling

PORCH

MAIN FLOOR

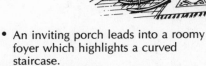

Plan HFL-1040-MB

Bedrooms: 4	Baths: 2½
Space:	
Upper floor	936 sq. ft.
Main floor	1,094 sq. ft.
Total Living Area	**2,030 sq. ft.**
Basement	1,022 sq. ft.
Garage	420 sq. ft.
Exterior Wall Framing	2x6

Foundation options:
Standard Basement
Slab
(Foundation & framing conversion diagram available—see order form.)

Blueprint Price Code	C

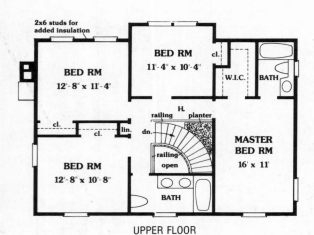

2x6 studs for added insulation

BED RM
12'-8" x 11'-4"

BED RM
11'-4" x 10'-4"

cl.

W.I.C.

BATH

cl.

cl.

lin.

railing H. planter
dn.
railing
open

BED RM
12'-8" x 10'-8"

MASTER
BED RM
16' x 11'

BATH

UPPER FLOOR

56' – 8"

34' – 2"

PATIO

sl. gl. dr.
cl.

DINETTE
10' x 8'

exposed beams

s.

cook-top

dw ov

closet

service entry

d w

STORAGE

FAMILY RM
16' x 11'-4"

KITCHEN
11'-4" x 10'

dn.

MUD RM

heat-circulating fireplace

LAV.

ref.

dn.
railing
open abv.

DINING RM
14' x 11'

TWO CAR
GARAGE
20' x 20'

up

LIVING RM
19'-6" x 12'-8"

FOYER

cl.

PORCH

MAIN FLOOR

Distinctive
Colonial
Farmhouse

- Although a casual living theme flows throughout this farmhouse, elegance is not forgotten.
- A beautiful circular stair ascends from the central foyer to the bedrooms on the upper level.
- Formal living and dining rooms flank the foyer.
- The informal family room at the rear captures an Early American style with exposed beams, wood paneling and a brick fireplace wall. Sliding glass doors provide access to the adjoining patio.
- A sunny dinette opens to an efficiently arranged kitchen with a handy laundry room near the garage entrance.
- A decorative railing and a planter adorn the second-floor balcony that overlooks the foyer below. Four generous-sized bedrooms and two baths share this level.

Plan HFL-1010-CR

Bedrooms: 4	Baths: 2 ½
Space:	
Upper floor	932 sq. ft.
Main floor	1,099 sq. ft.
Total Living Area	**2,031 sq. ft.**
Basement	998 sq. ft.
Garage and storage	476 sq. ft.
Exterior Wall Framing	2x4

Foundation options:
Standard Basement
Slab
(Foundation & framing conversion diagram available—see order form.)

Blueprint Price Code	C

Plan HFL-1010-CR

PRICES AND DETAILS ON PAGES 12-15

Big, Bright Country Kitchen

- Decorative dormers, shuttered windows and a large covered front porch give this charming two-story home a pleasant country flavor.
- Inside, the central Great Room is warmed by a handsome fireplace. The adjoining dining room offers sliding glass doors to a backyard deck.
- The enormous country kitchen features a sunny bay-windowed eating area and a convenient island counter. The nearby laundry/utility area accesses the garage and the backyard.
- The main-floor master bedroom boasts a roomy walk-in closet and private access to a compartmentalized bath with an oversized linen closet.
- Upstairs, two bedrooms with window seats share a full bath. An easy-to-access storage area is above the garage. Another convenient storage area can be reached from the garage.

Plan C-8040

Bedrooms: 3	Baths: 2
Living Area:	
Upper floor	718 sq. ft.
Main floor	1,318 sq. ft.
Total Living Area:	**2,036 sq. ft.**
Daylight basement	1,221 sq. ft.
Garage	436 sq. ft.
Exterior Wall Framing:	2x4

Foundation Options:

Daylight basement
Crawlspace
Slab
(All plans can be built with your choice of foundation and framing. A generic conversion diagram is available. See order form.)

BLUEPRINT PRICE CODE:	C

UPPER FLOOR

MAIN FLOOR

Attractive, Open Floor Plan

- Two-story ceilings in the foyer and living room add an attractive spatial dimension to this versatile two-story, finished in stucco.
- The spacious living areas include a sunken, formal living room with a large fireplace, front-facing bay

window and entrance from both the foyer and dining room.
- The family room, 3 steps below the main level, offers a second fireplace and a view of the nook through an open railing.
- The kitchen includes an island

work area, corner window, pantry and sliding doors to the attached deck.
- The home accommodates a master bedroom and two secondary bedrooms on the second floor and a single bedroom on the main level.

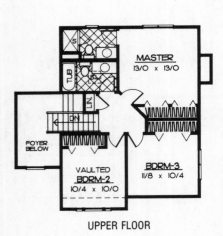

UPPER FLOOR

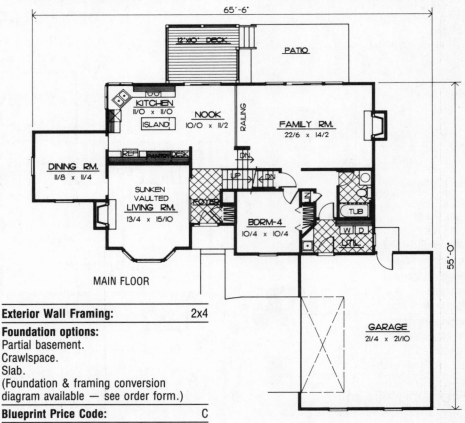

MAIN FLOOR

Plan U-89-403

Bedrooms: 4	Baths: 3

Space:

Upper floor:	656 sq. ft.
Main floor:	1,385 sq. ft.
Total living area:	**2,041 sq. ft.**
Basement:	704 sq. ft.
Garage:	466 sq. ft.

Exterior Wall Framing:	2x4

Foundation options:
Partial basement.
Crawlspace.
Slab.
(Foundation & framing conversion diagram available — see order form.)

Blueprint Price Code: C

Great Spaces

- Open, airy casual living spaces and intimate formal areas are the hallmarks of this intriguing home.
- A two-story-high foyer introduces the the living room, where French doors open to a veranda. On the opposite side of the foyer is a spacious dining room with a delightful bay window.
- The casual areas combine at the back of the home. The family room features a two-story-high ceiling and a fireplace framed with glass, including a French door that opens to the backyard.
- A half-wall is all that separates the family room from the inviting bay-windowed nook. An angled serving counter/snack bar keeps the kitchen open to the activity areas.
- A walk-in pantry and a laundry room are nearby, just off the garage entrance.
- Upstairs, the luxurious master suite features an elegant 9-ft. tray ceiling. The master bath boasts a 12-ft. vaulted ceiling, an oval garden tub, a private toilet compartment and a walk-in closet adorned with a plant shelf.
- Two more bedrooms, a versatile loft and a hall bath complete the upper floor.

Plan FB-5056-MAGU

Bedrooms: 3+	Baths: 2½
Living Area:	
Upper floor	1,019 sq. ft.
Main floor	1,034 sq. ft.
Total Living Area:	**2,053 sq. ft.**
Daylight basement	1,034 sq. ft.
Garage	415 sq. ft.
Exterior Wall Framing:	2x4

Foundation Options:

Daylight basement

(All plans can be built with your choice of foundation and framing. A generic conversion diagram is available. See order form.)

BLUEPRINT PRICE CODE: C

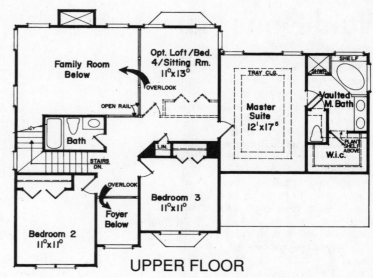

UPPER FLOOR

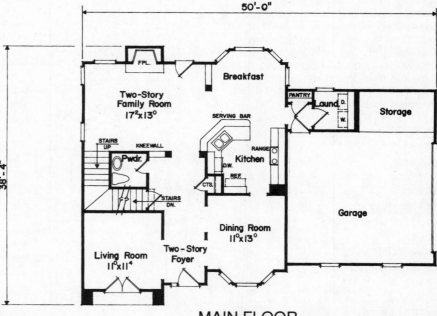

MAIN FLOOR

Fluid Floor Plan

- This updated 1½-story home features cathedral ceilings and a fluid floor plan that combine for easy family living.
- Several design options are offered, including a hutch space in the formal dining room, a 30-sq.-ft. extension off the family room, a window seat in the master bedroom, an alternate master bath layout and an alternate mudroom/entry design.
- A handsome fireplace and an 11½-ft. cathedral ceiling highlight the large family room, which opens to the dinette and the island kitchen. An 11-ft. cathedral ceiling is also found in the adjoining living room.
- The master suite features a 9-ft. tray ceiling, a large walk-in closet, a dressing area and a private bath.
- Upstairs, two more bedrooms share a hall bath. A window seat in the front bedroom offers storage space below.
- The blueprints also include an alternate upper-floor layout that adds another bedroom. The ceiling in the family room is lowered to 8 ft. to allow for a bedroom overhead.

Plan GL-2070

Bedrooms: 3	Baths: 2½
Living Area:	
Upper floor	509 sq. ft.
Main floor	1,561 sq. ft.
Total Living Area:	**2,070 sq. ft.**
Standard basement	1,561 sq. ft.
Garage	462 sq. ft.
Exterior Wall Framing:	2x6

Foundation Options:

Standard basement

(All plans can be built with your choice of foundation and framing. A generic conversion diagram is available. See order form.)

BLUEPRINT PRICE CODE: C

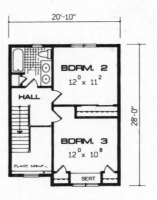

UPPER FLOOR

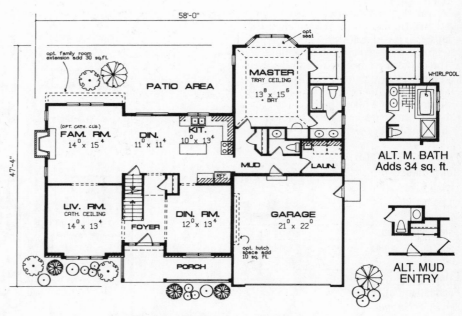

MAIN FLOOR

Plan GL-2070

Sun-Drenched Spaces

- Articulate rooflines and stone accents complement this two-story.
- Inside, radiant spaces stem from the use of glazed sun roofs and expansive windows and doors.
- The huge living room and dining room flow together for a spacious setting accentuated by a big fireplace and a cathedral ceiling. The dining room features a sunny bay and a rear sun roof and terrace.
- A second fireplace in the family room generates a warm and cozy atmosphere in the merging kitchen and bayed dinette.
- Four bedrooms and two skylighted baths share the upper level.

Plan K-651-U

Bedrooms: 4	Baths: 2 ½
Space:	
Upper floor	930 sq. ft.
Main floor	1,144 sq. ft.
Total Living Area	**2,074 sq. ft.**
Basement	1,082 sq. ft.
Garage	460 sq. ft.
Exterior Wall Framing	2x4 or 2x6

Foundation options:
Standard Basement
Slab
(Foundation & framing conversion diagram available—see order form.)

Blueprint Price Code	C

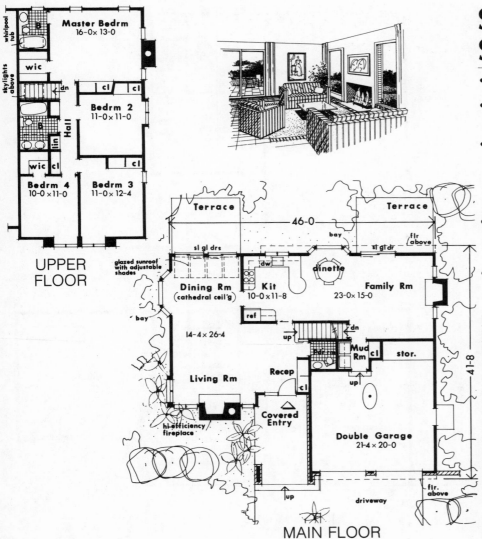

UPPER FLOOR

Master Bedrm 16-0 x 13-0
wic
whirlpool tub
B
skylights above
cl cl
Bedrm 2 11-0 x 11-0
dn
Hall
lin
B
wic cl
cl
Bedrm 4 10-0 x 11-0
Bedrm 3 11-0 x 12-4

MAIN FLOOR

Terrace
Terrace
46-0
bay
sl gl drs
dw
st gl dr
flr above
glazed sunroof with adjustable shades
Dining Rm (cathedral ceil'g)
Kit 10-0 x 11-8
dinette
Family Rm 23-0 x 15-0
ref
14-4 x 26-4
bay
up
dn
Mud Rm
cl
stor.
Living Rm
Recep
cl
up
41-8
hi-efficiency fireplace
Covered Entry
Double Garage 21-4 x 20-0
up
driveway
flr. above

Distinctive Family Design

- This beautiful, time-tested traditional design packs many features into a highly livable floor plan.
- To the left of the foyer, the 16½-ft. vaulted living room flows into the dining room, providing a huge space for both formal entertaining and family gatherings.
- The big kitchen includes a handy work island and a sunny dinette, which opens to the backyard. A half-bath, laundry facilities and garage access are nearby.
- The large family room adjoins the casual dinette area and boasts a handsome fireplace.
- Upstairs, the master bedroom features two large closets and a private bath. Three additional bedrooms share another full bath. A central balcony overlooks the foyer below.

Plan A-2109-DS

Bedrooms: 4	**Baths:** 2½
Living Area:	
Upper floor	942 sq. ft.
Main floor	1,148 sq. ft.
Total Living Area:	**2,090 sq. ft.**
Standard basement	1,148 sq. ft.
Garage	484 sq. ft.
Exterior Wall Framing:	2x4

Foundation Options:

Standard basement
(All plans can be built with your choice of foundation and framing. A generic conversion diagram is available. See order form.)

BLUEPRINT PRICE CODE:	C

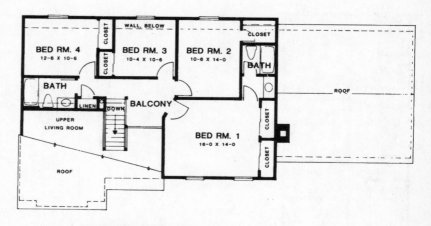

UPPER FLOOR

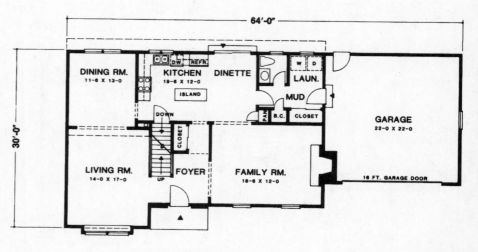

MAIN FLOOR

TO ORDER THIS BLUEPRINT, CALL TOLL-FREE 1-800-547-5570   **Plan A-2109-DS**   **PRICES AND DETAILS ON PAGES 12-15**

Classic Victorian

- This classic exterior is built around an interior that offers all the amenities desired by today's families.
- In from the covered front porch, the entry features a curved stairway and a glass-block wall to the dining room.
- A step down from the entry, the Great Room boasts a dramatic 24½-ft. cathedral ceiling and provides ample space for large family gatherings.
- The formal dining room is available for special occasions, while the 13-ft.-high breakfast nook serves everyday needs.
- The adjoining island kitchen offers plenty of counter space and opens to a handy utility room and a powder room.
- The deluxe main-floor master suite features a 14½-ft. cathedral ceiling and an opulent private bath with a garden spa tub and a separate shower.
- Upstairs, two secondary bedrooms share a full bath and a balcony overlooking the Great Room below.
- Detached two-car garage plans available upon request.

Plan DW-2112

Bedrooms: 3	Baths: 2½
Living Area:	
Upper floor	514 sq. ft.
Main floor	1,598 sq. ft.
Total Living Area:	**2,112 sq. ft.**
Standard basement	1,598 sq. ft.
Exterior Wall Framing:	2x4

Foundation Options:
Standard basement
Crawlspace
Slab
(All plans can be built with your choice of foundation and framing. A generic conversion diagram is available. See order form.)

BLUEPRINT PRICE CODE: C

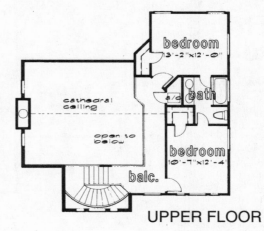

UPPER FLOOR

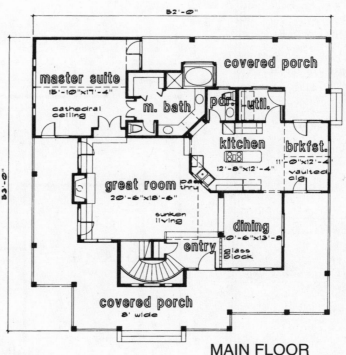

MAIN FLOOR

to detatched garage

TO ORDER THIS BLUEPRINT,
CALL TOLL-FREE 1-800-547-5570

Plan DW-2112

PRICES AND DETAILS
ON PAGES 12-15

109

Comfortable Country Home

- A central gable and a wide, welcoming front porch with columns give this design comfortable country charm.
- The large living room is open to the dining room, which features a tray ceiling and views to the backyard.
- The kitchen offers an oversized island counter with a snack bar. The adjoining breakfast area has a sliding glass door to the backyard and a half-wall that separates it from the family room. This inviting room includes a fireplace and a bay window with a cozy seat.
- Upstairs, the master suite boasts three windows, including a lovely arched window, that overlook the front yard. The private bath offers a whirlpool tub and a separate shower.
- Three more bedrooms, a second full bath and a multipurpose den make this a great family-sized home.

Plan OH-165

Bedrooms: 4+	Baths: 2½
Living Area:	
Upper floor	1,121 sq. ft.
Main floor	1,000 sq. ft.
Total Living Area:	**2,121 sq. ft.**
Standard basement	1,000 sq. ft.
Garage	400 sq. ft.
Exterior Wall Framing:	2x4

Foundation Options:

Standard basement

(All plans can be built with your choice of foundation and framing. A generic conversion diagram is available. See order form.)

BLUEPRINT PRICE CODE:	C

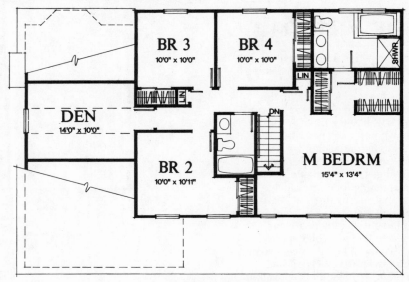

UPPER FLOOR

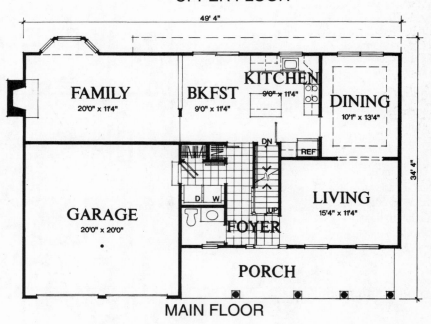

MAIN FLOOR

   Plan OH-165   **PRICES AND DETAILS ON PAGES 12-15**

Dramatic Family Room

- An impressive porch and simple, balanced rooflines make this warm and friendly farmhouse a classic beauty.
- The two-story foyer and formal living and dining rooms maintain the feeling of generous hospitality.
- The large and open country kitchen, with its big, bright breakfast area, pantry, wall oven and pass-through to the family room, is the perfect host for informal family gatherings.
- The step-down family room at the back of the home features a 15-ft. cathedral ceiling and a prominent fireplace.
- Three bedrooms and two full baths occupy the upper floor. The spacious and luxurious master suite has a big private bath and inherits a huge walk-in closet through the efficient use of the space above the garage.

Plan OH-163

Bedrooms: 3	Baths: 2½
Living Area:	
Upper floor	852 sq. ft.
Main floor	1,270 sq. ft.
Total Living Area:	**2,122 sq. ft.**
Partial basement	934 sq. ft.
Garage	576 sq. ft.
Exterior Wall Framing:	2x4

Foundation Options:

Partial basement

(All plans can be built with your choice of foundation and framing. A generic conversion diagram is available. See order form.)

BLUEPRINT PRICE CODE: C

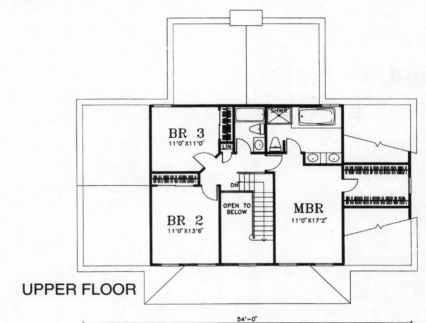

UPPER FLOOR

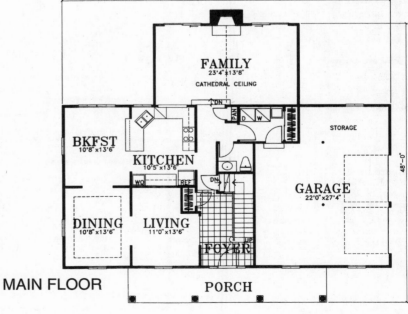

MAIN FLOOR

Upstairs Suite Creates Adult Retreat

● This multi-level design is ideal for a gently sloping site with a view to the rear.

● Upstairs master suite is a sumptuous "adult retreat" complete with magnificent bath, vaulted ceiling, walk-in closet, private deck and balcony loft.
● Living room includes wood stove area and large windows to the rear. Wood bin can be loaded from outside.
● Main floor also features roomy kitchen and large utility area.

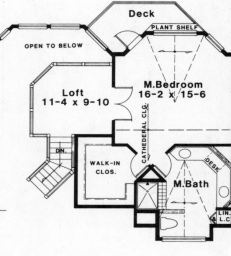

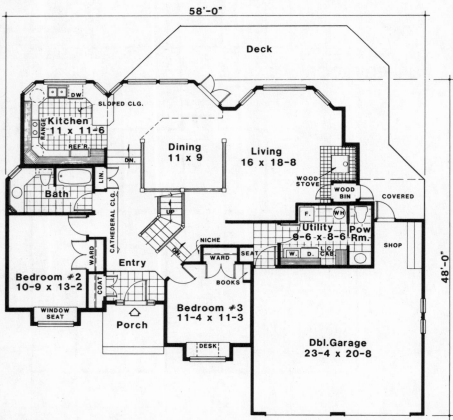

Plan NW-544-S

Plan NW-544-S	
Bedrooms: 3	**Baths:** 2½
Space:	
Upper floor:	638 sq. ft.
Main floor:	1,500 sq. ft.
Total living area:	2,138 sq. ft.
Garage:	545 sq. ft.
Exterior Wall Framing:	2x6
Foundation options: Crawlspace only. (Foundation & framing conversion diagram available — see order form.)	
Blueprint Price Code:	C

TO ORDER THIS BLUEPRINT, CALL TOLL-FREE 1-800-547-5570

Plan NW-544-S

PRICES AND DETAILS ON PAGES 12-15

Colonial for Today

- Designed for a growing family, this handsome traditional home offers four bedrooms plus a den and three complete baths. The Colonial exterior is updated by a covered front entry porch with a fanlight window above.
- The dramatic tiled foyer is two stories high and provides direct access to all of the home's living areas. The spacious living room has an inviting brick fireplace and sliding pocket doors to the adjoining dining room.
- Overlooking the backyard, the huge combination kitchen/family room is the home's hidden charm. The kitchen features a peninsula breakfast bar with seating for six. The family room has a window wall with sliding glass doors that open to an enticing terrace. A built-in entertainment center and bookshelves line another wall.
- The adjacent mudroom is just off the garage entrance and includes a pantry closet. A full bath and a large den complete the first floor.
- The second floor is highlighted by a beautiful balcony that is open to the foyer below. The luxurious master suite is brightened by a skylight and boasts two closets, including an oversized walk-in closet. The master bath has a whirlpool tub and a dual-sink vanity.

Plan AHP-7050	
Bedrooms: 4+	**Baths:** 3
Living Area:	
Upper floor	998 sq. ft.
Main floor	1,153 sq. ft.
Total Living Area:	**2,151 sq. ft.**
Standard basement	1,067 sq. ft.
Garage	439 sq. ft.
Exterior Wall Framing:	2x6

Foundation Options:
Standard basement
Crawlspace
Slab
(All plans can be built with your choice of foundation and framing. A generic conversion diagram is available. See order form.)

BLUEPRINT PRICE CODE:	C

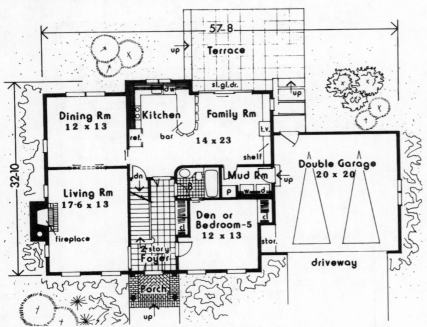

MAIN FLOOR

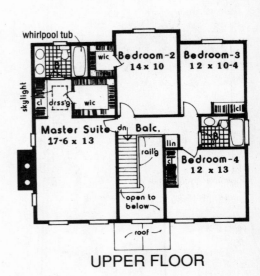

UPPER FLOOR

Down-Home Country Flavor!

- Open living areas, decorative dormers and a spacious wraparound porch give this charming home its country feel.
- The main entrance opens into an enormous living room, which boasts a handsome fireplace flanked by bright windows and built-in cabinets.
- The adjoining dining room is brightened by windows on three sides. A rear French door opens to the porch.
- The modern kitchen serves the dining room over an eating bar. A half-bath and a laundry/utility area with access to the garage and porch are nearby.
- The removed master bedroom includes a roomy walk-in closet and a private bath with a corner shower and a dual-sink vanity with knee space.
- All main-floor rooms have 9-ft. ceilings.
- Two upper-floor bedrooms share a hallway bath, which is enhanced by one of three dormer windows.

Plan J-90013

Bedrooms: 3	Baths: 2½
Living Area:	
Upper floor	823 sq. ft.
Main floor	1,339 sq. ft.
Total Living Area:	**2,162 sq. ft.**
Standard basement	1,339 sq. ft.
Garage	413 sq. ft.
Storage	106 sq. ft.
Exterior Wall Framing:	2x4

Foundation Options:

Standard basement

Crawlspace

Slab

(All plans can be built with your choice of foundation and framing. A generic conversion diagram is available. See order form.)

BLUEPRINT PRICE CODE:	C

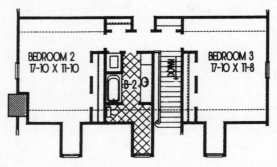

UPPER FLOOR

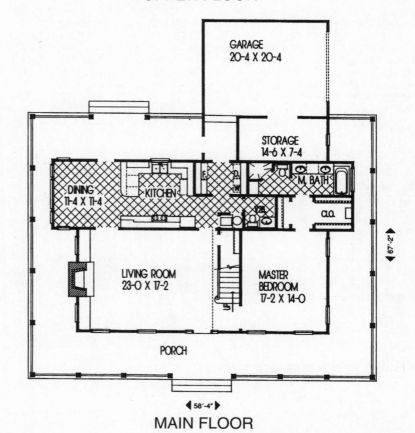

MAIN FLOOR

TO ORDER THIS BLUEPRINT, CALL TOLL-FREE 1-800-547-5570

Plan J-90013

PRICES AND DETAILS ON PAGES 12-15

Chalet for Town or Country

- Vertical siding, spacious viewing decks with cut-out railings and exposed beams in the interior give this home the look of a mountain chalet.
- The design of the home lends itself to year-round family living as well as to part-time recreational enjoyment.
- The expansive Great Room features exposed beams and an impressive fireplace. The large wraparound deck is accessed through sliding glass doors. The dining area is expanded by an 18-ft. vaulted ceiling.
- The well-planned kitchen is open and easily accessible.
- Two main-floor bedrooms share the hall bath between them.
- The upstairs offers an adult retreat: a fine master bedroom with a private deck and bath, plus a versatile loft area. An airy 13-ft. ceiling presides over the entire upper floor.
- The daylight-basement level includes a garage and a large recreation room with a fireplace and a half-bath.

Plan P-531-2D

Bedrooms: 3+	Baths: 2½
Living Area:	
Upper floor	573 sq. ft.
Main floor	1,120 sq. ft.
Daylight basement	532 sq. ft.
Total Living Area:	**2,225 sq. ft.**
Tuck-under garage	541 sq. ft.
Exterior Wall Framing:	2x6

Foundation Options:

Daylight basement
(All plans can be built with your choice of foundation and framing. A generic conversion diagram is available. See order form.)

BLUEPRINT PRICE CODE: C

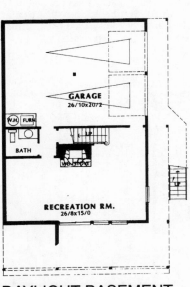

DAYLIGHT BASEMENT

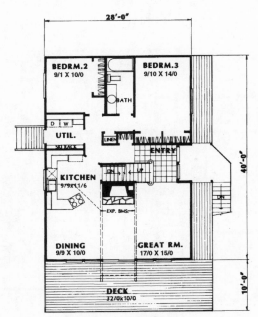

MAIN FLOOR

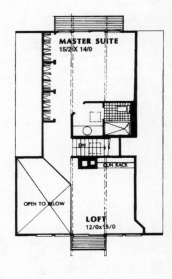

UPPER FLOOR

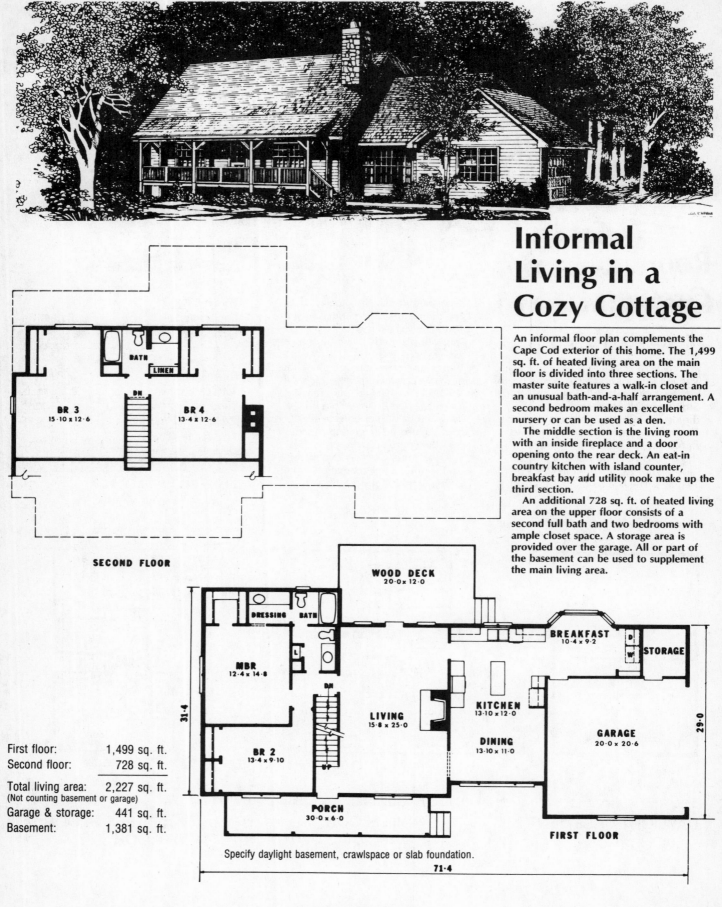

Informal Living in a Cozy Cottage

An informal floor plan complements the Cape Cod exterior of this home. The 1,499 sq. ft. of heated living area on the main floor is divided into three sections. The master suite features a walk-in closet and an unusual bath-and-a-half arrangement. A second bedroom makes an excellent nursery or can be used as a den.

The middle section is the living room with an inside fireplace and a door opening onto the rear deck. An eat-in country kitchen with island counter, breakfast bay and utility nook make up the third section.

An additional 728 sq. ft. of heated living area on the upper floor consists of a second full bath and two bedrooms with ample closet space. A storage area is provided over the garage. All or part of the basement can be used to supplement the main living area.

SECOND FLOOR

BATH
LINEN
BR 3 15·10 x 12·6
DN
BR 4 13·4 x 12·6

FIRST FLOOR

WOOD DECK 20·0 x 12·0
DRESSING BATH
MBR 12·4 x 14·8
BREAKFAST 10·4 x 9·2
STORAGE
KITCHEN 13·10 x 12·0
GARAGE 20·0 x 20·6
LIVING 15·8 x 25·0
DINING 13·10 x 11·0
BR 2 13·4 x 9·10
DN / UP
PORCH 30·0 x 6·0
31·4
29·0
71·4

First floor:	1,499 sq. ft.
Second floor:	728 sq. ft.
Total living area: (Not counting basement or garage)	2,227 sq. ft.
Garage & storage:	441 sq. ft.
Basement:	1,381 sq. ft.

Specify daylight basement, crawlspace or slab foundation.

Blueprint Price Code C
Plan C-8030

Room for a Growing Family

- Suitable for a narrow lot, this stylish home may have two, three or four bedrooms, depending on the needs of your family.
- The living room boasts a 13-ft.-high vaulted ceiling and a large bay window. Striking columns set off the formal dining room.
- The spacious family room features a handsome fireplace and a ceiling that vaults to 17 feet. Sliding glass doors provide access to an inviting deck.
- The efficiently designed kitchen offers an angled serving counter, a handy pantry and a sunny breakfast nook.
- A 10-ft. tray ceiling and private deck access highlight the master suite, which also includes his-and-hers closets and an opulent spa bath.
- A second bedroom is found upstairs, along with a nice loft that overlooks the family room and could serve as a third bedroom. The unfinished bonus room may be completed later as a fourth bedroom, a playroom or a home office.

Plan B-92001	
Bedrooms: 2+	**Baths: 2½**
Living Area:	
Upper floor	522 sq. ft.
Main floor	1,750 sq. ft.
Total Living Area:	**2,272 sq. ft.**
Bonus room (unfinished)	207 sq. ft.
Standard basement	1,750 sq. ft.
Garage	406 sq. ft.
Exterior Wall Framing:	2x6

Foundation Options:

Standard basement

(All plans can be built with your choice of foundation and framing. A generic conversion diagram is available. See order form.)

BLUEPRINT PRICE CODE:	**C**

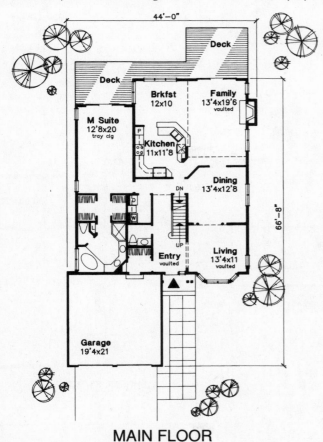

MAIN FLOOR

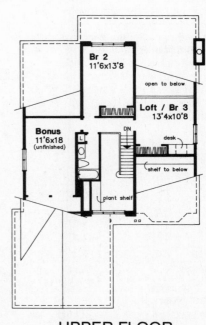

UPPER FLOOR

Classy Contemporary

- Steep rooflines accented by diagonal wood siding and tall windows give this home dramatic curb appeal.
- Inside, visitors are greeted by a view of the living room, with its 14½-ft. vaulted ceiling and inviting fireplace.
- The dining room is enhanced by a 12-ft. vaulted ceiling.
- The gourmet kitchen area flaunts an eating bar, a writing desk, a large recessed lighting panel, and a large utility room with a pantry.
- The adjacent breakfast nook offers access to the outdoors through lovely French doors.
- Brightened by three beautiful windows, the family room features a woodstove centered on a brick wall. The quiet den could double as an extra bedroom.
- Upstairs, the master suite is graced with a large window, a walk-in closet, a dressing area and a skylighted bath with a sunken tub.
- A hall bath serves the remaining two bedrooms.

Plans P-7627-4A & -4D

Bedrooms: 3+	Baths: 3
Living Area:	
Upper floor	900 sq. ft.
Main floor	1,389 sq. ft.
Total Living Area:	**2,289 sq. ft.**
Daylight basement	1,389 sq. ft.
Garage	462 sq. ft.
Exterior Wall Framing:	2x4
Foundation Options:	**Plan #**
Daylight basement	P-7627-4D
Crawlspace	P-7627-4A

(All plans can be built with your choice of foundation and framing. A generic conversion diagram is available. See order form.)

BLUEPRINT PRICE CODE: C

UPPER FLOOR

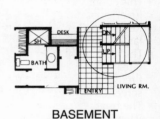

BASEMENT STAIRWAY LOCATION

MAIN FLOOR

TO ORDER THIS BLUEPRINT, CALL TOLL-FREE 1-800-547-5570

Plans P-7627-4A & -4D

PRICES AND DETAILS ON PAGES 12-15

Luxurious Country Home

- This country cottage hosts many luxuries, such as an expansive Great Room, good-sized sleeping areas and a large screened back porch.
- The rustic front porch opens into the Great Room, which offers a handsome fireplace and access to the large screened back porch.
- The bright kitchen features a huge work island, and unfolds to both the formal dining room and the breakfast bay. A handy laundry closet and access to the garage are also offered.
- The removed master suite has views of the front porch and offers a private bath with two walk-in closets, a dual-sink vanity, a spa tub and a separate shower.
- Upstairs are two oversized bedrooms, each with a dressing room that accesses a common bath.

Plan C-8535

Bedrooms: 3	Baths: 2½
Living Area:	
Upper floor	765 sq. ft.
Main floor	1,535 sq. ft.
Total Living Area:	**2,300 sq. ft.**
Daylight basement	1,535 sq. ft.
Garage	424 sq. ft.
Exterior Wall Framing:	2x4

Foundation Options:

Daylight basement

(All plans can be built with your choice of foundation and framing. A generic conversion diagram is available. See order form.)

BLUEPRINT PRICE CODE:	**C**

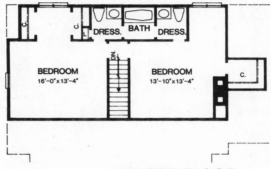

UPPER FLOOR

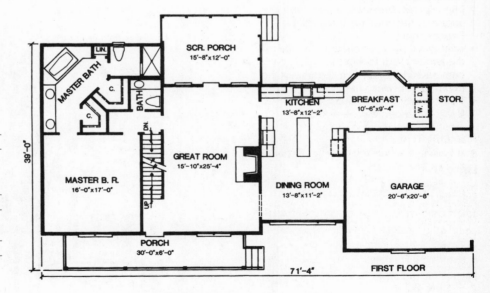

MAIN FLOOR

Grand Colonial Home

- This grand Colonial home boasts a porch entry framed by bay windows and gable towers.
- The two-story foyer flows to the dining room on the left and adjoins the bayed living room on the right, with its warm fireplace and flanking windows.
- At the rear, the family room features a 17-ft. ceiling, a media wall, a bar and terrace access through French doors.
- Connected to the family room is a high-tech kitchen with an island work area, a pantry, a work desk and a circular dinette.
- A private terrace, a romantic fireplace, a huge walk-in closet and a lavish bath with a whirlpool tub are featured in the main-floor master suite.
- Three bedrooms and two full baths share the upper floor.

Plan AHP-9120

Bedrooms: 4	**Baths:** 3
Living Area:	
Upper floor	776 sq. ft.
Main floor	1,551 sq. ft.
Total Living Area:	**2,327 sq. ft.**
Standard basement	1,580 sq. ft.
Garage	440 sq. ft.
Exterior Wall Framing:	2x4 or 2x6

Foundation Options:

Standard basement
Crawlspace
Slab
(All plans can be built with your choice of foundation and framing. A generic conversion diagram is available. See order form.)

BLUEPRINT PRICE CODE:	C

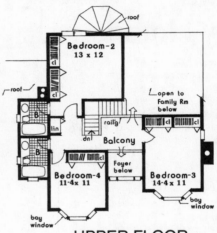

UPPER FLOOR

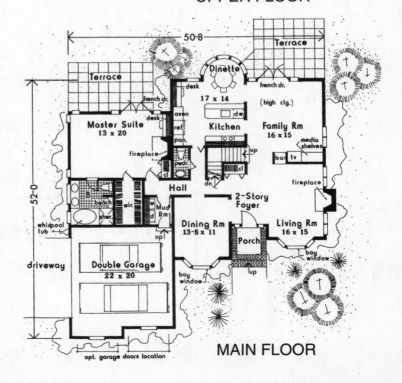

MAIN FLOOR

Plan AHP-9120

Magnificent Country Kitchen

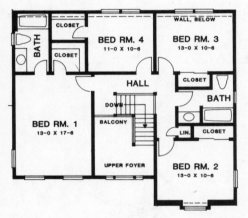

UPPER FLOOR

- Featuring ever-popular traditional design elements, this design offers a stunning interior loaded with amenities and space.
- A magnificent country kitchen includes a dinette area, work island, pantry and built-in desk.
- The combined formal living/dining area makes a spacious area for entertaining.
- For a more casual living area, the large family room includes a cozy fireplace, cathedral ceiling and a view to the back yard.
- A study off the two-story high foyer makes a great home office, guest room or den.
- A handy mudroom in the garage entry includes a utility area and half-bath.
- Upstairs, a large master suite includes a private bath and large closet.
- Three secondary bedrooms share another full bath and the upper hallway includes a balcony overlook into the entry below.

Plan A-2165-DS

Bedrooms: 4	Baths: 2½

Space:

Upper floor:	980 sq. ft.
Main floor:	1,362 sq. ft.
Total living area:	**2,342 sq. ft.**
Basement:	approx. 1,362 sq. ft.
Garage:	484 sq. ft.

Exterior Wall Framing:	2x4

Foundation options:
Standard basement only.
(Foundation & framing conversion diagram available — see order form.)

Blueprint Price Code:	C

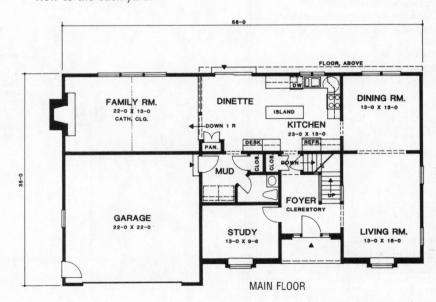

MAIN FLOOR

Loaded with Livability

- The attractive exterior of this home packages a marvelous floor plan that provides the utmost in livability.
- The gorgeous entry sports a 17-ft.-high vaulted ceiling. A 12-ft. vaulted ceiling presides over the spacious living room, which is enhanced by a dramatic boxed-out window. The adjoining dining room opens to a delightful covered patio.
- The kitchen features an island cooktop, a bright angled sink and a sunny nook that accesses another patio. A woodstove in the family room radiates warmth to the entire area.
- A half-bath, laundry facilities and garage access are nearby.
- Upstairs, the sumptuous master suite includes a deluxe bath and a large wardrobe closet.
- Two secondary bedrooms share a compartmentalized bath. A large bonus room above the garage offers a myriad of possible uses.

Plan R-2111

Bedrooms: 3+	Baths: 2½
Living Area:	
Upper floor	945 sq. ft.
Main floor	1,115 sq. ft.
Bonus room	285 sq. ft.
Total Living Area:	**2,345 sq. ft.**
Garage	851 sq. ft.
Exterior Wall Framing:	2x6

Foundation Options:

Crawlspace

(All plans can be built with your choice of foundation and framing. A generic conversion diagram is available. See order form.)

BLUEPRINT PRICE CODE: C

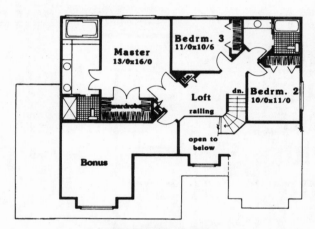

UPPER FLOOR

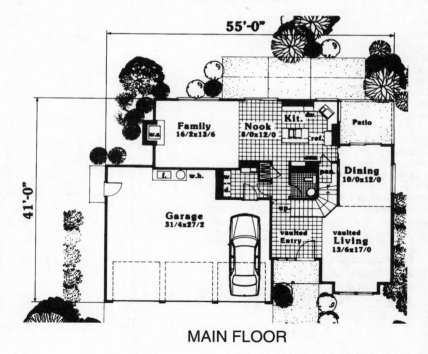

MAIN FLOOR

TO ORDER THIS BLUEPRINT, CALL TOLL-FREE 1-800-547-5570

Plan R-2111

PRICES AND DETAILS ON PAGES 12-15

Time-Tested Traditional Includes Deluxe Master Suite

This 2,360 square foot traditional design features a master suite with a walk-in closet as well as a deluxe compartmentalized bath with another walk-in closet, linen closet, double vanity, vaulted ceiling, large glass area, garden tub and separate shower stall. Two additional bedrooms with ample closets and a second full bath and linen closet are included on the 1,146 square foot upper floor.

The formal foyer is flanked by a dining room on one side and a study on the other. Behind the dining room is a U-shaped kitchen with breakfast bay. Double doors onto the rear patio, a raised-hearth fireplace, a half bath and a coat closet are included in the living room. The large utility room behind the garage completes the 1,214 square foot mainfloor.

Multi-paned windows, shutters, lap siding and a formal entrance combine for a traditional exterior.

First floor:	1,214 sq. ft.
Second floor:	1,146 sq. ft.
Total living area:	2,360 sq. ft.
(Not counting basement or garage)	

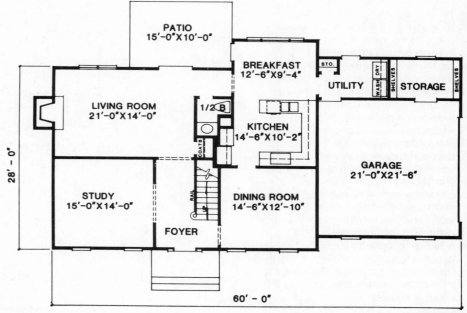

FIRST FLOOR

Specify daylight basement or crawlspace foundation.

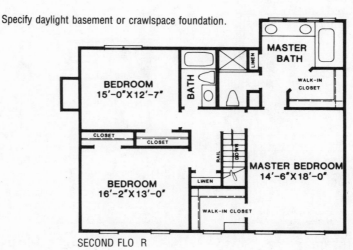

SECOND FLOOR

Blueprint Price Code C

Plan C-8350

One More Time!

- The character and excitement of our most popular plan in recent years, E-3000, has been recaptured in this smaller version of the design.
- The appealing facade is distinguished by a covered front porch accented with decorative columns, triple dormers and rail-topped corner windows.
- Off the foyer, a central gallery leads to the spacious family room, where a corner fireplace and a 17-ft. vaulted ceiling are found. Columns in the gallery introduce the kitchen and the dining areas.
- The kitchen showcases a walk-in pantry, a built-in desk and a long snack bar that serves the eating nook and the dining room.
- The stunning main-floor master suite offers a quiet sitting area and a private angled bath with dual vanities, a corner garden tub and a separate shower.
- A sweeping open stairway leads to a balcony that overlooks the family room. Two large bedrooms, a split bath and easy-to-access attic storage space are also found upstairs.

Plan E-2307-A

Bedrooms: 3	Baths: 2½
Living Area:	
Upper floor	595 sq. ft.
Main floor	1,765 sq. ft.
Total Living Area:	**2,360 sq. ft.**
Standard basement	1,765 sq. ft.
Garage	484 sq. ft.
Storage	44 sq. ft.
Exterior Wall Framing:	2x6

Foundation Options:
Standard basement
Crawlspace
Slab
(All plans can be built with your choice of foundation and framing. A generic conversion diagram is available. See order form.)

BLUEPRINT PRICE CODE: C

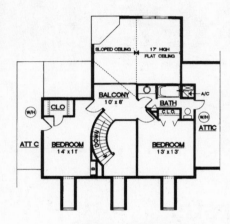

UPPER FLOOR

MAIN FLOOR

TO ORDER THIS BLUEPRINT,
CALL TOLL-FREE 1-800-547-5570

Plan E-2307-A

PRICES AND DETAILS
ON PAGES 12-15

Great Spaces

- The dynamic exterior of this unique home includes an eye-catching arched window and a cutout in the roof above the covered walkway.
- The impressive entry features a dramatic 15½-ft. vaulted ceiling and opens to the stunning sunken Great Room. A 9-ft. ceiling with wood beams and floor-to-ceiling windows enhance the sunken Great Room. A warm woodstove with a built-in wood bin and a nearby wet bar are other attractions found here.
- The skylighted kitchen offers a convenient snack bar, a greenhouse sink and an adjoining breakfast area.
- The main-floor master suite boasts a large walk-in closet, a private bath with a garden tub and private access to a covered patio or deck.
- A balcony hall upstairs leads to two more bedrooms and another bath.

Plan LRD-22884

Bedrooms: 3	**Baths:** 2½
Living Area:	
Upper floor	674 sq. ft.
Main floor	1,686 sq. ft.
Total Living Area:	**2,360 sq. ft.**
Standard basement	1,686 sq. ft.
Garage	450 sq. ft.
Exterior Wall Framing:	2x6

Foundation Options:

Standard basement

Crawlspace

(All plans can be built with your choice of foundation and framing. A generic conversion diagram is available. See order form.)

BLUEPRINT PRICE CODE:	C

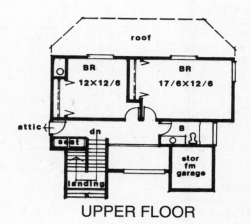

UPPER FLOOR

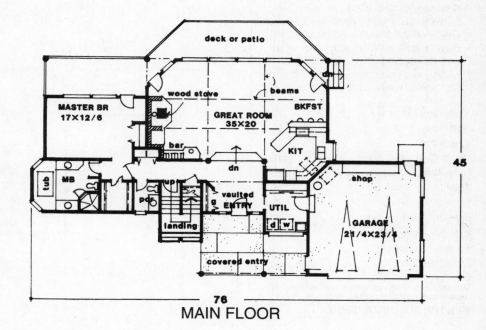

MAIN FLOOR

Arched Accents

- Elegant exterior arches add drama to the covered porch of this lovely home.
- Once inside, interior arches flank the two-story-high foyer, offering eye-catching entrances to the formal dining room and the intimate living room.
- A dramatic window-framed fireplace and a 17-ft. ceiling enhance the spacious family room. A columned archway leads into the island kitchen, which offers a convenient serving bar.
- The adjoining breakfast area features a pantry closet, open shelves and a French door to the backyard. A half-bath and a laundry room are close by.
- The ceilings in all main-floor rooms are 9 ft. high unless otherwise specified.
- Upstairs, a balcony overlooks the family room and the foyer below. The master bedroom flaunts a 10-ft. tray ceiling, a beautiful window showpiece and a private bath with 13-ft. vaulted ceiling and a garden tub. The bedroom may be extended to include a sitting area.
- Boasting its own dressing vanity, the rear-facing bedroom offers private access to a compartmentalized bath that also serves the two remaining bedrooms.

Plan FB-2368

Bedrooms: 4	Baths: 2½
Living Area:	
Upper floor	1,168 sq. ft.
Main floor	1,200 sq. ft.
Total Living Area:	**2,368 sq. ft.**
Daylight basement	1,200 sq. ft.
Garage	504 sq. ft.
Exterior Wall Framing:	2x4

Foundation Options:
Daylight basement
Slab
(All plans can be built with your choice of foundation and framing. A generic conversion diagram is available. See order form.)

BLUEPRINT PRICE CODE: C

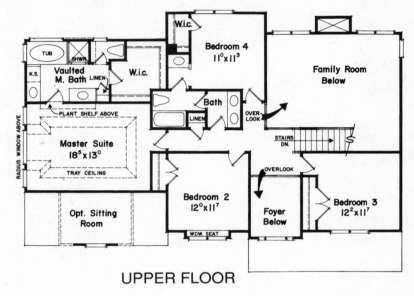

UPPER FLOOR

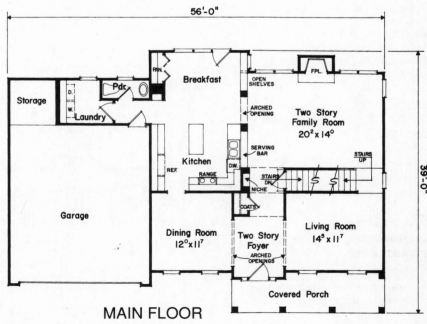

MAIN FLOOR

Plan FB-2368

PRICES AND DETAILS ON PAGES 292-295

Spacious Kitchen/Family Room Area

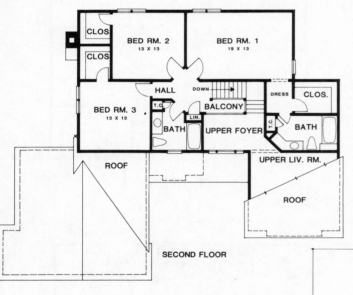

CLOS
CLOS
BED RM. 2
13 X 13
BED RM. 1
19 X 13
HALL
DOWN
CLOS.
BALCONY
DRESS
BED RM. 3
13 X 13
T.C.
T.C.
BATH
LIN.
UPPER FOYER
BATH
ROOF
UPPER LIV. RM.
ROOF

SECOND FLOOR

PLAN A-2181-DS
WITH BASEMENT

First floor:	1,356 sq. ft.
Second floor:	1,015 sq. ft.
Total living area:	2,371 sq. ft.

(Not counting basement or garage)

59-0

FAMILY RM.
13 X 18
DINETTE
KITCHEN
13 X 20
DW
DESK
REFR.
PAN.
CLOS.
B.C.
DOWN
UP
CLOS.
DINING RM.
13 X 13
MUD
CLOS
BALCONY
FOYER
DOWN
LAUN.
STUDY
10 X 11
DOWN
PORCH
VAULTED CLG.
48-0
GARAGE
22 X 22
LIVING RM.
16 X 14
ONE STEP DOWN

FIRST FLOOR

Blueprint Price Code C

Plan A-2181-DS

TO ORDER THIS BLUEPRINT,
CALL TOLL-FREE 1-800-547-5570

PRICES AND DETAILS
ON PAGES 12-15   **127**

Dignified and Stately

- Decorative corner quoins and a symmetrical hip roofline give a distinct European flavor to this dignified and stately brick home.
- Brightened by a high window, the two-story foyer bridges the formal dining room and living room and unfolds to the informal living areas at the rear.
- The spacious sunken family room has a large bay window and a cozy fireplace. An open rail separates the family room from the dinette and the island kitchen.
- The dinette's sliding glass doors open to the backyard and let the sun shine in. A pantry is convenient to the kitchen, as are a nice-sized laundry room and a powder room.
- Upstairs, the master suite boasts a walk-in closet and a separate dressing area with a vanity. The private bath has a garden tub and a towel closet.
- Three additional bathrooms share a second full bath. The balcony area overlooks the foyer below.

Plan A-2166-DS

Bedrooms: 4	Baths: 2½
Living Area:	
Upper floor	1,156 sq. ft.
Main floor	1,224 sq. ft.
Total Living Area:	**2,380 sq. ft.**
Standard basement	1,224 sq. ft.
Garage	484 sq. ft.
Exterior Wall Framing:	**2x4**

Foundation Options:

Standard basement

(All plans can be built with your choice of foundation and framing. A generic conversion diagram is available. See order form.)

BLUEPRINT PRICE CODE:	**C**

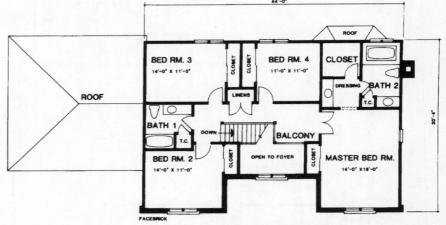

UPPER FLOOR

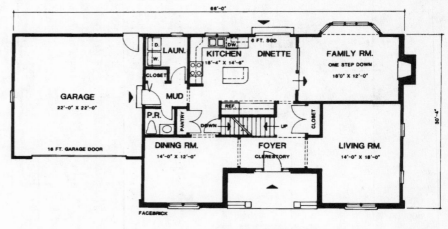

MAIN FLOOR

Plan A-2166-DS

A Glorious Blend of New and Old

This three-bedroom, two and one-half-bath home is a glorious blend of contemporary and traditional lines. Inside, its 2,035 sq. ft. are wisely distributed among amply proportioned, practically appointed rooms. A vaulted entry gives way to a second reception area bordering on a broad, vaulted living room nearly 20' long.

With its walls of windows overlooking the back yard, this grand room's centerpiece is a massive woodstove, whose central location contributes extra energy efficiency to the home — upstairs as well as down. The dining room offers quiet separation from the living room, while still enjoying the warmth from its woodstove. Its sliding door accesses a large wraparound covered patio to create a cool, shady refuge.

For sun-seeking, another wraparound patio at the front is fenced but uncovered, and elegantly accessed by double doors from a well-lighted, vaulted nook.

Placed conveniently between the two dining areas is a kitchen with all the trimmings: pantry, large sink window, and an expansive breakfast bar.

A stylish upstairs landing overlooks the living room on one side and the entry on the other, and leads to a master suite that rambles over fully half of the second floor.

Adjacent to the huge bedroom area is a spacious dressing area bordered by an abundance of closet space and a double-sink bath area. Unusual extras include walk-in wardrobe in the third bedroom and the long double-sink counter in the second upstairs bath.

Note also the exceptional abundance of closet space on both floors, and the separate utility room that also serves as a clean-up room connecting with the garage.

Upper floor:	1,085 sq. ft.
Main floor:	950 sq. ft.
Total living area: (Not counting basement or garage)	**2,035 sq. ft.**

Upper Floor

MASTER SUITE
17/8x15/8

OPEN TO LIVING BELOW

RAILING

DRESSING

DN

LIN

BATH

TUB

RAILING

SHWR

OPEN TO ENTRY BELOW

LIN

LIN

BATH

BEDRM. 3
10/6x12/8

BEDRM. 2
10/6x13/2

UPPER FLOOR

PLAN P-6597-2A
WITHOUT BASEMENT
(CRAWLSPACE FOUNDATION)

PLAN P-6597-2D
(WITH DAYLIGHT BASEMENT)

UP
DN

Main Floor

40'0"

54'0"

PATIO

BUILDING LINE ABOVE

VAULTED LIVING RM.
19/4x17/4

WOODSTOVE

DINING
12/0x10/0

CEILING LINE

OPEN

UP

KITCHEN
12/5x12/0

OV

DW

REF

PANTRY

BAR

VAULTED ENTRY

D
W

UTILITY

BATH

WH

F

VAULTED NOOK
40/0x11/0

GARAGE
21/4x28/0

PATIO

MAIN FLOOR

Plans P-6597-2A & -2D

PRICES AND DETAILS
ON PAGES 12-15

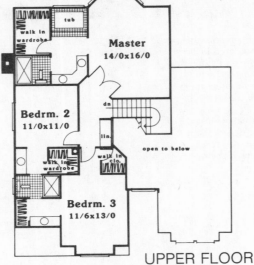

UPPER FLOOR

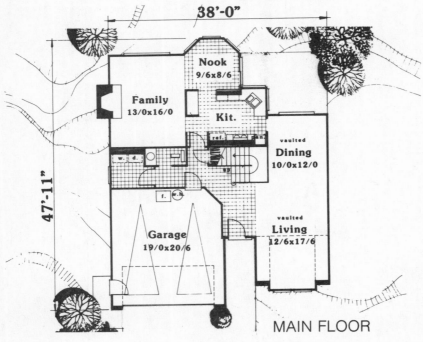

MAIN FLOOR

Spacious Narrow-Lot Design

- Soaring vaults and open living areas add to this spacious narrow-lot design.
- Sunlight streams through the many windows in the kitchen, nook and family room. This casual area boasts a pantry, a corner sink, a large fireplace, a bayed eating area and sliders to the backyard.
- Upstairs, all three bedrooms have walk-in closets. The master suite features a bayed sitting area and a luxurious bath. The remaining bedrooms share a connecting bath.

Plan R-2052

Bedrooms: 3	**Baths:** 2½
Living Area:	
Upper floor	974 sq. ft.
Main floor	1,078 sq. ft.
Total Living Area:	**2,052 sq. ft.**
Garage	387 sq. ft.
Exterior Wall Framing:	2x6
Foundation Options:	
Crawlspace	
(Typical foundation & framing conversion diagram available—see order form.)	
BLUEPRINT PRICE CODE:	**C**

TO ORDER THIS BLUEPRINT, CALL TOLL-FREE 1-800-547-5570

Plan R-2052

PRICES AND DETAILS ON PAGES 12-15

Photo by Mark Englund/HomeStyles

UPPER FLOOR

GREAT ROOM BELOW

BR 11/6 X 10/6

LIMITED STOR

STR

BALCONY

OPEN TO FOYER

DEN 10 X 11/6

BR 10/6 X 11/6

BATH

S

D

**NOTE: The above photographed home may have been modified by the homeowner. Please refer to floor plan and/or drawn elevation shown for actual blueprint details.

MAIN FLOOR

HOT TUB

DECK

VAULTED MBR 17/6 X 13/6

VAULTED GREAT ROOM 19 X 15/6 AVG

DINE 12/6 X 12

WI CLO

WI CLO

MB

FOYER

UTIL

KIT

P

L

W D

R

GARAGE 23/6 X 23/6

52'

50'

Vaulted Great Room

- While the exterior has traditional overtones, this plan is thoroughly modern both inside and out.
- The vaulted Great Room with adjacent kitchen and dining room gives the home an open and spacious feeling.
- The vaulted master suite on the first floor includes walk-in closets and a sumptuous master bath.
- The upper floor includes two more bedrooms, which share a continental bath.
- Also note the den and balcony overlooking the foyer and Great Room below.
- A huge deck with a hot tub can be reached easily from the master suite, the Great Room or the dining room.

Plan S-2100

Bedrooms: 3	Baths: 2½
Living Area:	
Upper floor:	660 sq. ft.
Main floor	1,440 sq. ft.
Total Living Area:	**2,100 sq. ft.**
Standard basement	1,440 sq. ft.
Garage	552 sq. ft.
Exterior Wall Framing:	2x6

Foundation Options:
Standard basement
Crawlspace
Slab
(Typical foundation & framing conversion diagram available—see order form.)

BLUEPRINT PRICE CODE:	C

Alluring Two-Story

- This dramatic contemporary is adorned with staggered rooflines that overlap and outline large expanses of glass.
- The interior features a floor plan that is both practical and functional, with individual rooms equally exciting.
- Flanking the two-story-high foyer are a formal dining room and a sunken living room. The living room boasts a cathedral ceiling and unfolds to a sunken family room with a fireplace and a patio overlook.
- A bright breakfast area and a U-shaped kitchen adjoin the family room.
- The second level features a spacious master bedroom with dual closets and a private bath. Two secondary bedrooms, another bath and an optional expansion room above the garage are also included.

Plan AX-8596-A

Bedrooms: 3+	Baths: 2½
Living Area:	
Upper floor	738 sq. ft.
Main floor	1,160 sq. ft.
Bonus room	226 sq. ft.
Total Living Area:	**2,124 sq. ft.**
Standard basement	1,160 sq. ft.
Garage	465 sq. ft.
Exterior Wall Framing:	2x4

Foundation Options:

Standard basement

(All plans can be built with your choice of foundation and framing. A generic conversion diagram is available. See order form.)

BLUEPRINT PRICE CODE:	C

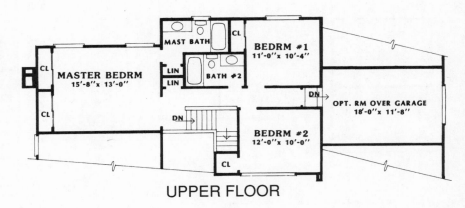

UPPER FLOOR

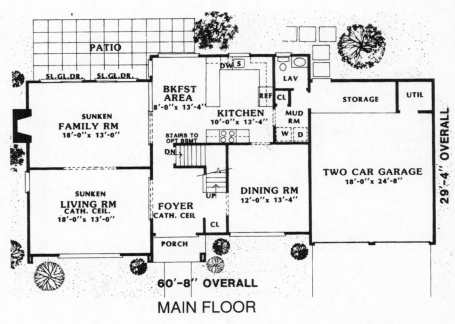

MAIN FLOOR

Today's Tradition

- The traditional two-story design is brought up to today's standards with this exciting new design.
- The front half of the main floor is devoted to formal entertaining. The living and dining rooms offer symmetrical bay windows overlooking the wrap-around front porch.
- The informal living zone faces the rear deck and yard. It includes a family room with fireplace and beamed ceiling as well as a modern kitchen with cooktop island and snack bar.
- There are four large bedrooms and two full baths on the upper sleeping level.

Plan AGH-2143

Bedrooms: 4	Baths: 2½
Space:	
Upper floor:	1,047 sq. ft.
Main floor:	1,096 sq. ft.
Total living area:	**2,143 sq. ft.**
Daylight basement:	1,096 sq. ft.
Garage:	852 sq. ft.
Exterior Wall Framing:	**2x6**

Foundation options:
Daylight basement.
(Foundation & framing conversion diagram available — see order form.)

Blueprint Price Code: C

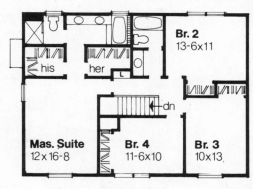

UPPER FLOOR

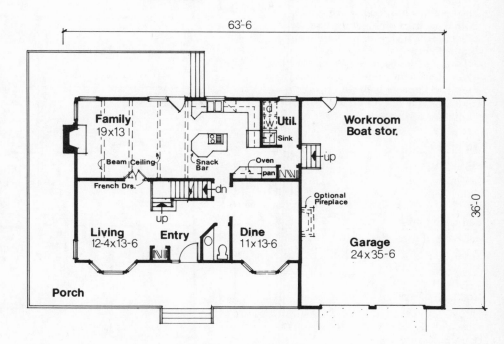

MAIN FLOOR

Colonial with a Contemporary Touch

- Open, flowing rooms highlighted by a two-story round-top window combine to give this colonial design a contemporary, today touch.
- To the left of the elegant, two-story foyer lies the living room, which flows into the rear-facing family room with fireplace.
- The centrally located kitchen serves both the formal dining room and the dinette, with a view of the family room beyond.
- All four bedrooms are located upstairs. The master suite includes a walk-in closet and private bath with double vanities, separate shower and whirlpool tub under skylights.

Plan AHP-9020	
Bedrooms: 4	**Baths:** 2 ½
Space:	
Upper floor	1,021 sq. ft.
Main floor	1,125 sq. ft.
Total Living Area	**2,146 sq. ft.**
Basement	1,032 sq. ft.
Garage	480 sq. ft.
Exterior Wall Framing	**2x6**

Foundation options:
Standard Basement
Slab
(Foundation & framing conversion diagram available—see order form.)

Blueprint Price Code	**C**

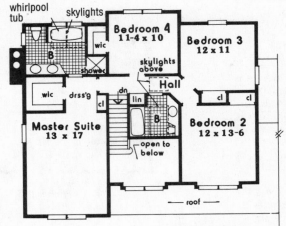

UPPER FLOOR

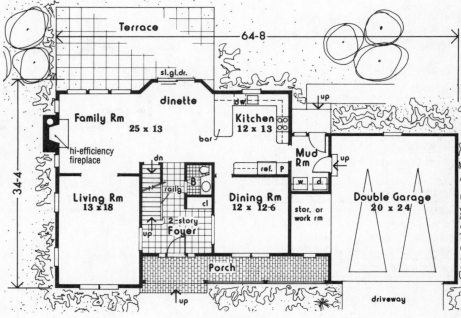

MAIN FLOOR

TO ORDER THIS BLUEPRINT, CALL TOLL-FREE 1-800-547-5570   Plan AHP-9020   **PRICES AND DETAILS ON PAGES 12-15**

Front Porch Invites Visitors

- This neat and well-proportioned design exudes warmth and charm.
- The roomy foyer connects the formal dining room and living room for special occasions, and the living and family rooms join together to create abundant space for large gatherings.
- The large kitchen, dinette and family room flow from one to the other for great casual family living.
- Upstairs, the roomy master suite is complemented by a master bath available in two configurations. The unique library is brightened by a beautiful arched window.

Plan GL-2161

Bedrooms: 3	**Baths:** 2½

Living Area:	
Upper floor	991 sq. ft.
Main floor	1,170 sq. ft.
Total Living Area	**2,161 sq. ft.**
Standard basement	1,170 sq. ft.
Garage	462 sq. ft.
Exterior Wall Framing	2x6

Foundation Options:

Standard basement

(All plans can be built with your choice of foundation and framing. A generic conversion diagram is available. See order form.)

BLUEPRINT PRICE CODE	C

UPPER FLOOR

OPT. MSTR. BATH

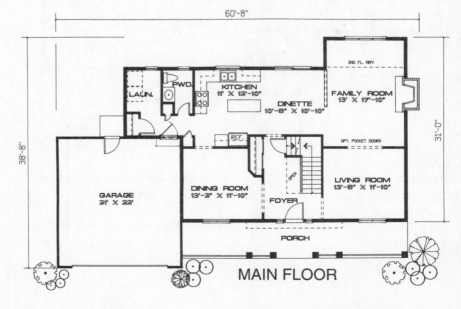

MAIN FLOOR

Country Kitchen and Deluxe Master Bath

- Front porch, dormers and shutters give this home a decidedly country look on the outside, which is complemented by an informal modern interior.
- The roomy country kitchen connects with a sunny breakfast nook and utility area on one hand and a formal dining room on the other.
- The central portion of the home consists of a large family room with a fireplace and easy access to a rear deck.
- The downstairs master suite is particularly impressive for a home of this size, a features a majestic master bath with two walk-in closets and double vanities.
- Upstairs, you will find two more ample-sized bedrooms, a double bath and a large storage area.

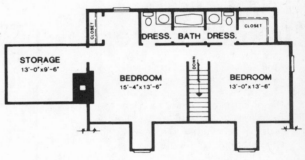

UPPER FLOOR

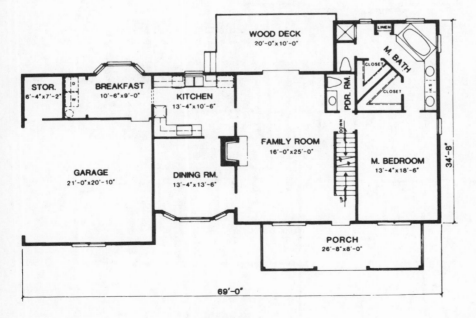

MAIN FLOOR

Plan C-8645

Bedrooms: 3	Baths: 2½

Living Area:	
Upper floor	704 sq. ft.
Main floor	1,477 sq. ft.

Total Living Area:	2,181 sq. ft.
Daylight basement	Approx. 1,400 sq. ft.
Garage	438 sq. ft.
Storage	123 sq. ft.

Exterior Wall Framing:	2x4

Foundation Options:
Daylight basement
Crawlspace
Slab
(Typical foundation & framing conversion diagram available—see order form.)

BLUEPRINT PRICE CODE:	C

Contemporary Elegance

- This striking contemporary design combines vertical siding with elegant traditional overtones.
- Inside, an expansive activity area is created with the joining of the vaulted living room, the family/dining room and the kitchen. The openness of the rooms creates a spacious, dramatic feeling, which extends to an exciting two-story sun space and a patio beyond.

- A convenient utility/service area near the garage includes a clothes-sorting counter, a deep sink and ironing space.
- Two main-floor bedrooms share a bright bath.
- The master suite includes a sumptuous skylighted bath with two entrances. The tub is uniquely positioned on an angled wall, while the shower and toilet are secluded behind a pocket door. An optional overlook provides views down into the sun space, which is accessed by a spiral staircase.
- A versatile loft area and a bonus room complete this design.

Plan LRD-1971

Bedrooms: 3+	**Baths:** 2
Living Area:	
Upper floor	723 sq. ft.
Main floor	1,248 sq. ft.
Sun space	116 sq. ft.
Bonus room	225 sq. ft.
Total Living Area:	**2,312 sq. ft.**
Standard basement	1,248 sq. ft.
Garage	483 sq. ft.
Exterior Wall Framing:	2x6

Foundation Options:

Standard basement
Crawlspace
(All plans can be built with your choice of foundation and framing. A generic conversion diagram is available. See order form.)

BLUEPRINT PRICE CODE: C

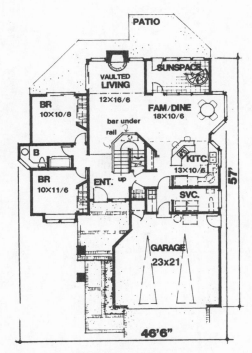

MAIN FLOOR

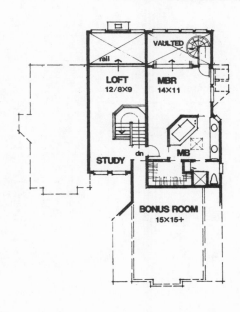

UPPER FLOOR

Fantastic Floor Plan!

- This is the famous house shown on the PBS "Hometime" television series.
- Impressive floor plan includes a deluxe master suite with a private courtyard, magnificent bath and large closet.
- The large island kitchen/nook combination includes a corner pantry and easy access to a rear deck.
- The spacious family room includes a fireplace and vaulted ceiling.
- The two upstairs bedrooms share a bath with double sinks.
- Note the convenient laundry room in the garage entry area.

Plan B-88015

Bedrooms: 3	Baths: 2½

Space:

Upper floor:	534 sq. ft.
Main floor:	1,689 sq. ft.

Total living area:	**2,223 sq. ft.**
Basement:	approx. 1,689 sq. ft.
Garage:	455 sq. ft.

Exterior Wall Framing:	2x4

Foundation options:
Standard basement only.
(Foundation & framing conversion diagram available — see order form.)

Blueprint Price Code:	C

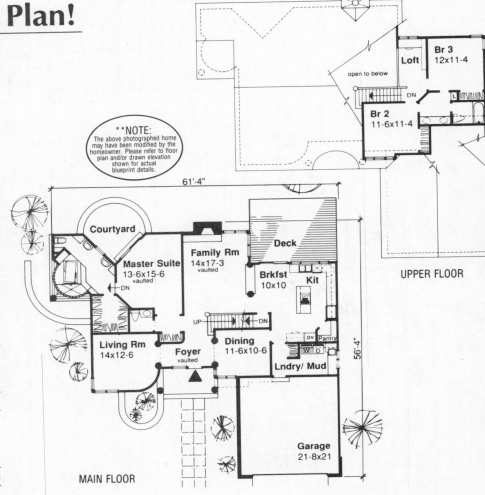

UPPER FLOOR

**NOTE:
The above photographed home may have been modified by the homeowner. Please refer to floor plan and/or drawn elevation shown for actual blueprint details.

MAIN FLOOR

Plan B-88015 **PRICES AND DETAILS**
ON PAGES 12-15

Affordable Country-Style

- This charming country-inspired home is economical to build and requires only a small lot.
- The powder room and the guest closet are conveniently located near the foyer and near the combination living/dining room with boxed-out window.
- A low partition visually separates the kitchen from the adjacent family room, which features an angled fireplace, a cathedral ceiling with skylight, and sliding glass doors that open to the rear yard.
- The second floor features an optional loft or fourth bedroom.

Plan AX-8923-A

Bedrooms: 3-4	Baths: 2½
Living Area:	
Upper floor	853 sq. ft.
Main floor	1,199 sq. ft.
Optional loft/bedroom	180 sq. ft.
Total Living Area:	**2,232 sq. ft.**
Standard basement	1,184 sq. ft.
Garage	420 sq. ft.
Exterior Wall Framing:	2x4

Foundation Options:
Standard basement
Slab
(Typical foundation & framing conversion diagram available—see order form.)

BLUEPRINT PRICE CODE:	C

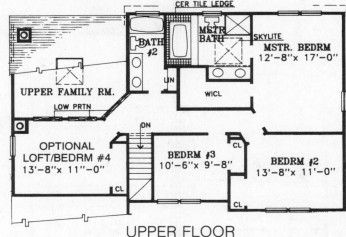

UPPER FLOOR

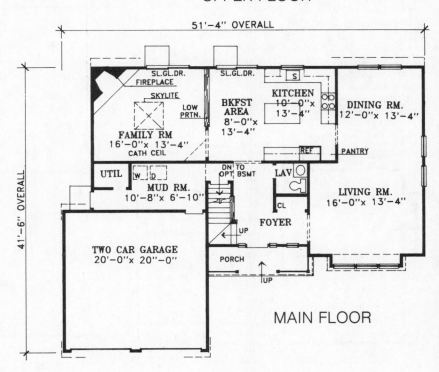

MAIN FLOOR

Distinctive Two-Story

- A playful and distinctive exterior invites you into a functional, contemporary interior.
- The sunken living room features a soaring cathedral ceiling open to the second floor balcony.
- The adjoining step-down family room is connected to allow for overflow and easy circulation of traffic.
- A luxurious master suite and room for three additional bedrooms are found on the second floor, with a dramatic balcony and a view of the foyer and the living room.

Plan AX-8922-A

Bedrooms: 3-4	Baths: 2½
Living Area:	
Upper floor	840 sq. ft.
Main floor	1,213 sq. ft.
Optional fourth bedroom	240 sq. ft.
Total Living Area:	**2,293 sq. ft.**
Standard basement	1,138 sq. ft.
Garage	470 sq. ft.
Exterior Wall Framing:	2x4

Foundation Options:
Standard basement
Slab
(Typical foundation & framing conversion diagram available—see order form.)

BLUEPRINT PRICE CODE: C

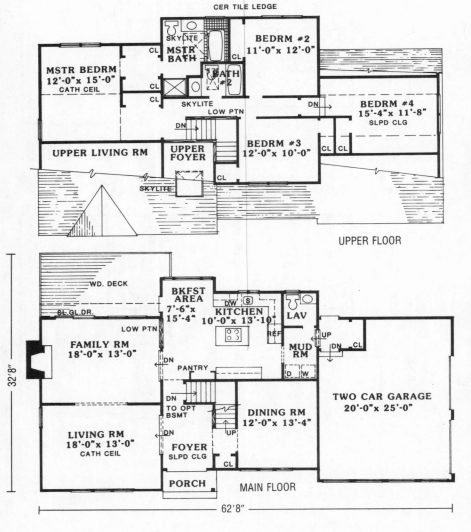

UPPER FLOOR

MAIN FLOOR

Charming Design for Hillside Site

- Split-level design puts living room on entry level, other rooms up or down a half-flight of steps.
- Kitchen includes work/eating island and combines with dining/family room for informal living.
- Vaulted master suite includes private bath and large closet.
- Daylight basement includes two bedrooms, bath, utility area and a rec room.

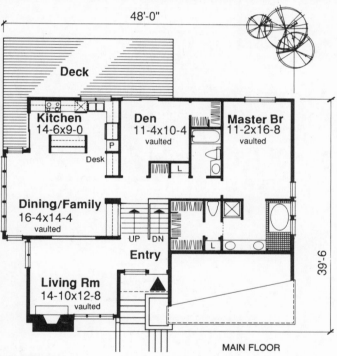

**NOTE: The above photographed home may have been modified by the homeowner. Please refer to floor plan and/or drawn elevation shown for actual blueprint details.

48'-0"

Deck

Kitchen 14-6x9-0

P

Desk

Den 11-4x10-4 vaulted

Master Br 11-2x16-8 vaulted

L

Dining/Family 16-4x14-4 vaulted

UP DN

Entry

Living Rm 14-10x12-8 vaulted

L

39'-6

MAIN FLOOR

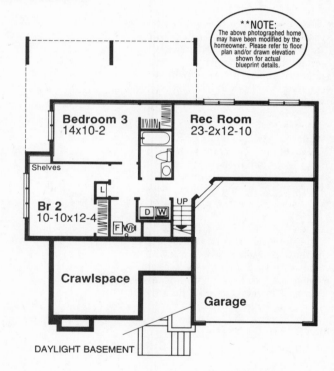

Bedroom 3 14x10-2

Rec Room 23-2x12-10

Shelves

L

Br 2 10-10x12-4

D W UP

F WH

Crawlspace

Garage

DAYLIGHT BASEMENT

Plan B-89037

Bedrooms: 3+	Baths: 3

Living Area:

Main floor	1,422 sq. ft.
Partial daylight basement	913 sq. ft.

Total Living Area:	**2,335 sq. ft.**
Garage	480 sq. ft.

Exterior Wall Framing:	2x6

Foundation Options:
Partial daylight basement
(Typical foundation & framing conversion diagram available—see order form.)

BLUEPRINT PRICE CODE:	**C**

TO ORDER THIS BLUEPRINT,
CALL TOLL-FREE 1-800-547-5570

Plan B-89037

PRICES AND DETAILS
ON PAGES 12-15
141

You Asked for It!

- Our most popular plan in recent years, E-3000, has now been downsized for affordability, without sacrificing character or excitement.
- Exterior appeal is created with a covered front porch with decorative columns, triple dormers and rail-topped bay windows.
- The floor plan has combined the separate living and family rooms available in E-3000 into one spacious family room with corner fireplace, which flows into the dining room through a columned gallery.
- The kitchen serves the breakfast room over an angled snack bar, and features a huge pantry.
- The stunning main-floor master suite offers a private sitting area, a walk-in closet and a dramatic, angled bath.
- There are two large bedrooms upstairs accessible via a curved staircase with bridge balcony.

Plan E-2307

Bedrooms: 3	Baths: 2½
Living Area:	
Upper floor	595 sq. ft.
Main floor	1,765 sq. ft.
Total Living Area:	**2,360 sq. ft.**
Standard basement	1,765 sq. ft.
Garage	484 sq. ft.
Storage	44 sq. ft.
Exterior Wall Framing:	2x6

Foundation Options:

Standard basement

Crawlspace

Slab

(All plans can be built with your choice of foundation and framing. A generic conversion diagram is available. See order form.)

BLUEPRINT PRICE CODE:	C

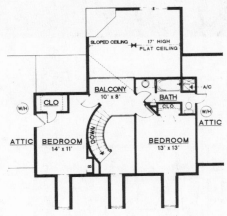

UPPER FLOOR

MAIN FLOOR

TO ORDER THIS BLUEPRINT, CALL TOLL-FREE 1-800-547-5570

Plan E-2307

PRICES AND DETAILS ON PAGES 12-15

Striking Countrypolitan Home

- An eye-catching exterior design encloses a modern interior to provide a great family plan for any setting.
- A pleasant covered porch leads into an entry which includes a half-bath and access to the stairs, dining room or hallway leading to the rest of the house.
- The large living room includes an impressive fireplace and a vaulted ceiling.
- The super country kitchen includes a work island and pantry, and is flanked by a large informal eating area, a formal dining room and a roomy utility area.
- The master bedroom suite is fit for a king and queen, with a deluxe bath and an entire wall of closets.

- Upstairs, three more bedrooms share another full bath and all have large closets.

UPPER FLOOR

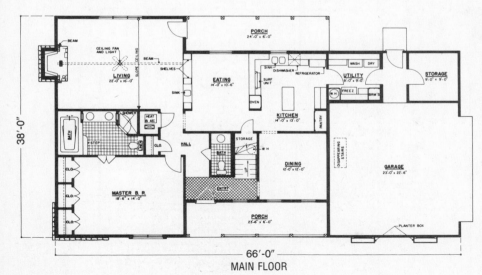

38'-0"

66'-0"

MAIN FLOOR

Plan E-2303

Bedrooms: 4	**Baths:** 2½
Space:	
Upper floor	814 sq. ft.
Main floor	1,553 sq. ft.
Total Living Area	**2,367 sq. ft.**
Basement	1,553 sq. ft.
Garage	517 sq. ft.
Storage	81 sq. ft.
Porches	285 sq. ft.
Exterior Wall Framing	2x6

Foundation options:
Standard Basement
Crawlspace
Slab
(Foundation & framing conversion diagram available—see order form.)

Blueprint Price Code	C

Photo by Mark Englund/HomeStyles

Classic Lines, Elegant Flair

- The rich brick arches and classic lines of this home lend an elegant air which will never be outdated.
- Inside, graceful archways lead from the vaulted entry to the living and dining rooms, which both feature heightened ceilings.
- The kitchen offers abundant counter space, an expansive window over the kitchen sink, large island, desk and pantry.
- The kitchen also is open to the nook and family room, which combine to make a great space for family living.
- The master suite is a pure delight, with a luxurious whirlpool tub and his-and-hers walk-in closets.
- The room marked for storage could also be an exercise or hobby room.

Plan R-2083	
Bedrooms: 3	**Baths:** 2½
Living Area:	
Upper floor	926 sq. ft.
Main floor	1,447 sq. ft.
Total Living Area:	**2,373 sq. ft.**
Garage	609 sq. ft.
Storage	138 sq. ft.
Exterior Wall Framing:	2x6
Foundation Options:	
Crawlspace (Typical foundation & framing conversion diagram available—see order form.)	
BLUEPRINT PRICE CODE:	C

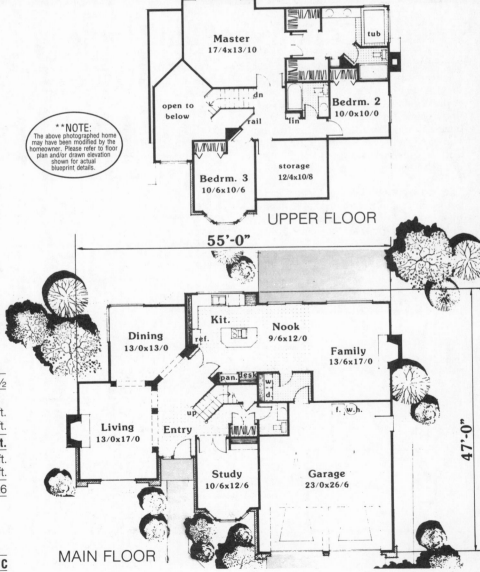

**NOTE: The above photographed home may have been modified by the homeowner. Please refer to floor plan and/or drawn elevation shown for actual blueprint details.

UPPER FLOOR

MAIN FLOOR

Plan R-2083

PRICES AND DETAILS ON PAGES 12-15

UPPER FLOOR

MAIN FLOOR

52'-0"

50'-0"

Plenty of Street Appeal

- This attractive home, with its painstaking attention to design detail, will be a pleasant addition to any neighborhood.

- The openness of the country kitchen establishes an expansive feeling that is echoed throughout the home.
- The vaulted living room and adjoining dining area make a great space for entertaining guests.
- A private den provides space for an office, guest room or library.
- The master suite includes a cozy sitting area, plus a private bath with double vanities, and a large closet.
- Two secondary upstairs bedrooms share a second full bath, and an upstairs sitting room/balcony overlooks the entry hall below.

Plan R-2108

Bedrooms: 3-4	Baths: 2½

Space:	
Upper floor:	1,048 sq. ft.
Main floor:	1,335 sq. ft.

Total living area:	2,383 sq. ft.
Bonus area:	445 sq. ft.
Garage:	652 sq. ft.

Exterior Wall Framing:	2x4

Foundation options:
Crawlspace only.
(Foundation & framing conversion diagram available — see order form.)

Blueprint Price Code:	C

Traditional Treat

- A covered front porch with ornamental columns and brackets provides a traditional treat on the exterior of this four-bedroom two-story home.
- Entering the front door, a dramatic view awaits guests of a vaulted foyer with double-back stairs leading up to a bridge overlook above.
- To the left of the foyer, through an arched, columned opening, lies the formal living room with fireplace and formal dining room beyond.
- To the right of the foyer is a double-doored den/guest room with built-in desk.
- The rear-facing family room opens to the island kitchen and breakfast nook.
- The four upstairs bedrooms include an exciting master suite with private bath highlighted by a spa tub.

UPPER FLOOR

Plan CDG-2026

Bedrooms: 4-5	Baths: 2½

Space:

Upper floor:	1,089 sq. ft.
Main floor:	1,295 sq. ft.

Total living area:	2,384 sq. ft.
Garage:	452 sq. ft.

Exterior Wall Framing:	2x4

Foundation options:
Crawlspace.
(Foundation & framing conversion diagram available — see order form.)

Blueprint Price Code:	C

MAIN FLOOR

Smooth Transitional

- An open floor plan and smooth lines punctuated with big windows give this transitional home its modern appeal.
- Illuminated by a large clerestory window, the inviting two-story-high entry flows into the living room.
- Enhanced by 12-ft.-high vaulted ceilings, the living and dining rooms are separated by a columned archway. All other main-floor rooms are expanded by 9-ft. ceilings.
- The adjacent island kitchen includes a sunny bay-windowed breakfast area, a pantry and a stylish angled counter.
- Warmed by a handsome fireplace, the spacious family room features a built-in media center and sliding glass doors to a backyard deck.
- Upstairs, the luxurious master bedroom boasts a bayed sitting area. The vaulted master bath has a spa tub, a sit-down shower and a dual-sink vanity.
- Two additional bedrooms share another full bath. The main-floor den can serve as a fourth bedroom, if needed.

Plan UDG-93004

Bedrooms: 3+	Baths: 3
Living Area:	
Upper floor	939 sq. ft.
Main floor	1,448 sq. ft.
Total Living Area:	**2,387 sq. ft.**
Standard basement	1,448 sq. ft.
Garage	420 sq. ft.
Exterior Wall Framing:	2x4

Foundation Options:

Standard basement

(All plans can be built with your choice of foundation and framing. A generic conversion diagram is available. See order form.)

BLUEPRINT PRICE CODE: C

UPPER FLOOR

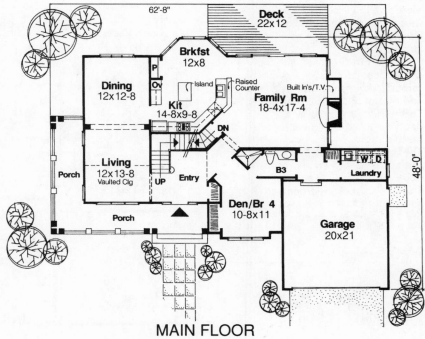

MAIN FLOOR

Spectacular Great Room!

- Open, light-filled spaces centered around a spectacular Great Room mark this updated traditional design.
- The tiled foyer opens to the dining room, which is defined by columns and an overhead plant shelf and enhanced by a 9½-ft.-high flat ceiling.
- The huge central Great Room features a wall of windows, a 17-ft.-high vaulted ceiling and a see-through fireplace with an adjacent wet bar. Sliding glass doors access a delightful deck.
- The kitchen offers a built-in desk, a large pantry, an angled snack bar and a gazebo-like breakfast nook.
- The master suite boasts a 9½-ft. ceiling and a spa bath that includes a separate shower and a huge walk-in closet.
- Double doors open to a quiet den or extra bedroom. The vaulted ceiling soars to a height of 12 ft. above a gorgeous arched window.
- An open, skylighted stairway leads to the upper floor, where two more bedrooms share another full bath.

Plan AG-2401

Bedrooms: 3+	Baths: 2½
Living Area:	
Upper floor	550 sq. ft.
Main floor	1,855 sq. ft.
Total Living Area:	**2,405 sq. ft.**
Standard basement	1,815 sq. ft.
Garage	441 sq. ft.
Exterior Wall Framing:	2x6
Foundation Options:	

Standard basement
(All plans can be built with your choice of foundation and framing. A generic conversion diagram is available. See order form.)

BLUEPRINT PRICE CODE:	C

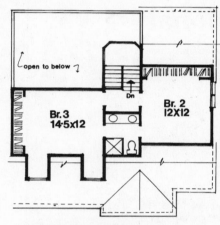

UPPER FLOOR

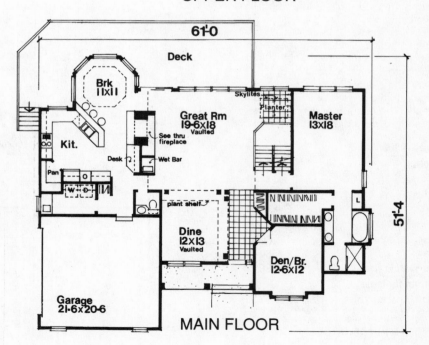

MAIN FLOOR

TO ORDER THIS BLUEPRINT, CALL TOLL-FREE 1-800-547-5570

Plan AG-2401

PRICES AND DETAILS ON PAGES 12-15

Dramatic Interior Spaces

- This home's design utilizes unique shapes and angles to create a dramatic and dynamic interior.
- Skylights brighten the impressive two-story entry from high above, as it flows to the formal living areas.
- The sunken Great Room features a massive stone-hearthed fireplace with flanking windows, plus a 19-ft. vaulted ceiling. Sliding glass doors open the formal dining room to a backyard patio.
- The spacious kitchen features an oversized island, plenty of counter space and a sunny breakfast nook.
- A den or third bedroom shares a full bath with another secondary bedroom to complete the main floor.
- An incredible bayed master suite takes up the entire upper floor of the home. The skylighted master bath features a bright walk-in closet, a dual-sink vanity, a sunken tub and a separate shower.

Plans P-6580-3A & -3D

Bedrooms: 2+	Baths: 2
Living Area:	
Upper floor	705 sq. ft.
Main floor	1,738 sq. ft.
Total Living Area:	**2,443 sq. ft.**
Daylight basement	1,738 sq. ft.
Garage	512 sq. ft.
Exterior Wall Framing:	2x4
Foundation Options:	Plan #
Daylight basement	P-6580-3D
Crawlspace	P-6580-3A

(All plans can be built with your choice of foundation and framing. A generic conversion diagram is available. See order form.)

BLUEPRINT PRICE CODE:	C

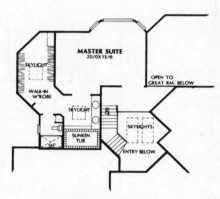

UPPER FLOOR

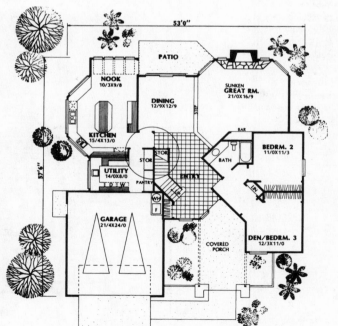

MAIN FLOOR

BASEMENT STAIRWAY LOCATION

Elegant Country Living

- Country elegance is found throughout this exciting two-story home.
- To the left of the central foyer, the living room and formal dining room combine to create a large entertainment area. An optional fireplace and rear bay window add flair.
- The spacious kitchen includes an island cooktop and a sunny bay-windowed breakfast area. A convenient main-floor laundry room and pantry are neatly positioned behind a half-bath.
- The huge sunken family room is open to the kitchen and features a 12-ft. vaulted ceiling, a dramatic fireplace, built-in storage space and outdoor access.
- Located at the front of the house is a quiet study that would make a great home office or extra bedroom.
- The large master suite on the upper floor has an 11-ft. vaulted ceiling, a walk-in closet and a skylighted bath.
- Two additional bedrooms and a second full bath complete the upper floor.

Plan CH-520-A

Bedrooms: 3+	Baths: 2½
Living Area:	
Upper floor	989 sq. ft.
Main floor	1,457 sq. ft.
Total Living Area:	**2,446 sq. ft.**
Basement	1,100 sq. ft.
Garage	455 sq. ft.
Exterior Wall Framing:	2x4

Foundation Options:

Daylight basement

Standard basement

Crawlspace

(All plans can be built with your choice of foundation and framing. A generic conversion diagram is available. See order form.)

BLUEPRINT PRICE CODE: C

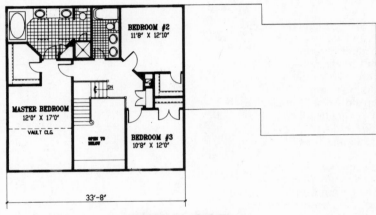

UPPER FLOOR

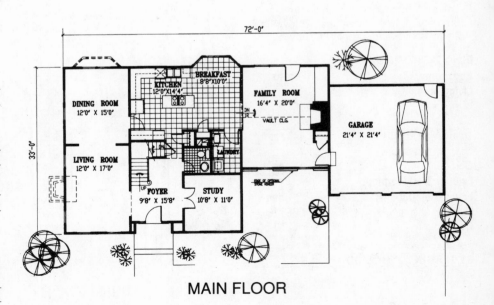

MAIN FLOOR

Plan CH-520-A

PRICES AND DETAILS
ON PAGES 12-15

Contemporary Colonial

- A Palladian window and a half-round window above the entry door give this Colonial a new look. Inside, the design maximizes space while creating an open, airy atmosphere.
- The two-story-high foyer flows between the formal areas at the front of the home. Straight ahead, the exciting family room features a built-in wet bar and a fireplace framed by French doors.
- A bay window brightens the adjoining breakfast nook and kitchen. An angled counter looks to the nook and the family room, keeping the cook in touch with the family activities.
- The four bedrooms on the upper floor include a luxurious master suite with an 11-ft. vaulted ceiling and a skylighted bathroom. The upper-floor laundry also makes this a great family home.
- The basement plan (not shown) has room for an optional den or bedroom, a recreation room with a fireplace, a storage room and a utility area.

Plan CH-320-A

Bedrooms: 4+	Baths: 3
Living Area:	
Upper floor	1,164 sq. ft.
Main floor	1,293 sq. ft.
Total Living Area:	**2,457 sq. ft.**
Basement	1,293 sq. ft.
Garage	462 sq. ft.
Exterior Wall Framing:	2x4

Foundation Options:

Daylight basement

Standard basement

Crawlspace

(All plans can be built with your choice of foundation and framing. A generic conversion diagram is available. See order form.)

BLUEPRINT PRICE CODE: C

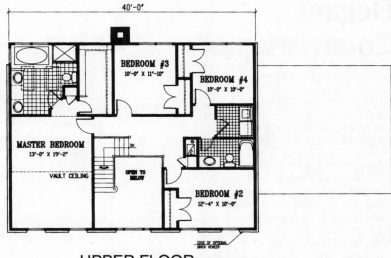

UPPER FLOOR

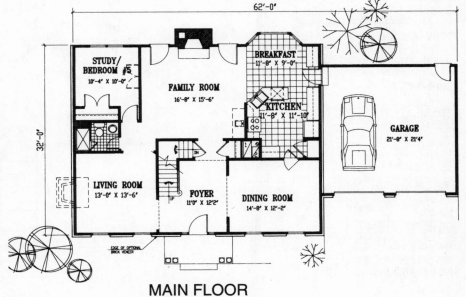

MAIN FLOOR

TO ORDER THIS BLUEPRINT,
CALL TOLL-FREE 1-800-547-5570

Plan CH-320-A

PRICES AND DETAILS
ON PAGES 12-15

151

Modern Elegance

- Half-round transom windows and a barrel-vaulted porch with paired columns lend elegance to the facade of this post-modern design.
- Inside, the two-story-high foyer leads past a den and a diagonal, open-railed stairway to the sunken living room.
- A 17-ft. vaulted ceiling and a striking fireplace enhance the living room, while square columns introduce the adjoining formal dining room.
- The adjacent kitchen is thoroughly modern, including an island cooktop and a large pantry. A sunny bay window defines the breakfast area, where a sliding glass door opens to the angled backyard deck.
- Columns preface the sunken family room, which also sports a 17-ft.-high vaulted ceiling and easy access to the deck. A half-bath, a laundry room and access to the garage are nearby.
- Upstairs, the master suite features a 10-ft. vaulted ceiling, a private bath and a large walk-in closet.

Plan B-89005

Bedrooms: 4	Baths: 2½

Living Area:	
Upper floor	1,083 sq. ft.
Main floor	1,380 sq. ft.
Total Living Area:	**2,463 sq. ft.**
Standard basement	1,380 sq. ft.
Garage	483 sq. ft.
Exterior Wall Framing:	2x4

Foundation Options:

Standard basement

(All plans can be built with your choice of foundation and framing. A generic conversion diagram is available. See order form.)

BLUEPRINT PRICE CODE:	**C**

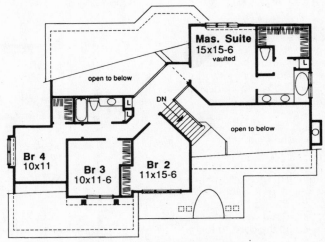

UPPER FLOOR

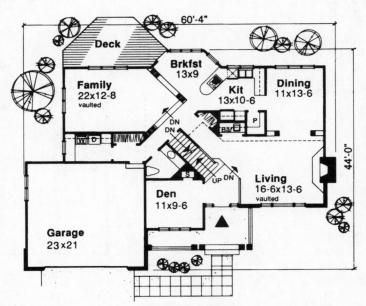

MAIN FLOOR

TO ORDER THIS BLUEPRINT, CALL TOLL-FREE 1-800-547-5570   Plan B-89005   *PRICES AND DETAILS ON PAGES 12-15*

Light-Hearted, Open Elegance

- Tradition takes a few twists with arched brickwork and a two-story-high foyer in this transitional three-bedroom home.
- Large windows and a 10½-ft. vaulted ceiling add light and drama to the formal living room. A warm fireplace is the focal point.
- A 9-ft. vaulted ceiling expands the dining room, which offers easy access to the outdoors.
- Skylights, a windowed nook, a handy pantry and an angled island make the sunny kitchen perfect for both family cooking and formal entertaining.
- Off the kitchen, the generous-sized family room with a practical wood-stove is the center of family activity.
- A secluded study provides a quiet work retreat or extra bedroom.
- Upstairs, all three bedrooms are enhanced by 9½-ft. ceilings. The elegant master suite features an octagonal sitting area to capture the view, plus a large walk-in closet and a skylighted bath with a step-up tub.

Plan R-2117

Bedrooms: 3+	Baths: 3
Living Area:	
Upper floor	1,005 sq. ft.
Main floor	1,460 sq. ft.
Total Living Area:	**2,465 sq. ft.**
Garage	626 sq. ft.
Exterior Wall Framing:	2x6

Foundation Options:

Crawlspace

(All plans can be built with your choice of foundation and framing. A generic conversion diagram is available. See order form.)

BLUEPRINT PRICE CODE: C

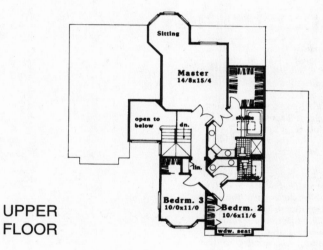

UPPER FLOOR

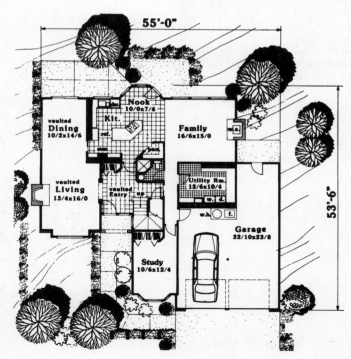

MAIN FLOOR

Rustic Four-Bedroom Home

This 2,467 sq. ft. rustic design includes a deluxe master suite with walk-in and walk-thru closets, linen closet, large double vanity and both a tub and separate shower stall.

The U-shaped kitchen features a counter bar open to the Great Room, which has a raised-hearth fireplace. A large utility room and a second bedroom and full bath with linen closet are located on the 1,694 sq. ft. main floor.

Two additional bedrooms and a third full bath with linen closet are located upstairs. A built-in bookcase, window seats and access to attic storage areas are also included on the 773 sq. ft. upper floor.

Front porch, dormers, shutters, multi-paned windows and a combination of wood and stone materials combine for a rustic exterior. The screened-in porch doubles as a covered breezeway connecting house and garage.

Specify crawlspace or daylight basement foundation when ordering.

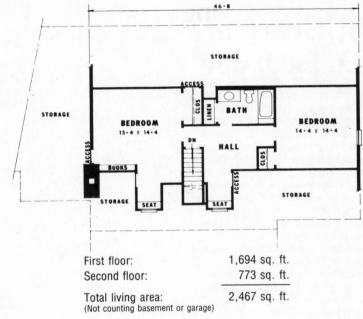

First floor: 1,694 sq. ft.
Second floor: 773 sq. ft.

Total living area: 2,467 sq. ft.
(Not counting basement or garage)

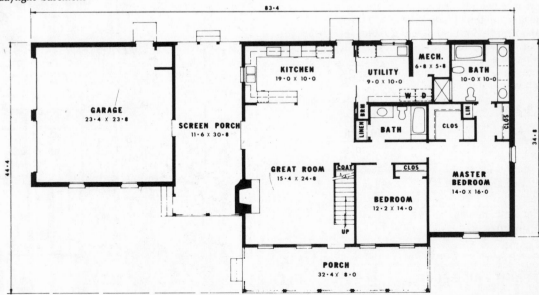

Blueprint Price Code C

Plan C-7746

Large-Scale Living

- Eye-catching windows and an appealing wraparound porch highlight the exterior of this outstanding home.
- High ceilings and large-scale living spaces prevail inside, beginning with the two-story-high foyer.
- The spacious living room flows into the formal dining room, which accesses the front porch as well as an optional backyard deck.
- The island kitchen combines with a bright breakfast room, also with deck access. The fabulous family room offers a warm corner fireplace, a soaring 18-ft. vaulted ceiling, a wall of windows and a view of the balcony hall above.
- Upstairs, the luxurious master bedroom boasts an 11-ft. vaulted ceiling, a magnificent arched window and two walk-in closets. The skylighted master bath features a spa tub, a separate shower and a dual-sink vanity.
- The three remaining bedrooms are reached via a balcony hall, which offers stunning views of the family room.

Plan AX-93309

Bedrooms: 4	Baths: 2½
Living Area:	
Upper floor	1,180 sq. ft.
Main floor	1,290 sq. ft.
Total Living Area:	**2,470 sq. ft.**
Basement	1,290 sq. ft.
Garage	421 sq. ft.
Exterior Wall Framing:	2x4

Foundation Options:

Daylight basement

Standard basement

Slab

(All plans can be built with your choice of foundation and framing. A generic conversion diagram is available. See order form.)

BLUEPRINT PRICE CODE: C

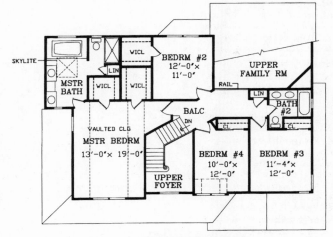

UPPER FLOOR

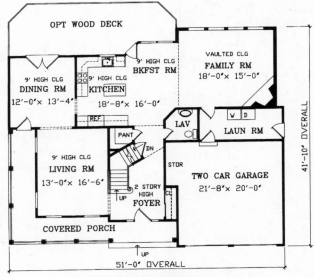

MAIN FLOOR

Pillars of Success

- A stunning two-story entry porch with heavy support pillars creates a look of success for this exciting new design.
- The covered entrance gives way to an open entry foyer with closets for coats and general storage. A powder room is just steps away.
- Straight ahead, the Great Room features a fireplace, a TV niche and a 16-ft. vaulted ceiling. A French door gives access to a view deck that wraps around much of the home.
- The kitchen's island boasts a cooktop and a convenient snack counter. The adjacent dining bay offers great views.
- The main-floor master suite has a 10-ft. coved ceiling, private deck access, built-in shelves, a dressing area and a private skylighted bath.
- A den or guest room includes a 9-ft. vaulted ceiling and deck access.
- The upper floor has a central hobby area with a 13-ft. vaulted ceiling. Two bedrooms feature views to the Great Room below.

Plan LRD-32190

Bedrooms: 3+	Baths: 3
Living Area:	
Upper floor	606 sq. ft.
Main floor	1,865 sq. ft.
Total Living Area:	**2,471 sq. ft.**
Standard basement	1,865 sq. ft.
Garage	529 sq. ft.
Exterior Wall Framing:	2x6

Foundation Options:

Standard basement
Crawlspace
Slab

(All plans can be built with your choice of foundation and framing. A generic conversion diagram is available. See order form.)

BLUEPRINT PRICE CODE: C

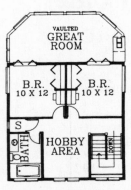

UPPER FLOOR

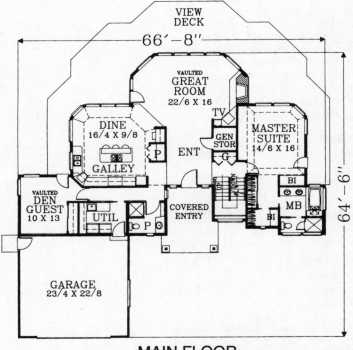

MAIN FLOOR

Plan LRD-32190

PRICES AND DETAILS ON PAGES 12-15

Fantastic Facade, Stunning Spaces

- Matching dormers and a generous covered front porch give this home its fantastic facade. Inside, the open living spaces are just as stunning.
- A two-story foyer bisects the formal living areas. The living room offers three bright windows, an inviting fireplace and sliding French doors to the Great Room. The formal dining room overlooks the front porch and has easy access to the kitchen.
- The Great Room is truly grand, featuring a fireplace and a TV center flanked by French doors that lead to a large deck.
- A circular dinette connects the Great Room to the kitchen, which is handy to a mudroom and a powder room.
- The main-floor master suite boasts a 14-ft. cathedral ceiling, a walk-in closet and a private bath with a whirlpool tub.
- Upstairs, four large bedrooms share another whirlpool bath. One bedroom offers a 12-ft. sloped ceiling.

Plan AHP-9397

Bedrooms: 5	Baths: 2½
Living Area:	
Upper floor	928 sq. ft.
Main floor	1,545 sq. ft.
Total Living Area:	**2,473 sq. ft.**
Standard basement	1,165 sq. ft.
Garage and storage	432 sq. ft.
Exterior Wall Framing:	2x4 or 2x6

Foundation Options:

Standard basement
Crawlspace
Slab
(All plans can be built with your choice of foundation and framing. A generic conversion diagram is available. See order form.)

BLUEPRINT PRICE CODE:	C

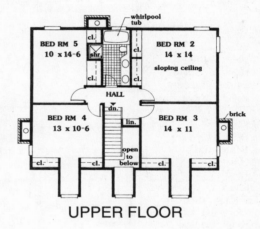

UPPER FLOOR

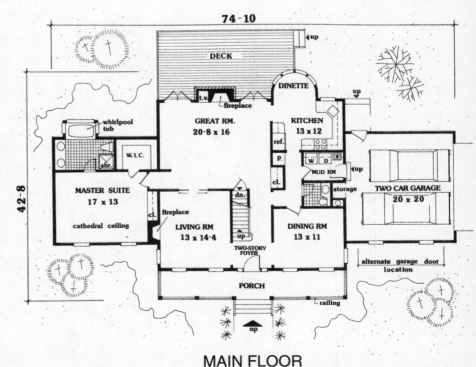

MAIN FLOOR

TO ORDER THIS BLUEPRINT,
CALL TOLL-FREE 1-800-547-5570

Plan AHP-9397

PRICES AND DETAILS
ON PAGES 12-15

157

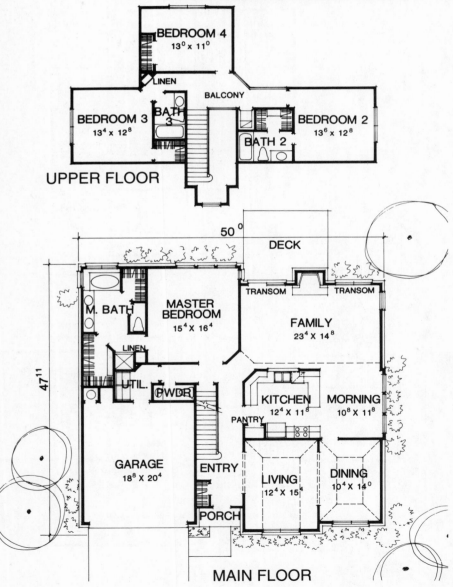

BEDROOM 4
13⁰ x 11⁰

LINEN

BALCONY

BEDROOM 3
13⁴ x 12⁸

BATH 3

BEDROOM 2
13⁶ x 12⁸

BATH 2

UPPER FLOOR

50⁰

DECK

TRANSOM   TRANSOM

M. BATH

MASTER BEDROOM
15⁴ x 16⁴

FAMILY
23⁴ x 14⁸

LINEN

UTIL.

PWDR

KITCHEN
12⁴ x 11⁸

MORNING
10⁸ x 11⁸

47¹¹

PANTRY

GARAGE
18⁸ x 20⁴

ENTRY

LIVING
12⁴ x 15⁴

DINING
10⁴ x 14⁰

PORCH

MAIN FLOOR

Easy Building, Easy Living

- This stylish 1½ story home is easy to build, economical and compact.
- Gambrel ceilings adorn the formal living and dining rooms.
- An open atmosphere flows through the large family room with fireplace, sloped ceiling, spectacular rear view and attached deck, the morning room and the kitchen with counter bar and pantry.
- The private master bedroom is on the main level; it offers a generous rear view and private bath with twin vanities, garden luxury tub, separate shower and his 'n her closets.
- Three nice-sized extra bedrooms are found on the upper level. Two baths shared between them offer plenty of time-savings.

Plan DD-2514

Bedrooms: 4	Baths: 3 ½
Space:	
Upper floor	776 sq. ft.
Main floor	1,738 sq. ft.
Total Living Area	**2,514 sq. ft.**
Basement	1,738 sq. ft.
Garage	380 sq. ft.
Exterior Wall Framing	2x4

Foundation options:
Standard Basement
Crawlspace
Slab
(Foundation & framing conversion diagram available—see order form.)

Blueprint Price Code	D

Plan DD-2514

Formal Meets Informal

- The charming, columned front porch of this appealing home leads visitors into a two-story-high foyer with a beautiful turned staircase.
- The gracious formal living room shares a 15-ft. cathedral ceiling and a dramatic see-through fireplace with the adjoining family room.
- A railing separates the family room from the spacious breakfast area and the island kitchen. A unique butler's pantry joins the kitchen to the dining room, which is enhanced by a tray ceiling.
- A convenient laundry room is located between the kitchen and the entrance to the garage.
- All four bedrooms are located on the upper level. The master suite boasts an 11-ft. cathedral ceiling, a walk-in closet and a large, luxurious bath.

Plan OH-132

Bedrooms: 4	Baths: 2½
Living Area:	
Upper floor	1,118 sq. ft.
Main floor	1,396 sq. ft.
Total Living Area:	**2,514 sq. ft.**
Standard basement	1,396 sq. ft.
Garage	413 sq. ft.
Storage/workshop	107 sq. ft.
Exterior Wall Framing:	2x4

Foundation Options:

Standard basement

(All plans can be built with your choice of foundation and framing. A generic conversion diagram is available. See order form.)

BLUEPRINT PRICE CODE: D

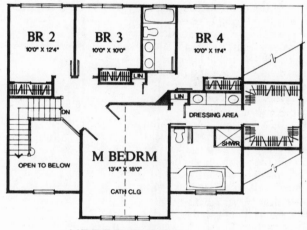

UPPER FLOOR

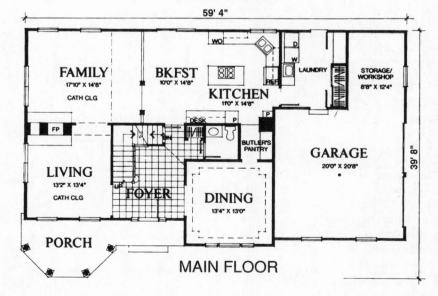

MAIN FLOOR

TO ORDER THIS BLUEPRINT,
CALL TOLL-FREE 1-800-547-5570

Plan OH-132

PRICES AND DETAILS
ON PAGES 12-15

159

All the Best

- This unique home offers the best of both worlds, with its charming, old-time exterior and modern, luxurious interior.
- The covered front porch leads to a two-story foyer with a beautiful open staircase. To the right, the large formal dining room showcases a boxed-out window. To the left, the living room overlooks the front porch and has the option of a cased opening or a solid wall facing the family room.
- The expansive family room is brightened by a dramatic window wall and has a French door to the backyard. The fireplace is positioned so it can be enjoyed from the adjoining kitchen.
- The deluxe kitchen boasts a double oven, a huge walk-in pantry and a long serving bar. The 11½-ft.-high vaulted breakfast room is illuminated by a gorgeous arched window.
- The upper floor includes a dynamite master suite, which features a 9½-ft. tray ceiling in the sleeping area and a 16-ft. vaulted ceiling in the luxurious bath.
- The big bonus room could serve as a playroom or an extra bedroom.

Plan FB-2516

Bedrooms: 3+	Baths: 2½
Living Area:	
Upper floor	1,057 sq. ft.
Main floor	1,212 sq. ft.
Bonus room	247 sq. ft.
Total Living Area:	**2,516 sq. ft.**
Daylight basement	1,212 sq. ft.
Garage and storage	504 sq. ft.
Exterior Wall Framing:	2x4

Foundation Options:
Daylight basement
Crawlspace
(All plans can be built with your choice of foundation and framing. A generic conversion diagram is available. See order form.)

BLUEPRINT PRICE CODE: D

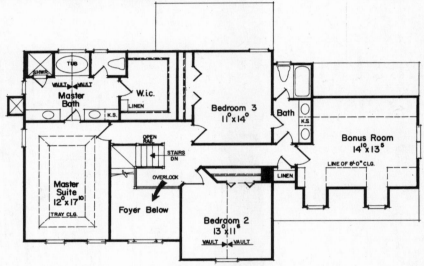

UPPER FLOOR

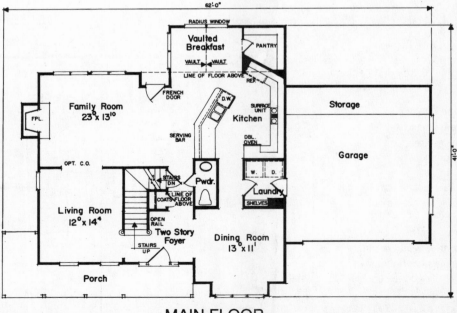

MAIN FLOOR

160   *TO ORDER THIS BLUEPRINT,*
CALL TOLL-FREE 1-800-547-5570   Plan FB-2516   **PRICES AND DETAILS**
ON PAGES 12-15

Solid Character

- A dramatic, stately roofline and a distinguished brick facade give a solid look to this distinctive family home.
- The impressive two-story-high foyer boasts an elegant tray ceiling.
- A columned arch introduces the formal dining room, where French doors bring the outside in.
- The central kitchen includes a pantry and features an arched opening over the sink. The nearby breakfast bay offers a built-in serving shelf with an arched pass-through to the family room.
- Flanked by tall windows, a handsome fireplace is the focal point of the two-story-high family room.
- Ceilings in all main-floor rooms are 9 ft. high unless otherwise specified.
- Upstairs, a railed balcony overlooks the family room and the foyer. The tray-ceilinged master suite boasts a morning kitchen and a vaulted sitting room. The master bath has a 13-ft. vaulted ceiling and showcases a corner garden tub, a separate shower and a dual-sink vanity.
- Three additional bedrooms, a second full bath and a laundry room complete the upper floor.

Plan FB-5048-NELS

Bedrooms: 4	Baths: 2½
Living Area:	
Upper floor	1,309 sq. ft.
Main floor	1,240 sq. ft.
Total Living Area:	**2,549 sq. ft.**
Daylight basement	1,240 sq. ft.
Garage	400 sq. ft.
Exterior Wall Framing:	2x4

Foundation Options:

Daylight basement

(All plans can be built with your choice of foundation and framing. A generic conversion diagram is available. See order form.)

BLUEPRINT PRICE CODE: D

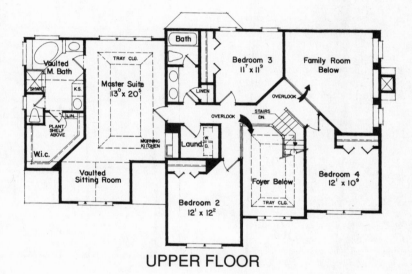

UPPER FLOOR

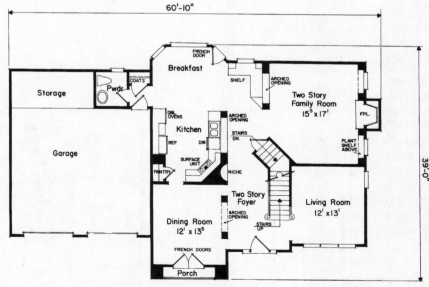

MAIN FLOOR

Stately Colonial

- This stately Colonial features a covered front entry and a secondary entry near the garage and the utility room.
- The main foyer opens to a comfortable den with elegant double doors.
- The formal living areas adjoin to the left of the foyer and culminate in a lovely bay window overlooking the backyard.
- The open island kitchen has a great central location, easily accessed from each of the living areas. Informal dining can be extended to the outdoors through sliding doors in the dinette.
- A half-wall introduces the big family room, which boasts a high 16-ft., 9-in. vaulted ceiling, an inviting fireplace and optional built-in cabinets.
- The upper floor is shared by four bedrooms, including a spacious master bedroom with a large walk-in closet, a dressing area for two and a private bath. An alternate bath layout is included in the blueprints.
- A bonus room may be added above the garage for additional space.

Plan A-2283-DS

Bedrooms: 4+	Baths: 2½
Living Area:	
Upper floor	1,137 sq. ft.
Main floor	1,413 sq. ft.
Total Living Area:	**2,550 sq. ft.**
Optional bonus room	280 sq. ft.
Standard basement	1,413 sq. ft.
Garage	484 sq. ft.
Exterior Wall Framing:	2x6

Foundation Options:

Standard basement

(All plans can be built with your choice of foundation and framing. A generic conversion diagram is available. See order form.)

BLUEPRINT PRICE CODE: D

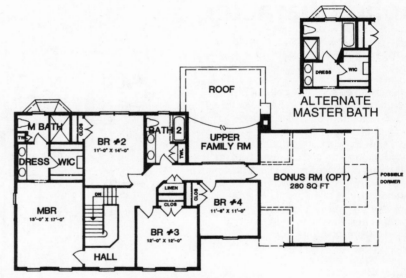

UPPER FLOOR

ALTERNATE MASTER BATH

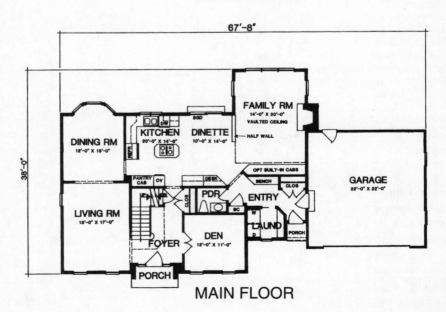

MAIN FLOOR

Plan A-2283-DS

PRICES AND DETAILS ON PAGES 12-15

Elegant Interior

- An inviting covered porch welcomes guests into the elegant interior of this spectacular country home.
- Just past the entrance, the formal dining room boasts a stepped ceiling and a nearby server with a sink.
- The adjoining island kitchen has an eating bar that serves the breakfast room, which is enhanced by a 12-ft. cathedral ceiling and a bayed area of 8- and 9-ft.-high windows. Sliding glass doors lead to a covered side porch.
- Brightened by a row of 8-ft.-high windows and a glass door to the backyard, the spacious Great Room features a stepped ceiling, a built-in media center and a corner fireplace.
- The master bedroom has a tray ceiling and a cozy sitting area. The skylighted master bath boasts a whirlpool tub, a separate shower and a walk-in closet.
- A second main-floor bedroom offers private access to a compartmentalized bath. Two more bedrooms share a third bathroom on the upper floor.

Plan AX-3305-B

Bedrooms: 3+	Baths: 3
Living Area:	
Upper floor	550 sq. ft.
Main floor	2,017 sq. ft.
Total Living Area:	**2,567 sq. ft.**
Upper-floor storage	377 sq. ft.
Standard basement	2,017 sq. ft.
Garage	415 sq. ft.
Exterior Wall Framing:	2x4

Foundation Options:
Standard basement
Crawlspace
Slab
(All plans can be built with your choice of foundation and framing. A generic conversion diagram is available. See order form.)

BLUEPRINT PRICE CODE: D

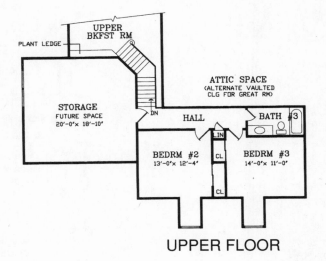

UPPER FLOOR

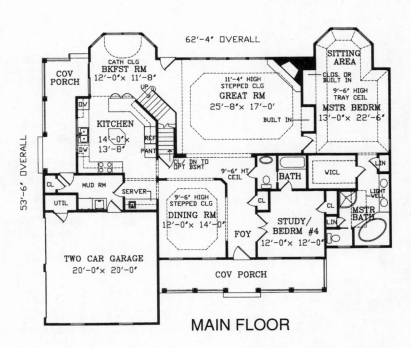

MAIN FLOOR

Nostalgic Exterior Appeal

- A covered front porch, large half-round windows and Victorian gable details give this nostalgic home classic appeal.
- A stunning two-story foyer awaits guests at the entry, which is flooded with light from the half-round window above.
- The central island kitchen is brightened by the bay-windowed breakfast room, which looks into the family room over a low partition.
- Highlighted by a skylight and a corner fireplace, the cathedral-ceilinged family room is sure to be a high-traffic area. Sliding glass doors allow activities to be extended to the backyard patio.
- Upstairs, the master bedroom boasts a unique sloped ceiling and a lovely boxed-out window. The master bath has a spa tub, a corner shower and a dual-sink vanity. A dressing area and a walk-in closet are also offered.
- Three more upstairs bedrooms share two linen closets and a hallway bath. A railed balcony bridge overlooks the foyer and the family room.

Plan AX-90305

Bedrooms: 4	Baths: 2½
Living Area:	
Upper floor	1,278 sq. ft.
Main floor	1,237 sq. ft.
Total Living Area:	**2,515 sq. ft.**
Standard basement	1,237 sq. ft.
Garage	400 sq. ft.
Exterior Wall Framing:	2x4

Foundation Options:

Standard basement

Slab

(All plans can be built with your choice of foundation and framing. A generic conversion diagram is available. See order form.)

BLUEPRINT PRICE CODE: D

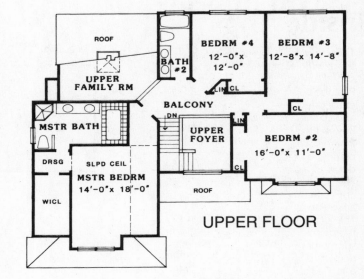

UPPER FLOOR

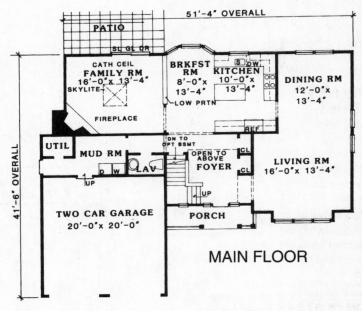

MAIN FLOOR

 TO ORDER THIS BLUEPRINT, CALL TOLL-FREE 1-800-547-5570   Plan AX-90305   **PRICES AND DETAILS ON PAGES 12-15**

Inside Angles

- This cleverly designed home offers a space-efficient floor plan that is well suited for building on a narrow lot.
- Past the columned porch, the vaulted entry orients guests to the home's angled interior.
- Beyond the entry, the spectacular Great Room features a 17-ft.-high vaulted ceiling, a corner fireplace and glass doors to a patio.
- The adjoining formal dining room is convenient to the kitchen and has access to a rear deck.
- The kitchen serves the Great Room via a handy pass-through above the sink. The sunny morning room accesses the rear deck through sliding glass doors.
- A turned stairway brightened by tall windows leads to the upper floor. The elegant master bedroom is enhanced by a 10-ft. gambrel ceiling. The master bath showcases a spa tub, a separate shower, a dual-sink vanity and his-and-hers walk-in closets.

Plan DD-2594

Bedrooms: 2+	Baths: 2½
Living Area:	
Upper floor	1,127 sq. ft.
Main floor	1,467 sq. ft.
Total Living Area:	**2,594 sq. ft.**
Standard basement	1,467 sq. ft.
Garage	488 sq. ft.
Exterior Wall Framing:	2x4

Foundation Options:

Standard basement

Crawlspace

Slab

(All plans can be built with your choice of foundation and framing. A generic conversion diagram is available. See order form.)

BLUEPRINT PRICE CODE: D

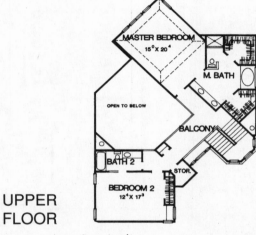

UPPER FLOOR

MAIN FLOOR

Fine Details

- Elegant window treatments, eye-catching gables and a finely detailed stucco facade give this home a distinctive look.
- The spacious interior begins with an 18-ft.-high foyer and a dramatic two-way stairway with open railings.
- Decorative columns introduce the formal living room. Straight ahead, the spacious family room features a focal-point fireplace framed by windows.
- A French door between the family room and the breakfast room provides easy access to the backyard. The gourmet kitchen is highlighted by an angled serving bar/snack counter.
- Upstairs, the luxurious master bedroom features a 10-ft. tray ceiling and an intimate sitting room with a two-sided fireplace. Double doors open to the opulent master bath, which includes a huge walk-in closet and a 13½-ft.-high bathing area with an oval tub.
- Three more bedrooms share a compartmentalized bath. A balcony overlook with a beautiful plant shelf is open to the foyer below.

Plan FB-2600

Bedrooms: 4	Baths: 2½
Living Area:	
Upper floor	1,348 sq. ft.
Main floor	1,252 sq. ft.
Total Living Area:	**2,600 sq. ft.**
Daylight basement	1,252 sq. ft.
Garage	448 sq. ft.
Storage	36 sq. ft.
Exterior Wall Framing:	2x4

Foundation Options:
Daylight basement
Crawlspace
(All plans can be built with your choice of foundation and framing. A generic conversion diagram is available. See order form.)

BLUEPRINT PRICE CODE: D

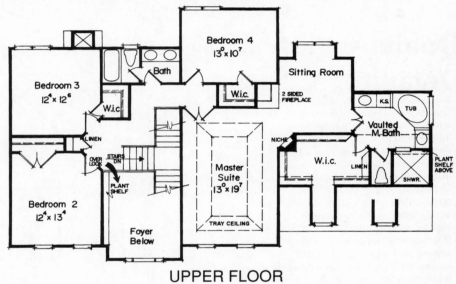

UPPER FLOOR

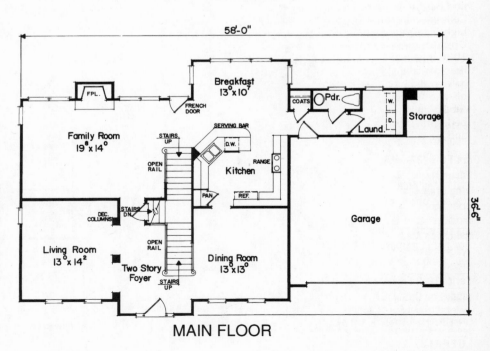

MAIN FLOOR

TO ORDER THIS BLUEPRINT, CALL TOLL-FREE 1-800-547-5570

Plan FB-2600

PRICES AND DETAILS ON PAGES 12-15

Quaint Detailing

- Quaint windows accented by keystones and shutters exemplify the detailing found through this stately brick home.
- The columned front entry leads to the two-story foyer that flows between the front-oriented formal areas.
- The 18-ft. ceiling extends past an open-railed stairway to the expansive family room, which boasts a fireplace and a French door to the backyard.
- The bayed breakfast nook features an angled serving counter/desk that wraps around to the adjoining island kitchen. A pantry, a laundry room, a half-bath and the garage entrance are all nearby.
- Ceilings in all main-floor rooms are 9 ft. high unless otherwise specified.
- Upstairs, the master suite includes a 10-ft. tray ceiling, a see-through fireplace and a luxurious bath with a garden spa tub, a separate shower and his-and-hers walk-in closets.
- A balcony bridge leads to three more bedrooms, two with walk-in closets, and another full bath.

Plan FB-5237-NORW

Bedrooms: 4	Baths: 2½
Living Area:	
Upper floor	1,353 sq. ft.
Main floor	1,248 sq. ft.
Total Living Area:	**2,601 sq. ft.**
Daylight basement	1,248 sq. ft.
Garage	528 sq. ft.
Exterior Wall Framing:	2x4

Foundation Options:

Daylight basement

(All plans can be built with your choice of foundation and framing. A generic conversion diagram is available. See order form.)

BLUEPRINT PRICE CODE:	D

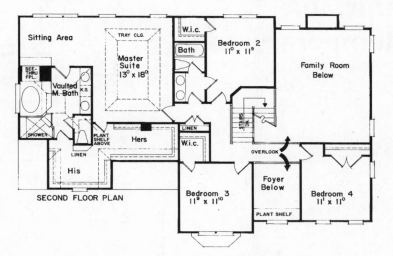

UPPER FLOOR

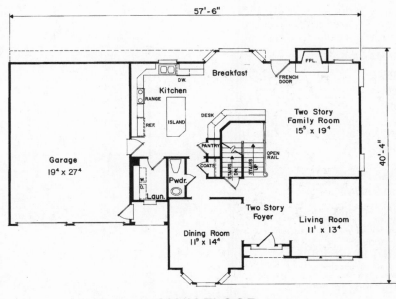

MAIN FLOOR

Comfortable Contemporary

- Contemporary lines give this home a bold facade. Its interior is both innovative and comfortable.
- Graced with a beautiful fireplace and three large windows, the living room is open to the dining room. The dining room features a sliding glass door that accesses a partially covered patio.
- The U-shaped kitchen boasts a writing desk, a pantry, a cooktop island and a breakfast nook with patio access.
- Showcasing a beautiful fireplace flanked by windows, the sunken family room is perfect for casual entertaining.
- Double doors introduce a quiet den or extra bedroom. A full bath is nearby.
- The master bedroom is highlighted by a private deck, a walk-in wardrobe, a sunken tub and a dual-sink vanity.
- The three remaining upper-floor bedrooms share another full bath.

Plans P-7644-2A & -2D

Bedrooms: 4+	**Baths:** 3

Living Area:	
Upper floor	1,101 sq. ft.
Main floor	1,523 sq. ft.
Total Living Area:	**2,624 sq. ft.**
Daylight basement	1,286 sq. ft.
Garage	935 sq. ft.
Exterior Wall Framing:	2x4

Foundation Options:	**Plan #**
Daylight basement	P-7644-2D
Crawlspace	P-7644-2A

(All plans can be built with your choice of foundation and framing. A generic conversion diagram is available. See order form.)

BLUEPRINT PRICE CODE:	**D**

BASEMENT STAIRWAY LOCATION

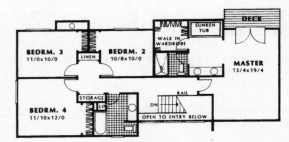

UPPER FLOOR

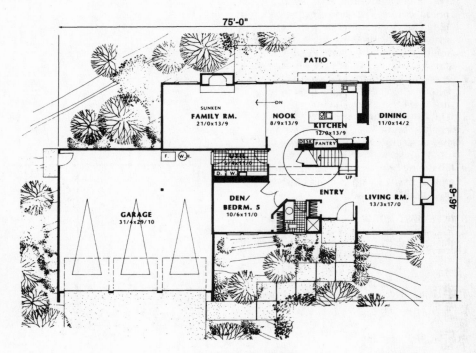

MAIN FLOOR

Plans P-7644-2A & -2D

PRICES AND DETAILS ON PAGES 12-15

Innovative Floor Plan

- The wide, covered front porch, arched windows and symmetrical lines of this traditional home conceal the modern, innovative floor plan found within.
- A two-story-high foyer guides guests to the front-oriented formal areas, which have views to the front porch.
- The hotspot of the home is the Great Room, with one of the home's three fireplaces and a media wall. Flanking doors open to a large backyard deck.
- The island kitchen and glassed-in eating nook overlook the deck and access a handy mudroom. High 9-ft. ceilings add to the aura of warmth and hospitality found on the main floor of this home.
- Another of the fireplaces is offered in the master suite. This private oasis also boasts a 13-ft.-high cathedral ceiling and a delicious bath with a garden tub.
- Upstairs, one bedroom has a sloped ceiling and a private bath. Three more bedrooms share another full bath.

Plan AHP-9360

Bedrooms: 5	Baths: 3½
Living Area:	
Upper floor	970 sq. ft.
Main floor	1,688 sq. ft.
Total Living Area:	**2,658 sq. ft.**
Standard basement	1,550 sq. ft.
Garage and utility area	443 sq. ft.
Exterior Wall Framing:	2x6

Foundation Options:

Standard basement
Crawlspace
Slab
(All plans can be built with your choice of foundation and framing. A generic conversion diagram is available. See order form.)

BLUEPRINT PRICE CODE:	D

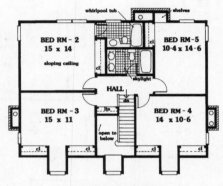

UPPER FLOOR

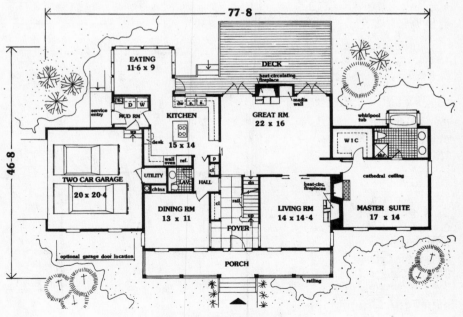

MAIN FLOOR

Fantastic Front Entry

- A fantastic arched window presides over the 18-ft.-high entry of this two-story, giving guests a bright welcome.
- The spacious living room is separated from the dining room by a pair of boxed columns with built-in shelves.
- The kitchen offers a walk-in pantry, a serving bar and a sunny breakfast room with a French door to the backyard.
- A boxed column accents the entry to the 18-ft. vaulted family room, which boasts a dramatic window bank and an inviting fireplace.
- The main-floor den is easily converted into an extra bedroom or guest room.
- The master suite has a 10-ft. tray ceiling, a huge walk-in closet and decorative plant shelves. The 15½-ft. vaulted bath features an oval tub and two vanities, one with knee space.
- Three additional bedrooms share another full bath near the second stairway to the main floor.

Plan FB-2680

Bedrooms: 4+	Baths: 3
Living Area:	
Upper floor	1,256 sq. ft.
Main floor	1,424 sq. ft.
Total Living Area:	**2,680 sq. ft.**
Daylight basement	1,424 sq. ft.
Garage	496 sq. ft.
Exterior Wall Framing:	2x4

Foundation Options:

Daylight basement

(All plans can be built with your choice of foundation and framing. A generic conversion diagram is available. See order form.)

BLUEPRINT PRICE CODE: D

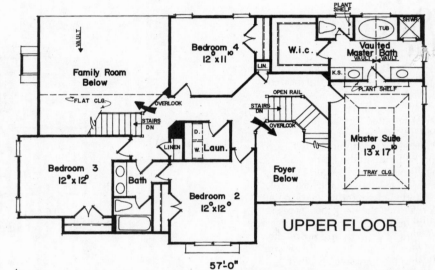

UPPER FLOOR

57'-0"

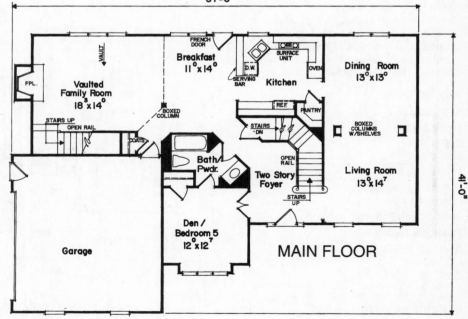

MAIN FLOOR

41'-0"

TO ORDER THIS BLUEPRINT, CALL TOLL-FREE 1-800-547-5570

Plan FB-2680

PRICES AND DETAILS ON PAGES 12-15

Two-Story Palace

- Decorative brick borders, a columned porch and dramatic arched windows give a classy look to this magnificent two-story palace.
- The open, sidelighted entry is flanked by the formal dining and living rooms, both of which feature elegant paned-glass windows. A coat closet and a powder room are just steps away.
- The spacious family room is warmed by a fireplace and brightened by a beautiful arched window set into a high-ceilinged area.
- The well-planned kitchen, highlighted by an island worktop and a windowed sink, is centrally located to provide easy

service to both the dining room and the bayed morning room. The morning room offers access to a large, inviting backyard deck.
- A bright and heartwarming sun room also overlooks the deck, and is a perfect spot to read or just relax.
- A handy laundry/utility area is located at the entrance to the two-car garage.
- Windows surround the main-floor master suite, which boasts a luxurious bath with a garden tub, a separate shower and a dual-sink vanity. Three walk-in closets provide plenty of space for wardrobe storage.
- Ceilings in all main-floor rooms are 9 ft. high for added spaciousness.
- Upstairs, three good-sized bedrooms share a compartmentalized bath. A large and convenient attic area offers additional storage possibilities.

Plan DD-2689	
Bedrooms: 4	**Baths:** 2½
Living Area:	
Upper floor	755 sq. ft.
Main floor	1,934 sq. ft.
Total Living Area:	**2,689 sq. ft.**
Standard basement	1,934 sq. ft.
Garage	436 sq. ft.
Exterior Wall Framing:	2x4

Foundation Options:
Standard basement
Crawlspace
Slab
(All plans can be built with your choice of foundation and framing. A generic conversion diagram is available. See order form.)

BLUEPRINT PRICE CODE:	D

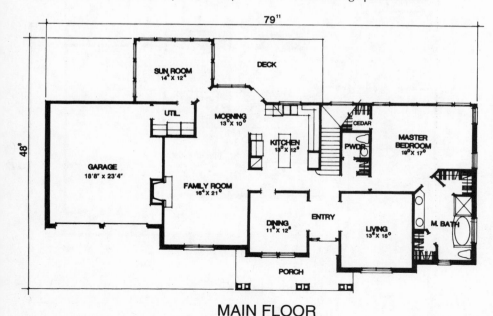

MAIN FLOOR

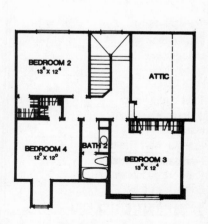

UPPER FLOOR

TO ORDER THIS BLUEPRINT,
CALL TOLL-FREE 1-800-547-5570

Plan DD-2689

PRICES AND DETAILS
ON PAGES 12-15

171

Classic Cape Cod

- Six eye-catching dormer windows and a charming front porch create a stately, dignified look for this handsome home.
- An elegant open staircase is the focal point of the inviting foyer, which is set off from the formal dining room by decorative wood columns.
- A swinging door leads to the exciting kitchen, which includes an angled counter overlooking the breakfast room.
- The spectacular skylighted family room boasts a soaring 17-ft.-high ceiling. A cozy fireplace is flanked by tall windows and a set of French doors to the backyard.
- The deluxe master bedroom offers a vaulted ceiling and a charming bay window. The skylighted master bath has a spa tub, a separate shower, two walk-in closets and a dual sink vanity.
- Upstairs, a railed balcony overlooks the family room and foyer. Three bright bedrooms share a hallway bath.

Plan CH-445-A

Bedrooms: 4	Baths: 2½
Living Area:	
Upper floor	988 sq. ft.
Main floor	1,707 sq. ft.
Total Living Area:	**2,695 sq. ft.**
Basement	1,118 sq. ft.
Garage	802 sq. ft.
Exterior Wall Framing:	2x4

Foundation Options:
Partial daylight basement
Partial basement
Crawlspace
(All plans can be built with your choice of foundation and framing. A generic conversion diagram is available. See order form.)

BLUEPRINT PRICE CODE: D

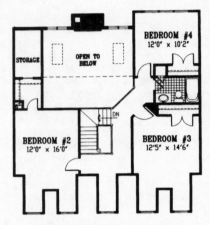

UPPER FLOOR

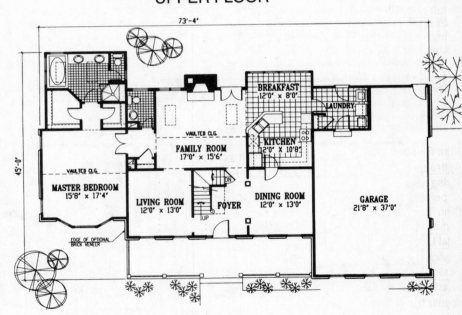

MAIN FLOOR

Plan CH-445-A

PRICES AND DETAILS ON PAGES 12-15

Striking Stucco

- The facade of this striking stucco home is adorned with elegant window treatments and eye-catching gables.
- Inside, a two-story-high foyer views to an open-railed staircase and is brightened by an arched window.
- To the right of the foyer, an arched opening connects the living room to the formal dining room.
- The casual living areas consist of an open kitchen, a sunny breakfast nook and a family room with a fireplace. The kitchen boasts a island cooktop, while the nook offers a French door leading to the backyard. A second stairway in the family room accesses the upper floor.
- Just off the foyer, a den with access to a full bath may serve as a guest room.
- Ceilings in all main-floor rooms are 9 ft. high unless otherwise specified.
- Upstairs, the master suite features a 9-ft. tray ceiling and a private bath with a 12-ft. vaulted ceiling over a garden tub.
- Three additional bedrooms, one with an 11-ft. vaulted ceiling, share two more full baths. A versatile bonus room is also included.

Plan FB-5081-AVER

Bedrooms: 4+	Baths: 4
Living Area:	
Upper floor	1,325 sq. ft.
Main floor	1,447 sq. ft.
Bonus room	301 sq. ft.
Total Living Area:	**3,073 sq. ft.**
Daylight basement	1,447 sq. ft.
Garage	465 sq. ft.
Exterior Wall Framing:	2x4

Foundation Options:

Daylight basement

(All plans can be built with your choice of foundation and framing. A generic conversion diagram is available. See order form.)

BLUEPRINT PRICE CODE: E

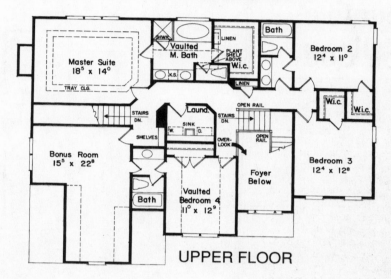

UPPER FLOOR

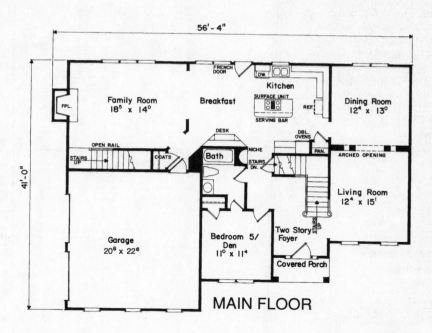

MAIN FLOOR

Executive Excellence

- This executive home with a stucco exterior has a bright interior with flowing spaces and lots of windows.
- The two-story-high entry opens to the formal living and dining rooms, which are defined by decorative columns and enhanced by a shared 11-ft. ceiling.
- The island kitchen offers a corner windowed sink and a bayed morning room that merges with the family room.
- A fireplace warms the entire family area. Plenty of glass provides views of a large covered deck.
- A guest bedroom/study, a full bath and a utility room with a washer and dryer complete the main level.
- Upstairs, the master suite boasts an enormous walk-in closet and a lavish master bath with a boxed-out window, a spa tub and a separate shower.
- Two more bedrooms share another full bath. The third bedroom is expanded by an 11-ft. cathedral ceiling.
- Ceilings in all main-floor rooms are at least 9 ft. high for added spaciousness.

Plan DD-2725

Bedrooms: 3+	Baths: 3
Living Area:	
Upper floor	1,152 sq. ft.
Main floor	1,631 sq. ft.
Total Living Area:	**2,783 sq. ft.**
Standard basement	1,631 sq. ft.
Garage	600 sq. ft.
Storage	100 sq. ft.
Exterior Wall Framing:	2x4

Foundation Options:

Standard basement
Crawlspace
Slab
(All plans can be built with your choice of foundation and framing. A generic conversion diagram is available. See order form.)

BLUEPRINT PRICE CODE: D

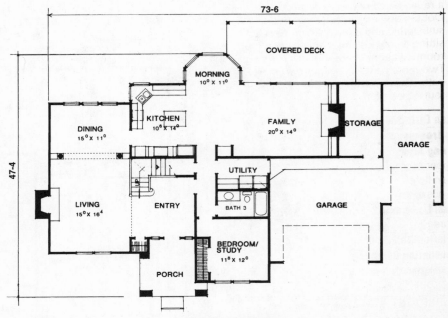

UPPER FLOOR

MAIN FLOOR

TO ORDER THIS BLUEPRINT, CALL TOLL-FREE 1-800-547-5570

Plan DD-2725

PRICES AND DETAILS ON PAGES 12-15

Impressive and Distinguished

- Beyond the columned porch of this stylish home is an impressive two-story entry with an arched transom window.
- A series of elegant arches leads into the living room, which boasts a charming bay window, a handsome fireplace and an expansive 10-ft. vaulted ceiling.
- The adjoining formal dining room features a 10-ft. vaulted ceiling, built-in cabinetry and French doors to a backyard patio. A pocket door leads to the adjacent island kitchen, which includes a sunny bayed breakfast nook.
- The spacious family room offers an inviting woodstove and patio access.
- Just off the entry, double doors open to the den, which is furnished with built-in shelves and a boxed-out window.
- A curved stairway leads upstairs, where a railed balcony overlooks the entry. Double doors open into the master suite, which includes a bright bayed sitting area and a luxurious bath with a roomy walk-in closet.
- Two more bedrooms share a skylighted bath. The bonus area can be used as a fourth bedroom.

Plan CDG-2007

Bedrooms: 3+	Baths: 2½

Living Area:	
Upper floor	1,036 sq. ft.
Main floor	1,563 sq. ft.
Bonus room	225 sq. ft.
Total Living Area:	**2,824 sq. ft.**
Garage	841 sq. ft.
Exterior Wall Framing:	2x6

Foundation Options:

Crawlspace

(All plans can be built with your choice of foundation and framing. A generic conversion diagram is available. See order form.)

BLUEPRINT PRICE CODE:	D

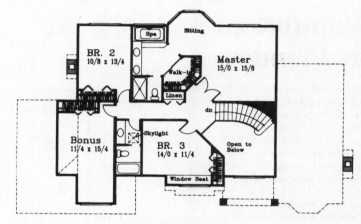

UPPER FLOOR

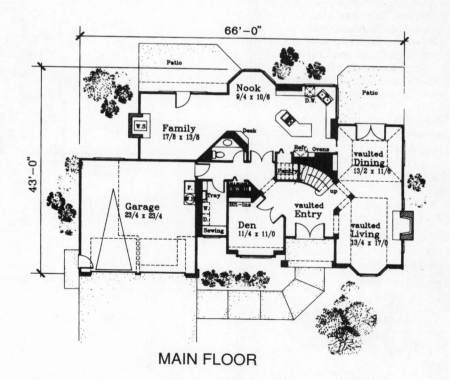

MAIN FLOOR

TO ORDER THIS BLUEPRINT,
CALL TOLL-FREE 1-800-547-5570

Plan CDG-2007

PRICES AND DETAILS
ON PAGES 12-15

175

Symmetrical Bay Windows

- This home's ornate facade proudly displays a pair of symmetrical copper-topped bay windows.
- A bright, two-story-high foyer stretches to the vaulted Great Room, with its fireplace and backyard deck access.
- The island kitchen offers a snack bar and a breakfast nook that opens to the deck and the garage.
- The main-floor master suite features private deck access, dual walk-in closets and a personal bath with a corner garden tub. A laundry room and a bayed study are nearby.
- Upstairs, three secondary bedrooms and another full bath are located off the balcony bridge, which overlooks both the Great Room and the foyer.
- A second stairway off the breakfast nook climbs to a bonus room, which adjoins an optional full bath and closet.

Plan C-9010

Bedrooms: 4+	Baths: 2½-3½
Living Area:	
Upper floor	761 sq. ft.
Main floor	1,637 sq. ft.
Bonus room	347 sq. ft.
Optional bath and closet	106 sq. ft.
Total Living Area:	**2,851 sq. ft.**
Daylight basement	1,637 sq. ft.
Garage	572 sq. ft.
Exterior Wall Framing:	2x4

Foundation Options:

Daylight basement
Crawlspace
(All plans can be built with your choice of foundation and framing. A generic conversion diagram is available. See order form.)

BLUEPRINT PRICE CODE:	**D**

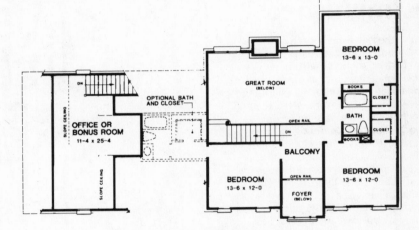

UPPER FLOOR

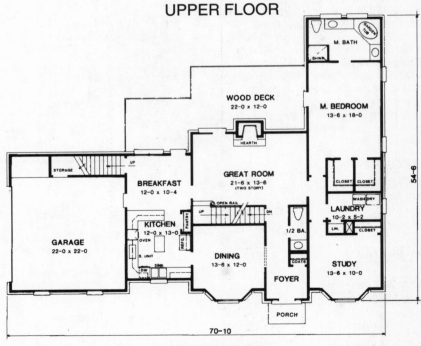

MAIN FLOOR

TO ORDER THIS BLUEPRINT, CALL TOLL-FREE 1-800-547-5570

Plan C-9010

PRICES AND DETAILS ON PAGES 12-15

Simple, Economical, Comfortable Space

- It's hard to beat a design like this for economical comfort.
- The large, welcoming front porch dresses up the basic rectangle of the home, adding grace and eye appeal.
- Inside, the large country kitchen includes a spacious and sunny breakfast area, which adjoins a convenient utility room.
- A formal dining room opens off the foyer, which leads to a large living room with a fireplace.
- The deluxe master bedroom suite includes a luxurious master bath with two walk-in closets and double vanities.
- Upstairs, two dormered bedrooms share a double bath and are connected by a balcony loft overlooking the living room below.

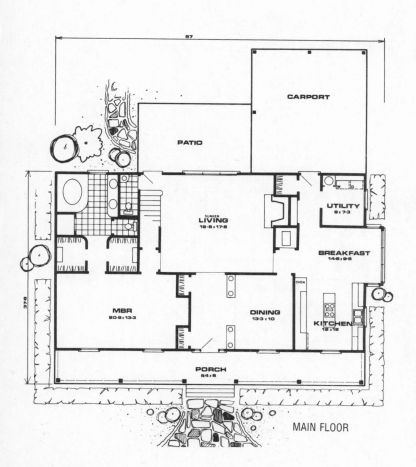

MAIN FLOOR

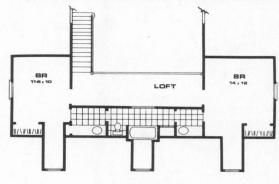

UPPER FLOOR

Plan J-86113

Bedrooms: 3	Baths: 2½

Space:	
Upper floor:	658 sq.ft.
Main floor:	1,740 sq.ft.

Total living area:	2,398 sq.ft.
Basement:	Approx. 1,740 sq.ft.
Carport:	440 sq.ft.
Porch:	324 sq.ft.

Exterior Wall Framing:	2x4

Foundation options:
Standard basement.
Crawlspace.
Slab.
(Foundation & framing conversion diagram available — see order form.)

Blueprint Price Code:	C

Photo by Mark Englund/HomeStyles

Old-Fashioned Charm

- A trio of dormers add old-fashioned charm to this modern design.
- Both the living room and the dining room offer vaulted celings, and the two rooms flow together to create a sense of even more spaciousness.
- The open kitchen, nook and family room combination features a sunny alcove, a walk-in pantry and an inviting wood stove.
- A first-floor den and a walk-through utility room are other big bonuses.
- Upstairs, the master suite includes a walk-in closet and a deluxe bath with a spa tub and a separate shower and water closet.
- Two more bedrooms, each with a window seat, and a bonus room complete this stylish design.

Plan CDG-2004

Bedrooms: 4	Baths: 2½
Living Area:	
Upper floor	928 sq. ft.
Main floor	1,317 sq. ft.
Bonus room	192 sq. ft.
Total Living Area:	**2,437 sq. ft.**
Partial daylight basement	780 sq. ft.
Garage	537 sq. ft.
Exterior Wall Framing:	2x6

Foundation Options:

Partial daylight basement
Crawlspace
(Typical foundation & framing conversion diagram available—see order form.)

BLUEPRINT PRICE CODE: C

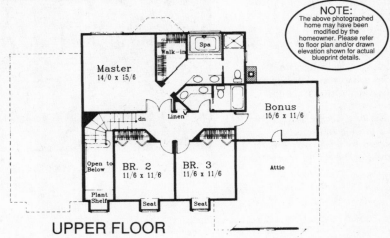

NOTE:
The above photographed home may have been modified by the homeowner. Please refer to floor plan and/or drawn elevation shown for actual blueprint details.

UPPER FLOOR

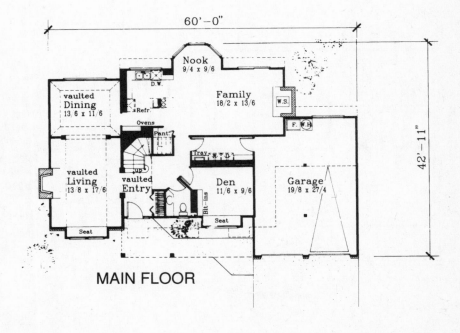

MAIN FLOOR

TO ORDER THIS BLUEPRINT, CALL TOLL-FREE 1-800-547-5570

Plan CDG-2004

PRICES AND DETAILS ON PAGES 12-15

Design Exudes Warmth and Comfort

- This plan represents a return to traditional styling with the open-concept interior so much in demand today.
- A vaulted entry and living room with an adjacent dining room make up the formal portion of this plan.
- A spacious hall leads to the large informal entertaining area composed of the kitchen, nook and family room.

- The second floor offers a large master suite and two additional bedrooms with a bonus room that can be left unfinished until needed.
- Exterior rooflines are all gabled for ease of construction and lower framing costs. The brick veneer garage face echoes the brick columns supporting the covered entry.

Plan S-8389	
Bedrooms: 3-4	**Baths:** 2½
Living Area:	
Upper floor	932 sq. ft.
Main floor	1,290 sq. ft.
Bonus room	228 sq. ft.
Total Living Area:	**2,450 sq. ft.**
Standard basement	1,290 sq. ft.
Garage	429 sq. ft.
Exterior Wall Framing:	2x6

Foundation Options:
Standard basement
Crawlspace
Slab
(Typical foundation & framing conversion diagram available—see order form.)

BLUEPRINT PRICE CODE:	C

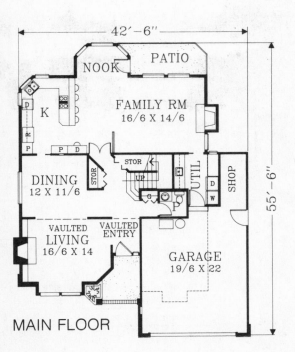

MAIN FLOOR

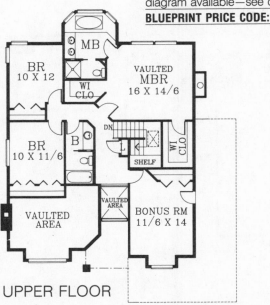

UPPER FLOOR

Panoramic Porch

- A gracious, ornate rounded front porch and a two-story turreted bay lend a Victorian charm to this home.
- A two-story foyer with round-top transom windows and plant ledge above greets guests at the entry.
- The living room enjoys a panoramic view overlooking the front porch and yard.
- The formal dining room and den each feature a bay window for added style.
- The kitchen/breakfast room incorporates an angled island cooktop, from which the sunken family room with corner fireplace can be enjoyed.
- The three bedrooms and two full baths upstairs are highlighted by a stunning master suite. The master bath offers a quaint octagonal sitting area within the turret bay.

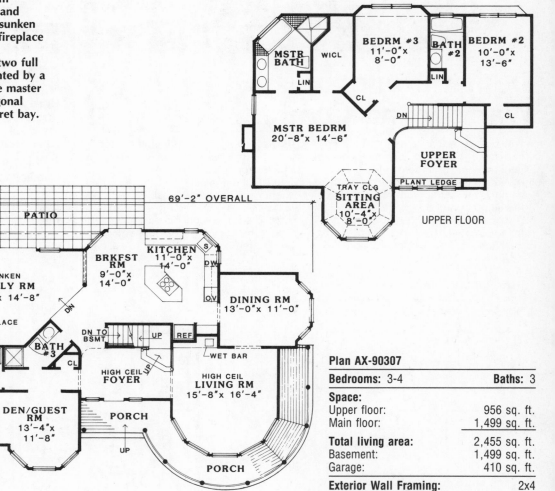

UPPER FLOOR

MAIN FLOOR

Plan AX-90307

Bedrooms: 3-4	Baths: 3

Space:	
Upper floor:	956 sq. ft.
Main floor:	1,499 sq. ft.

Total living area:	**2,455 sq. ft.**
Basement:	1,499 sq. ft.
Garage:	410 sq. ft.

Exterior Wall Framing:	2x4

Foundation options:
Standard basement.
Slab.
(Foundation & framing conversion diagram available — see order form.)

Blueprint Price Code:	C

PLANS H-3711-1 & H-3711-1A
(WITH GARAGE)

All-American Country Home

- Romantic, old-fashioned and spacious living areas combine to create this modern home.
- Off the entryway is the generous living room with fireplace and French doors which open onto the traditional rear porch.
- Country kitchen features an island table for informal occasions, while the adjoining family room is ideal for family gatherings.
- Practically placed, a laundry/mud room lies off the garage for immediate disposal of soiled garments.
- This plan is available with garage (H-3711-1) or without garage (H-3711-2) and with or without basement.

UPPER FLOOR

WALK-IN CLOSET 7'-6" x 7'-6"

BATH

BEDROOM 13'-3" x 15'-0"

LINEN 6'-0"

BATH

STOR.

CLOSET 4'-9" CLOSET 4'-9"

UP TO ATTIC

CLOSET 4'-0"

BEDROOM 13'-0" x 19'-0"

CLOSET 4'-0"

BEDROOM 15'-0" x 10'-0"

BEDROOM 10'-0" x 13'-3"

Plans H-3711-1/1A & -2/2A

Bedrooms: 4	Baths: 2½

Space:

Upper floor:	1,176 sq. ft.
Main floor:	1,288 sq. ft.
Total living area:	**2,464 sq. ft.**
Basement:	approx. 1,288 sq. ft.
Garage:	505 sq. ft.

Exterior Wall Framing:	2x6

Foundation options:
Standard basement (Plans H-3711-1 & -2).
Crawlspace (Plans H-3711-1A & -2A).
(Foundation & framing conversion diagram available — see order form.)

Blueprint Price Code:	C

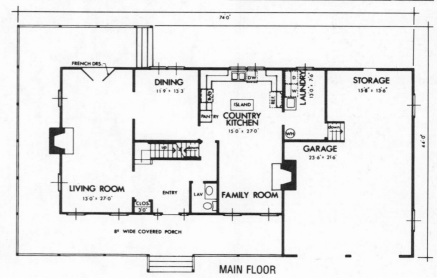

74'-0"

44'-0"

FRENCH DRS.

DINING 11'-9" x 13'-3"

DW

LAUNDRY 13'-0" x 7'-6"

STORAGE 15'-8" x 13'-6"

PANTRY

ISLAND

COUNTRY KITCHEN 15'-0" x 27'-0"

REF.

WH

down

GARAGE 23'-6" x 21'-6"

LIVING ROOM 13'-0" x 27'-0"

CLOS. 3'-0"

ENTRY

LAV.

FAMILY ROOM

8' WIDE COVERED PORCH

MAIN FLOOR

Luxury Home with Outdoor Orientation

- Courtyards, patios and a sun room orient this multi-level home to the outdoors.
- Interior design is carefully zoned for informal family living and formal entertaining.
- Expansive kitchen includes large island and plenty of counter space, and a sunny nook adjoins the kitchen.
- Soaring entry area leads visitors to the vaulted living room with fireplace, or to the more casual family room.
- An optional fourth bedroom off the foyer would make an ideal home office.
- Upstairs master suite includes luxury bath and big walk-in closet.
- Daylight basement version adds nearly 1,500 more square feet of space.

Plans P-7659-3A & -3D

Bedrooms: 3-4	Baths: 3

Space:

Upper floor:	1,050 sq. ft.
Main floor:	1,498 sq. ft.
Total living area:	**2,548 sq. ft.**
Basement:	1,490 sq. ft.
Garage:	583 sq. ft.

Exterior Wall Framing:	2x4

Foundation options:
Daylight basement, Plan P-7659-3D.
Crawlspace, Plan P-7659-3A.
(Foundation & framing conversion diagram available — see order form.)

Blueprint Price Code:	D

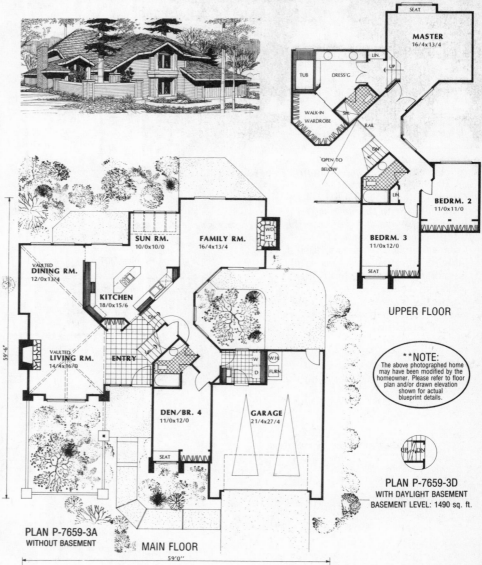

SUN RM. 10/0x10/0

FAMILY RM. 16/4x13/4

VAULTED DINING RM. 12/0x13/4

KITCHEN 18/0x15/6

VAULTED LIVING RM. 14/4x16/0

ENTRY

DEN/BR. 4 11/0x12/0

GARAGE 21/4x27/4

59'-6"

59'0"

PLAN P-7659-3A
WITHOUT BASEMENT

MAIN FLOOR

SEAT

MASTER 16/4x13/4

TUB   DRESS'G   LIN.

WALK-IN WARDROBE

OPEN TO BELOW

BEDRM. 2 11/0x11/0

BEDRM. 3 11/0x12/0

SEAT

UPPER FLOOR

**NOTE:
The above photographed home may have been modified by the homeowner. Please refer to floor plan and/or drawn elevation shown for actual blueprint details.

PLAN P-7659-3D
WITH DAYLIGHT BASEMENT
BASEMENT LEVEL: 1490 sq. ft.

TO ORDER THIS BLUEPRINT, CALL TOLL-FREE 1-800-547-5570

Plans P-7659-3A & -3D

PRICES AND DETAILS ON PAGES 12-15

Gracious Open-Concept Floor Plan

- A striking and luxurious contemporary, this home offers great space and modern styling.
- A covered entry leads to a spacious foyer, which flows into the sunken dining and Great Room area.
- The vaulted Great Room boasts a spectacular two-story-high fireplace, dramatic window walls and access to a rear deck or patio.
- A bright nook adjoins the open kitchen, which includes a corner window above the sink.
- The den, which could be a guest bedroom, features a bay window overlooking the deck.
- The majestic master bedroom on the second floor offers a 10-ft.-high coved ceiling, a splendid bath, a large closet and a private deck.
- Two other upstairs bedrooms share a second bath and a balcony hallway overlooking the Great Room and entry below.

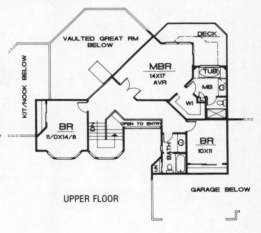

UPPER FLOOR

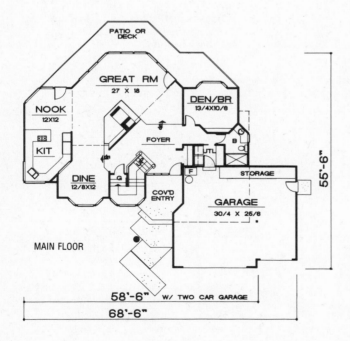

MAIN FLOOR

58'-6" W/ TWO CAR GARAGE

68'-6"

Plan S-41587	
Bedrooms: 3-4	**Baths:** 3
Living Area:	
Upper floor:	1,001 sq. ft.
Main floor	1,550 sq. ft.
Total Living Area:	**2,551 sq. ft.**
Basement	1,550 sq. ft.
Garage (three-car)	773 sq. ft.
Exterior Wall Framing:	2x6

Foundation Options:
Daylight basement
Standard basement
Crawlspace
Slab
(Typical foundation & framing conversion diagram available—see order form.)

BLUEPRINT PRICE CODE: D

PLAN H-2114-1B REAR VIEW

Designed for Outdoor Living

- Dining room, living room, and spa are oriented toward the full-width deck extending across the rear of the home.
- Floor-to-ceiling windows, vaulted ceilings, and a fireplace are featured in the living room.
- Spa room has tile floor, operable skylights, and private access through connecting master suite.
- Upper level offers two bedrooms, spacious bathroom, and a balcony view of the living room and scenery beyond.

MAIN FLOOR

70' - 2"

DECK

LIVING ROOM
23/0 x 13/10

DINING
14/0 x 14/0

SPA ROOM
13/6 x 10/0

SPA

SKYLIGHTS ABOVE

KITCHEN
11/0 x 11/0

PANTRY

STORAGE

BATH

REF

NOOK
12/0 x 11/0

ENTRY

GUEST

LAV

SH

LINEN

GARAGE
23/4 x 21/4

WALK IN CLOSET
8/0 x 7/6

BEDROOM
13/6 x 20/6

SEAT

STORAGE

LAUNDRY ROOM FOR PLAN W/O BSMT

PLAN H-2114-1A
WITHOUT BASEMENT

PLAN H-2114-1B
WITH DAYLIGHT BASEMENT

RECREATION ROOM
23/0 x 12/0

BEDROOM
13/0 x 11/6

STORAGE
13/0 x 9/6

furnace

CLOSET
4/6

CLOSET
4/6

LAUNDRY

BATH

STORAGE

BENCH

SAUNA

BENCH

GAME ROOM
13/0 x 20/0

UPPER FLOOR

OPEN TO LIVING ROOM

CLOSET
6/6

CLOSET
6/6

RAIL

down

BATH

LINEN

BEDROOM
13/0 x 16/0

CLOSET
8/0

BEDROOM
12/0 x 11/0

Plans H-2114-1A & -1B

Bedrooms: 3-4	Baths: 2½-3½
Space:	
Upper floor:	732 sq. ft.
Main floor:	1,682 sq. ft.
Spa room:	147 sq. ft.
Total living area:	**2,561 sq. ft.**
Basement:	approx. 1,386 sq. ft.
Garage:	547 sq. ft.
Exterior Wall Framing:	2x6

Foundation options:
Daylight basement (Plan H-2114-1B).
Crawlspace (Plan H-2114-1A).
(Foundation & framing conversion diagram available — see order form.)

Blueprint Price Code:

Without basement:	D
With basement:	F

TO ORDER THIS BLUEPRINT, CALL TOLL-FREE 1-800-547-5570

Plans H-2114-1A & -1B

PRICES AND DETAILS ON PAGES 12-15

Classic Country-Style

- Almost completely surrounded by an expansive porch, this classic plan exudes warmth and grace.
- The foyer is liberal in size and leads guests to a formal dining room to the left or the large living room to the right.
- A large country kitchen includes a sunny, bay-windowed breakfast nook.
- The main floor also includes a utility area and full bath.
- Upstairs, the master suite is impressive, with its large sleeping area, big closet and magnificent bath.
- Three secondary bedrooms with ample closets share a full bath with double sinks.
- Also note the stairs leading up to an attic, which is useful for storage space.

Plan J-86134

Bedrooms: 4	Baths: 3
Living Area:	
Upper floor	1,195 sq. ft.
Main floor	1,370 sq. ft.
Total Living Area	**2,565 sq. ft.**
Basement	1,370 sq. ft.
Garage	576 sq. ft.
Storage	144 sq. ft.
Exterior Wall Framing	2x4

Foundation Options:

Standard basement

Crawlspace

Slab

(Typical foundation & framing conversion diagram available—see order form.)

BLUEPRINT PRICE CODE   **D**

NOTE: The above photographed home may have been modified by the homeowner. Please refer to floor plan and/or drawn elevation shown for actual blueprint details.

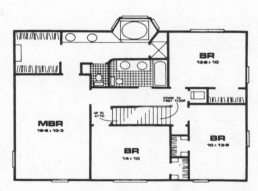

UPPER FLOOR

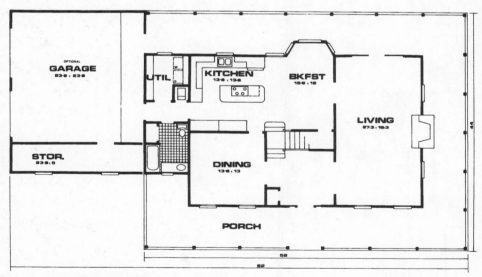

MAIN FLOOR

Photo by Kevin Haslip

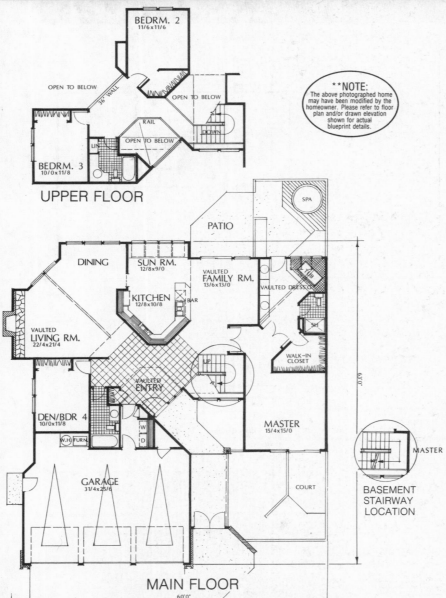

BEDRM. 2
11/6 x 11/6

OPEN TO BELOW

3/6' WALL

OPEN TO BELOW

RAIL

OPEN TO BELOW

LIN

DOWN

BEDRM. 3
10/0 x 11/8

UPPER FLOOR

NOTE:
The above photographed home may have been modified by the homeowner. Please refer to floor plan and/or drawn elevation shown for actual blueprint details.

SPA

PATIO

DINING

SUN RM.
12/8 x 9/0

KITCHEN
12/8 x 10/8

VAULTED FAMILY RM.
13/6 x 13/0

VAULTED DRESS

BAR

VAULTED LIVING RM.
22/4 x 21/4

SH

HP

WALK-IN CLOSET

VAULTED ENTRY

DEN/BDR 4
10/0 x 11/8

W.H. FURN

W D

MASTER
15/4 x 15/0

63'0"

GARAGE
31/4 x 25/6

COURT

MASTER

BASEMENT STAIRWAY LOCATION

MAIN FLOOR
60'0"

Privacy and Luxury

- This home's large roof planes and privacy fences enclose a thoroughly modern, open floor plan.
- A beautiful courtyard greets guests on their way to the secluded entrance. Inside, a vaulted entry area leads directly into the living and dining rooms, which also boast a vaulted ceiling, plus floor-to-ceiling windows, a fireplace and a wall-length stone hearth.
- A sun room next to the spacious, angular kitchen offers passive solar heating and natural brightness.
- The vaulted family room features access to a rear patio through sliding glass doors.
- The main-floor master bedroom boasts sliders to a secluded portion of the front courtyard. The vaulted master bath includes a walk-in closet, a raised tub, a separate shower and access to a private sun deck with a hot tub.
- Upstairs, two bedrooms are separated by a bridge hallway that overlooks the rooms below.

Plans P-7663-3A & -3D

Bedrooms: 3+	Baths: 3
Living Area:	
Upper floor	569 sq. ft.
Main floor	2,039 sq. ft.
Total Living Area:	**2,608 sq. ft.**
Daylight basement	2,039 sq. ft.
Garage	799 sq. ft.
Exterior Wall Framing:	2x4
Foundation Options:	**Plan #**
Daylight basement	P-7663-3D
Crawlspace	P-7663-3A
(Typical foundation & framing conversion diagram available—see order form.)	
BLUEPRINT PRICE CODE:	D

Sunlit Elegance

- This elegant contemporary design offers just about all the amenities today's families expect in a home.
- The formal dining room is large enough for a good-sized dinner party.
- The living room is sunken and vaulted and includes a handsome fireplace.
- The spacious kitchen includes a large island and a pantry, and is open to the vaulted family room.
- Upstairs, the master bedroom is impressive, with a private master bath, large closets and easy access to a private deck. (If the greenhouse is built, stairs go from the master bath down to the hot tub.)
- The second floor also includes a roomy library and a bonus room or extra bedroom.
- The plan also offers an optional solar greenhouse, which may contain a hot tub or simply offer a great space for green plants and sunbathing.

Plan S-8217

Bedrooms: 3-4	Baths: 2
Living Area:	
Upper floor	789 sq. ft.
Main floor	1,709 sq. ft.
Bonus room	336 sq. ft.
Total Living Area:	**2,834 sq. ft.**
Partial basement	1,242 sq. ft.
Garage	441 sq. ft.
Exterior Wall Framing:	2x6

Foundation Options:
Partial basement
Crawlspace
Slab
(Typical foundation & framing conversion diagram available—see order form.)

BLUEPRINT PRICE CODE:	D

UPPER FLOOR

MAIN FLOOR

62'

50'-6"

Photo by Mark Englund/HomeStyles

Take the Plunge!

- From the elegant porte cochere to the striking rooflines, this home's facade is magnificent. But the rear area is equally fine, with its spa, waterfall and pool.
- Double doors lead from the entry into a columned foyer. Beyond the living room is a sunken wet bar that extends into the pool area, allowing guests to swim up to the bar for refreshments.
- The stunning master suite offers views of the pool through a curved window wall, access to the patio and an opulent bath.
- A secluded den, study or guest room is conveniently close to the hall bath.
- The dining room boasts window walls and a tiered pedestal ceiling. The island kitchen easily services both the formal and the informal areas of the home.
- A large breakfast room flows into a warm family room with a fireplace and sliders to the patio and pool.
- A railed staircase leads to the upper floor, where there are two bedrooms, a continental bath and a shared balcony deck overlooking the pool area.
- The observatory features high windows to accommodate an amateur stargazer's telescope. This room could also be used as an activity area for hobbies or games.

Plan HDS-99-154

Bedrooms: 3-4	Baths: 3
Living Area:	
Upper floor	675 sq. ft.
Main floor	2,212 sq. ft.
Total Living Area:	**2,887 sq. ft.**
Garage	479 sq. ft.
Exterior Wall Framing:	2x4

Foundation Options:

Slab
(Typical foundation & framing conversion diagram available—see order form.)

BLUEPRINT PRICE CODE: **D**

NOTE:
The above photographed home may have been modified by the homeowner. Please refer to floor plan and/or drawn elevation shown for actual blueprint details.

UPPER FLOOR

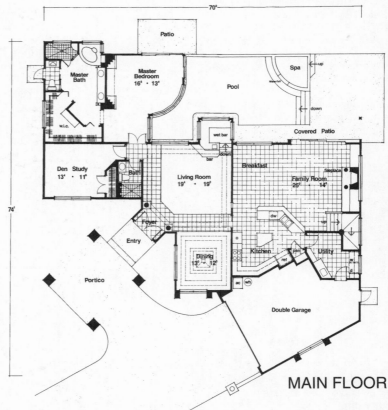

MAIN FLOOR

Photo by Mark Englund/HomeStyles

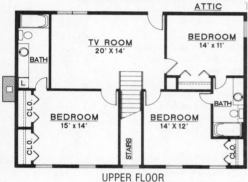

TV ROOM 20' X 14'

BEDROOM 14' x 11'

BATH

BATH

CLO. CLO.

BEDROOM 15' x 14'

BEDROOM 14' X 12'

STAIRS

CLO.

ATTIC

UPPER FLOOR

Plantation Perfected

- The stately plantation style with two-story columns, triple dormers, full-width porch and shuttered windows, is perfected with a modern, exciting floor plan.
- A vast living room lies to the left of the entry and stairs, complete with a fireplace and access to the rear porch and deck.
- The formal dining room is located to the right of the entry.
- The island kitchen overlooks the eating bay, and has glimpses of the living room through columns.
- The stunning main floor master suite features sloped ceilings, a garden bath overlooking a private courtyard, and a bay windowed sitting room.
- The three bedrooms upstairs share a large TV/playroom.

Plan E-2800	
Bedrooms: 4	**Baths:** 3

Space:	
Upper floor:	1,120 sq. ft.
Main floor:	1,768 sq. ft.

Total living area:	2,888 sq. ft.
Basement:	1,768 sq. ft.
Garage:	726 sq. ft.

Exterior Wall Framing:	2x6

Ceiling Heights:	
Upper floor:	8'
Main floor:	9'

Foundation options:
Crawlspace.
Standard basement.
Slab.
(Foundation & framing conversion diagram available — see order form.)

Blueprint Price Code:	D

MAIN FLOOR

72'

58'

DECK

MASTER SUITE 18' x 14'

SITTING 9' x 8'

SHV'S.

CLO.

S

PORCH

A/C

HALL

BATH

BATH

LIN

COURT YARD

3 CAR GARAGE 22' x 32'

EATING 13' x 10'

SINK

D.W.

REF.

P

W

D

UTIL.

F

STOR. 10' x 8'

PORCH

BAR

KITCHEN 14' x 12'

CT. OVEN

P

P

LIVING 28' x 18'

CLO.

DINING 18' X 14'

ENTRY

PORCH 39' x 5'

**NOTE:
The above photographed home may have been modified by the homeowner. Please refer to floor plan and/or drawn elevation shown for actual blueprint details.

Wrap-around Porch Accents Victorian Farmhouse

- Fish-scale shingles and horizontal siding team with the detailed front porch to create this look of yesterday. The sides and rear are brick.
- The main level features a center section of informal family room and formal living and dining rooms. They can all be connected via French doors.
- A separate workshop is located on the main level and connected to the main house by a covered breezeway.
- The master bath ceiling is sloped and has built-in skylights. The kitchen and eating area have high sloped ceilings also. Typical ceiling heights are 8' on the basement and upper level and 10' on the main level.
- This home is energy efficient.
- This home is designed on a full daylight basement. The two-car garage is located under the workshop.

MAIN LEVEL

UPPER LEVEL
PLAN E-3103
WITH DAYLIGHT BASEMENT

Exterior walls are 2x6 construction.

Heated area:	3,153 sq. ft.
Unheated area	2,066 sq. ft.
Total area: (Not counting basement)	5,219 sq. ft.

Blueprint Price Code E

Plan E-3103

TO ORDER THIS BLUEPRINT,
CALL TOLL-FREE 1-800-547-5570

PRICES AND DETAILS
ON PAGES 12-15

Splendor of the Old South

- Designed after "Monteigne," an Italianate home from the Natchez area, this reproduction utilizes modern stucco finishes for the exterior.
- The formal foyer is accented by the large circular stairwell. The foyer is open to the upper-floor balcony.
- The sun room stretches across the rear of the main house and overlooks the center courtyard.
- A uniquely located entertainment center serves the main activity rooms.
- The master suite and bath are super-plush and contain every imaginable feature — including his and hers vanities, a separate mirrored make-up vanity, large walk-in closets and a glassed-in garden tub. The king-sized bedroom suite even utilizes the adjoining study.
- Two additional bedrooms with private baths are located on the upper level. They share a study and a veranda. On the main floor, a fourth bedroom serves as a guest room or nursery.
- The living room and study have 14' ceilings. Typical ceiling heights are 9' on the main floor and 8' on the upper floor.

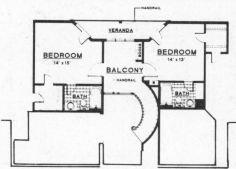

UPPER FLOOR

Plan E-3200	
Bedrooms: 4	**Baths:** 4
Living Area:	
Upper floor	629 sq. ft.
Main floor	2,655 sq. ft.
Total Living Area:	**3,284 sq. ft.**
Standard basement	2,655 sq. ft.
Garage and storage	667 sq. ft.
Exterior Wall Framing:	2x6
Foundation Options:	
Standard basement	
Crawlspace	
Slab	
(Typical foundation & framing conversion diagram available—see order form.)	
BLUEPRINT PRICE CODE	E

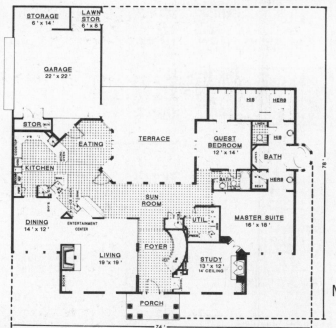

MAIN FLOOR

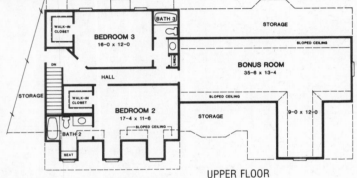

UPPER FLOOR

MAIN FLOOR

Deluxe Main-Floor Master Suite

- Traditional-style exterior with modern floor plan. Dormers and stone add curb appeal to this home.
- Formal entry with staircase leads to formal living or large family room.
- Large kitchen is conveniently located between formal dining room and secluded breakfast nook with bay window.
- Private master suite has tray ceiling and walk-in closet. Master bath has corner tub, shower, and dual vanities.
- Large screened porch off family room is perfect for outdoor living.
- Large utility room with pantry and toilet are conveniently located off the garage.
- Second floor features two large bedrooms with walk-in closets and two full baths.
- Optional bonus room (624 sq. ft.) can be finished as a large game room, bedroom, office, etc.

Plan C-8915

Bedrooms: 3		Baths: 3½
Space:		
Upper floor:		832 sq. ft.
Main floor:		1,927 sq. ft.
Bonus area:		624 sq. ft.
Total living area:		**3,383 sq. ft.**
Basement:		1,674 sq. ft.
Garage:		484 sq. ft.
Exterior Wall Framing:		2x4

Ceiling Heights:
First floor: 9'
Second floor: 8'

Foundation options:
Daylight basement.
Crawlspace.
(Foundation & framing conversion diagram available — see order form.)

Blueprint Price Code: E

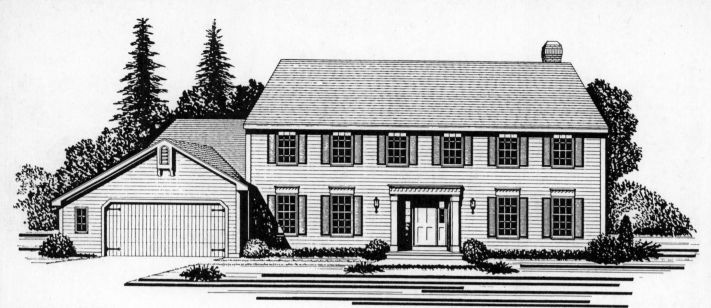

A Family Tradition

- This traditional design has clean, sharp styling, with family-sized areas for formal and casual gatherings.
- The sidelighted foyer is graced with a beautiful open staircase and a wide coat closet. Flanking the foyer are the spacious formal living areas.
- The everyday living areas include an island kitchen, a bayed dinette and a large family room with a fireplace.
- Just off the entrance from the garage, double doors open to the quiet study, which boasts built-in bookshelves.
- A powder room and a deluxe laundry room with cabinets are convenient to the active areas of the home.
- Upstairs, the master suite features a roomy split bath and a large walk-in closet. Three more bedrooms share another split bath.

Plan A-118-DS

Bedrooms: 4+	Baths: 2½
Living Area:	
Upper floor	1,344 sq. ft.
Main floor	1,556 sq. ft.
Total Living Area:	**2,900 sq. ft.**
Standard basement	1,556 sq. ft.
Garage	576 sq. ft.
Exterior Wall Framing:	2x4

Foundation Options:

Standard basement

(All plans can be built with your choice of foundation and framing. A generic conversion diagram is available. See order form.)

BLUEPRINT PRICE CODE:	D

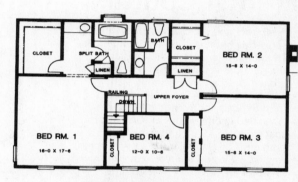

UPPER FLOOR

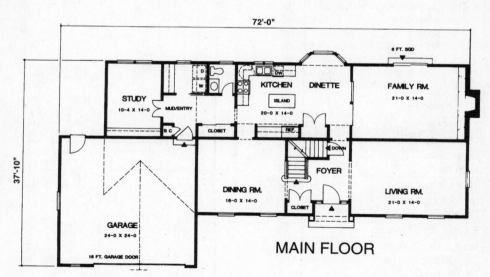

MAIN FLOOR

TO ORDER THIS BLUEPRINT,
CALL TOLL-FREE 1-800-547-5570

Plan A-118-DS

PRICES AND DETAILS
ON PAGES 12-15

193

Sprawling French Country

- A hip roof and gable accents give this sprawling home a country, French look.
- To the left of the entry, the formal dining room is illuminated with a tall arched window arrangement.
- The spectacular living room stretches from the entry of the home to the rear. A vaulted ceiling in this expansive space rises to 19 ft., and windows at both ends offer light and a nice breeze.
- Angled walls add interest to the roomy informal areas, which overlook the covered lanai. The island kitchen opens to the adjoining morning room and the sunny family room.
- The spacious main-floor master suite is highlighted by a 13-ft. vaulted ceiling and a bayed sitting area. The master bath features dual walk-in closets, a large spa tub and a separate shower.
- Three extra bedrooms and two more baths share the upper level.

Plan DD-2889

Bedrooms: 4	Baths: 3½
Living Area:	
Upper floor	819 sq. ft.
Main floor	2,111 sq. ft.
Total Living Area:	**2,930 sq. ft.**
Standard basement	2,111 sq. ft.
Garage	622 sq. ft.
Exterior Wall Framing:	2x4

Foundation Options:
Standard basement
Crawlspace
Slab
(All plans can be built with your choice of foundation and framing. A generic conversion diagram is available. See order form.)

BLUEPRINT PRICE CODE: D

UPPER FLOOR

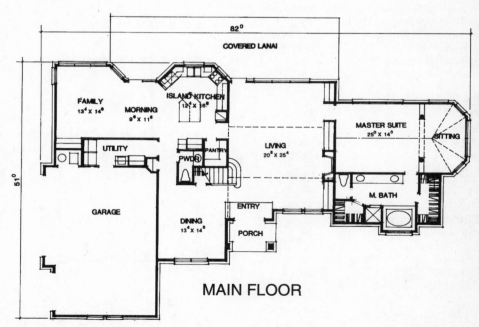

MAIN FLOOR

Plan DD-2889

PRICES AND DETAILS ON PAGES 12-15

Set In Stone

- Sure to impress, this home features a stucco finish set off by a two-story entry faced with stone.
- Inside, a stunning 18-ft. vaulted foyer separates the formal living spaces. The secluded living room has a 15-ft. vaulted ceiling and a boxed-out window. Columns outline the dining room, which has French doors to a covered porch.
- The casual spaces begin with a wonderful Great Room that features a two-story-high ceiling and a fireplace flanked by tall arched windows.
- Window walls and a French door to the backyard brighten the breakfast nook, which has a 14-ft. vaulted ceiling. The adjoining kitchen offers a work island, a corner sink and a walk-in pantry.
- The superb master suite includes a 10½-ft. tray ceiling in the angled sleeping area and a 16-ft. vaulted ceiling in the luxurious master bath.
- Ceilings in all main-floor rooms are 9 ft. high unless otherwise specified.
- Upstairs, a balcony hall leads to three nice-sized bedrooms, each with a walk-in closet and private access to one of two compartmentalized baths.

Plan FB-5348-BARR

Bedrooms: 4	Baths: 3½
Living Area:	
Upper floor	1,057 sq. ft.
Main floor	2,165 sq. ft.
Total Living Area:	**3,222 sq. ft.**
Daylight basement	2,165 sq. ft.
Garage	400 sq. ft.
Exterior Wall Framing:	2x4

Foundation Options:

Daylight basement

(All plans can be built with your choice of foundation and framing. A generic conversion diagram is available. See order form.)

BLUEPRINT PRICE CODE: E

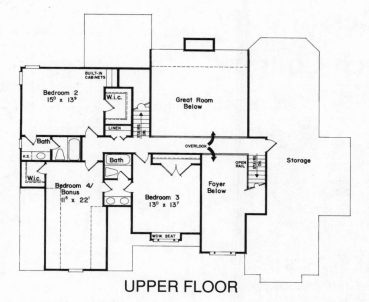

UPPER FLOOR

MAIN FLOOR

TO ORDER THIS BLUEPRINT,
CALL TOLL-FREE 1-800-547-5570

Plan FB-5348-BARR

PRICES AND DETAILS
ON PAGES 12-15

195

Timeless Beauty

- Reflected in its lovely windows and stone and stucco facade, this home has timeless beauty and lasting appeal.
- Past the inviting covered front porch, the two-story-high entry is flanked by the intimate formal areas.
- Warmed by a handsome fireplace, the large family room features a window wall with views to a backyard patio.
- The good-sized kitchen includes a pantry and an angled serving bar. The adjoining morning room opens to the partially covered patio.
- The main-floor bedroom is a perfect guest or in-law suite, with easy access to the bathroom, utility room and garage. All main-floor ceilings are 10 ft. high for added spaciousness.
- Upstairs, a versatile game room boasts a 10-ft. ceiling and access to a nice deck.
- The master bedroom also has a 10-ft. ceiling and enjoys a private covered porch, a roomy walk-in closet and a luxurious bath with a garden tub.
- Three additional upper-floor bedrooms and a full bath all have 9-ft. ceilings.

Plan DD-2952

Bedrooms: 5	Baths: 3
Living Area:	
Upper floor	1,721 sq. ft.
Main floor	1,394 sq. ft.
Total Living Area:	**3,115 sq. ft.**
Standard basement	1,394 sq. ft.
Garage	442 sq. ft.
Exterior Wall Framing:	2x4

Foundation Options:

Standard basement
Crawlspace
Slab

(All plans can be built with your choice of foundation and framing. A generic conversion diagram is available. See order form.)

BLUEPRINT PRICE CODE:	E

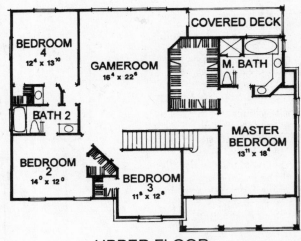

UPPER FLOOR

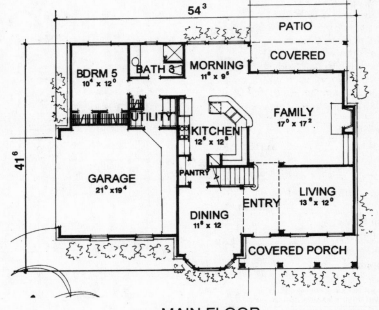

MAIN FLOOR

TO ORDER THIS BLUEPRINT, CALL TOLL-FREE 1-800-547-5570   Plan DD-2952   *PRICES AND DETAILS ON PAGES 12-15*

Dramatic Rear Views

- Columned front and rear porches offer country styling to this elegant two-story.
- The formal dining room and living room flank the two-story-high foyer.
- A dramatic array of windows stretches along the informal, rear-oriented living areas, where the central family room features a 17-ft.-high vaulted ceiling and a striking fireplace.
- The modern kitchen features an angled snack counter, a walk-in pantry and a work island, in addition to the bayed morning room.
- The exciting and secluded master suite has a sunny bayed sitting area with its own fireplace. Large walk-in closets lead to a luxurious private bath with angled dual vanities, a garden spa tub and a separate shower.
- The centrally located stairway leads to three extra bedrooms and two full baths on the upper floor.

Plan DD-2912

Bedrooms: 4	Baths: 3½
Living Area:	
Upper floor	916 sq. ft.
Main floor	2,046 sq. ft.
Total Living Area:	**2,962 sq. ft.**
Standard basement	1,811 sq. ft.
Garage	513 sq. ft.
Exterior Wall Framing:	2x4

Foundation Options:

Standard basement

Crawlspace

Slab

(All plans can be built with your choice of foundation and framing. A generic conversion diagram is available. See order form.)

BLUEPRINT PRICE CODE: D

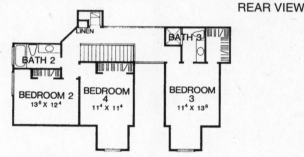

REAR VIEW

UPPER FLOOR

MAIN FLOOR

TO ORDER THIS BLUEPRINT,
CALL TOLL-FREE 1-800-547-5570

Plan DD-2912

PRICES AND DETAILS
ON PAGES 12-15

197

Stately Elegance

- The elegant interior of this home is introduced by a dramatic barrel-vaulted entry with stately columns.
- Double doors open to the 19-ft.-high foyer, where a half-round transom window brightens an attractive open-railed stairway.
- Off the foyer, the living room is separated from the sunny dining room by impressive columns.
- The island kitchen offers a bright corner sink, a walk-in pantry and a bayed breakfast area with backyard views.
- The adjoining family room offers a door to a backyard patio, while a wet bar and a fireplace enhance the whole area.
- Upstairs, the master suite boasts a private bath with two walk-in closets, a garden spa tub and a separate shower.
- Three secondary bedrooms have private bathroom access.
- Ceilings in all rooms are 9 ft. high for added spaciousness.

Plan DD-2968-A

Bedrooms: 4+	Baths: 3½
Living Area:	
Upper floor	1,382 sq. ft.
Main floor	1,586 sq. ft.
Total Living Area:	**2,968 sq. ft.**
Standard basement	1,586 sq. ft.
Garage	521 sq. ft.
Exterior Wall Framing:	2x4

Foundation Options:

Standard basement

Crawlspace

Slab

(All plans can be built with your choice of foundation and framing. A generic conversion diagram is available. See order form.)

BLUEPRINT PRICE CODE:	D

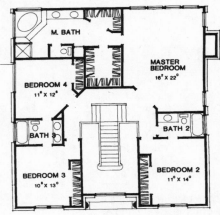

UPPER FLOOR

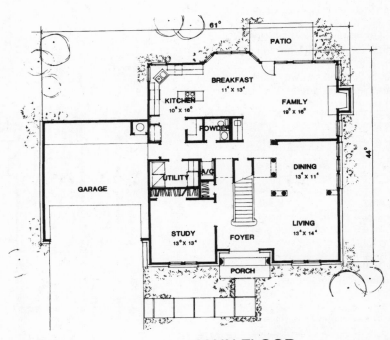

MAIN FLOOR

Oriented for Scenic Rear View

- That elegant look of the past is found in this expansive post-modern design.
- A two-story vaulted entry leads to spacious formal entertaining areas.
- A dining room with built-in China closet is to the left.
- To the right is a formal living room with a strikingly elegant bow window.
- The family room and living room share an interesting corner fireplace.
- A convenient powder room is tucked away behind the sweeping curved staircase.
- A see-through wine rack is an eye-catcher in the kitchen, along with its green-house window, island chopping block and abundant counter space.
- The living and family rooms are defined by decorative columns and arches and are a step-down from the foyer/hallway.
- Upstairs, a luxurious master suite boasts a sunny bow window, deluxe bath and enormous closet.
- Three other bedrooms, a full bath and a large unfinished "bonus space" complete the second floor.

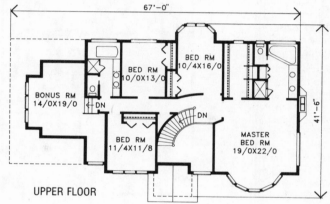

UPPER FLOOR

67'—0"

41'—6"

BONUS RM 14/0X19/0

BED RM 10/0X13/0

BED RM 10/4X16/0

BED RM 11/4X11/8

MASTER BED RM 19/0X22/0

DN

DN

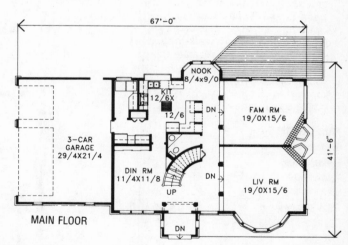

MAIN FLOOR

67'—0"

41'—6"

3-CAR GARAGE 29/4X21/4

DIN RM 11/4X11/8

KIT 12/6X 12/6

NOOK 8/4X9/0

FAM RM 19/0X15/6

LIV RM 19/0X15/6

UP

DN

DN

DN

Plan SD-8819

Bedrooms: 4-5	**Baths:** 2½

Space:
Upper floor:	1,500 sq. ft.
Main floor:	1,476 sq. ft.

Total living area:	**2,976 sq. ft.**
Bonus area:	266 sq. ft.
Basement:	approx. 1,476 sq. ft.
Garage:	626 sq. ft.

Exterior Wall Framing: 2x6

Foundation options:
Standard basement.
Crawlspace.
(Foundation & framing conversion diagram available — see order form.)

Blueprint Price Code: D

Spacious and Stately

- This popular home design boasts a classic Creole exterior and a symmetrical layout, with 9-ft.-high ceilings on the main floor.
- French doors lead from the formal living and dining rooms to the large family room. The central fireplace is flanked by French doors that open to a covered rear porch and an open-air deck.
- The kitchen is reached easily from the family room, the dining room and the rear entrance. An island cooktop and a window-framed eating area are other features found here.
- The real seller, though, is the main-floor master suite with its spectacular bath. Among its many extras are a built-in vanity, a spa tub and a 16-ft. sloped ceiling with a skylight.
- Three upstairs bedrooms, each with double closets and private bath access, make this the perfect family-sized home.

Plan E-3000

Bedrooms: 4	Baths: 3½
Living Area:	
Upper floor	1,027 sq. ft.
Main floor	2,008 sq. ft.
Total Living Area:	**3,035 sq. ft.**
Standard basement	2,008 sq. ft.
Garage	484 sq. ft.
Storage	96 sq. ft.
Exterior Wall Framing:	2x6

Foundation Options:

Standard basement
Crawlspace
Slab

(All plans can be built with your choice of foundation and framing. A generic conversion diagram is available. See order form.)

BLUEPRINT PRICE CODE:	E

UPPER FLOOR

MAIN FLOOR

Plan E-3000

PRICES AND DETAILS ON PAGES 12-15

Attractive Options

- This two-story traditional has an attractive facade and a modern floor plan with plenty of enticing options.
- Inside, the foyer flows to the formal living areas. On the left, the living room has windows on three sides and the option of a fireplace and a wet bar. To the right, the large dining room is easily served from the kitchen.
- With an island cooktop and a built-in desk, the kitchen merges with a sunny breakfast room at the rear of the home.
- Overlooking the rear deck, the spacious family room features a fireplace, a skylight and an 11-ft. cathedral ceiling that opens up to an optional loft area over the garage.
- The nice-sized master bedroom on the upper level offers a private sitting area with an 11½-ft. sloped ceiling and a luxurious skylighted bath with a garden tub and a separate shower.
- The optional area above the garage includes an extra bedroom and another full bath as well as a loft area.

Plan AX-91310

Bedrooms: 4+	Baths: 2½-3½
Living Area:	
Upper floor	1,083 sq. ft.
Main floor	1,377 sq. ft.
Optional upper loft	597 sq. ft.
Total Living Area:	**3,057 sq. ft.**
Standard basement	1,377 sq. ft.
Garage	640 sq. ft.
Exterior Wall Framing:	2x4

Foundation Options:

Standard basement

Slab

(All plans can be built with your choice of foundation and framing. A generic conversion diagram is available. See order form.)

BLUEPRINT PRICE CODE: E

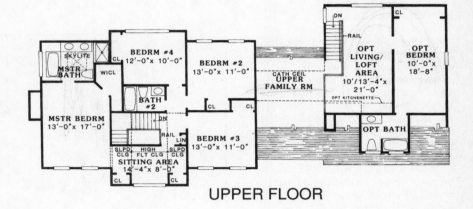

UPPER FLOOR

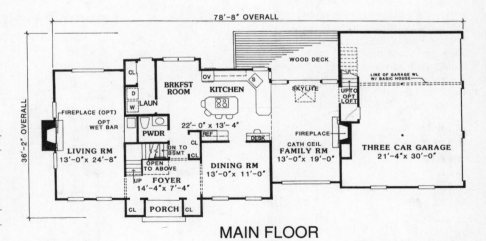

MAIN FLOOR

Stately and Roomy

- The exquisite exterior of this two-story home opens to a very roomy interior.
- The magnificent two-story-high foyer shows off a curved, open-railed stairway to the upper floor and opens to a study on the right and the formal living areas on the left.
- The spacious living room flows into a formal dining room that overlooks the outdoors through a lovely bay window.
- A large work island and snack counter sit at the center of the open kitchen and breakfast room. An oversized pantry closet, a powder room and a laundry room are all close at hand.
- Adjoining the breakfast room is the large sunken family room, featuring a 12-ft.-high vaulted ceiling, a cozy fireplace and outdoor access.
- The upper floor includes a stunning master bedroom with an 11-ft. vaulted ceiling and a luxurious private bath.
- Three additional bedrooms share a second full bath.

Plan CH-280-A

Bedrooms: 4+	Baths: 2½
Living Area:	
Upper floor	1,262 sq. ft.
Main floor	1,797 sq. ft.
Total Living Area:	**3,059 sq. ft.**
Basement	1,797 sq. ft.
Garage	462 sq. ft.
Exterior Wall Framing:	2x4

Foundation Options:

Daylight basement

Standard basement

Crawlspace

(All plans can be built with your choice of foundation and framing. A generic conversion diagram is available. See order form.)

BLUEPRINT PRICE CODE: E

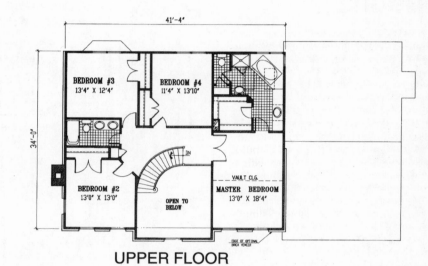

UPPER FLOOR

MAIN FLOOR

TO ORDER THIS BLUEPRINT, CALL TOLL-FREE 1-800-547-5570

Plan CH-280-A

PRICES AND DETAILS ON PAGES 12-15

Spacious and Striking

- Alluring angles and an open, airy floor plan distinguish this impressive home, designed to take advantage of a sloping lot.
- A gorgeous covered deck and patio give guests a royal welcome.
- Designed for both entertaining and family gatherings, the home's main floor features a bright family room with an 11-ft.-high vaulted ceiling and fabulous windows. A two-way fireplace with a lovely semi-round planter is shared with the adjoining dining room.
- The combination kitchen and breakfast area features a 10-ft. vaulted ceiling, a center island and a high pot shelf.
- The roomy master suite boasts a 10-ft. vaulted ceiling and double doors to a private balcony. The sumptuous master bath includes a beautiful Jacuzzi, a separate shower and a walk-in closet.
- Three more bedrooms and three full baths are located on the lower floor.
- A second family room includes a wet bar and double doors to a large covered patio.

Plan Q-3080-1A

Bedrooms: 4	Baths: 4½
Living Area:	
Main floor	1,575 sq. ft.
Lower floor	1,505 sq. ft.
Total Living Area:	**3,080 sq. ft.**
Garage	702 sq. ft.
Exterior Wall Framing:	2x4
Foundation Options:	

Slab
(All plans can be built with your choice of foundation and framing. A generic conversion diagram is available. See order form.)

BLUEPRINT PRICE CODE:	E

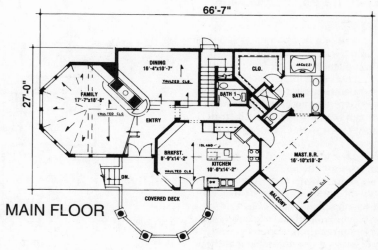

MAIN FLOOR

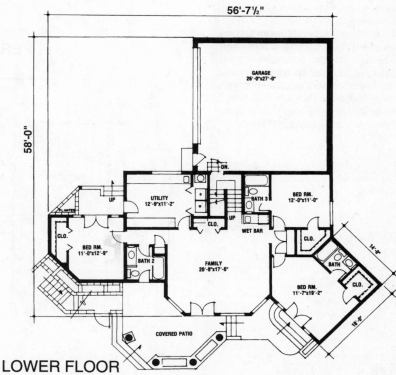

LOWER FLOOR

Tall Two-Story

- This gorgeous two-story is introduced by a barrel-vaulted entry and supporting columns. Inside, a spectacular curved staircase leads to a balcony overlook.
- Off the two-story-high foyer, a library with a 16-ft.-high vaulted ceiling is perfect for reading or study.
- A formal dining room opposite the library opens to the fabulous island kitchen. The kitchen offers an angled serving bar to the bayed breakfast area and adjoining living room.
- The spacious living room, with an 18-ft. vaulted ceiling, opens to a backyard patio. A fireplace flanked by built-in shelving warms the whole family area.
- The master bedroom boasts a 10-ft. gambrel ceiling, a sunny bay window and patio access. The spacious master bath offers his-and-hers walk-in closets, an oval tub and a separate shower.
- A second stairway near the utility room leads to the upper floor, where there are three more bedrooms, two baths and a bonus room above the garage. The bonus room could be finished as a game room, a media center or a hobby area.

Plan DD-3125

Bedrooms: 4+	Baths: 3½
Living Area:	
Upper floor	982 sq. ft.
Main floor	2,147 sq. ft.
Total Living Area:	**3,129 sq. ft.**
Unfinished Bonus	196 sq. ft.
Standard basement	1,996 sq. ft.
Garage	771 sq. ft.
Exterior Wall Framing:	2x4

Foundation Options:

Standard basement
Crawlspace
Slab

(All plans can be built with your choice of foundation and framing. A generic conversion diagram is available. See order form.)

BLUEPRINT PRICE CODE: E

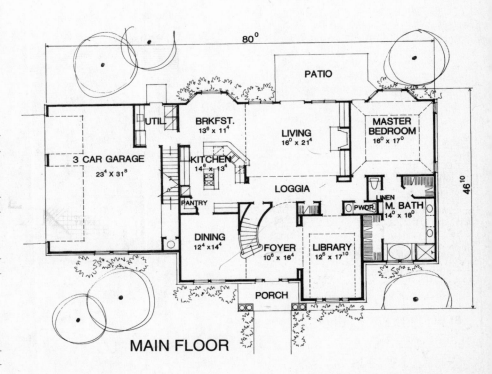

UPPER FLOOR

MAIN FLOOR

Plan DD-3125

PRICES AND DETAILS ON PAGES 12-15

Creative Spaces

- This expansive home uses vaulted ceilings and multiple levels to create a functional, airy floor plan.
- The broad, vaulted entry foyer leads to the bayed living room, which is warmed by a striking fireplace. A few steps down, the dining room opens to a wide backyard deck.
- The island kitchen features a sunny sink area and a breakfast nook with deck access. A laundry room, a half-bath and a den or extra bedroom are also found on this level.
- Adjacent to the nook, the sunken family room boasts a wet bar, a second fireplace and a bright window wall with sliding glass doors to a lovely patio.
- Upstairs, the master suite includes a sunken bedroom with a private deck. The lavish master bath offers a sunken garden tub, a dual-sink vanity and a skylight near the private shower.
- Three large secondary bedrooms share another skylighted bath. Each bedroom has its own unique design feature.

Plans P-7664-4A & -4D

Bedrooms: 4+	Baths: 2½
Living Area:	
Upper floor	1,301 sq. ft.
Main floor	1,853 sq. ft.
Total Living Area:	**3,154 sq. ft.**
Daylight basement	1,486 sq. ft.
Garage	668 sq. ft.
Exterior Wall Framing:	2x4
Foundation Options:	**Plan #**
Daylight basement	P-7664-4D
Crawlspace	P-7664-4A

(All plans can be built with your choice of foundation and framing. A generic conversion diagram is available. See order form.)

BLUEPRINT PRICE CODE:	E

UPPER FLOOR

BASEMENT STAIRWAY LOCATION

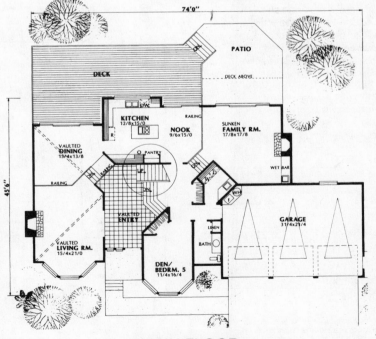

MAIN FLOOR

Ornate Design

- This exciting home is distinguished by an ornate facade with symmetrical windows and a columned entry.
- A beautiful arched window highlights the two-story-high foyer and its open-railed stairway. The foyer separates the two formal rooms and flows back to the huge family room.
- With an 18-ft. ceiling, the family room is brightened by corner windows and warmed by a central fireplace.
- Columns introduce the sunny breakfast area and the gourmet kitchen, which features an angled island/serving bar and a butler's pantry near the dining room. A laundry room and a second stairway to the upper floor are nearby.
- Ceilings in all main-floor rooms are 9 ft. high unless otherwise specified.
- Upstairs, a dramatic balcony overlooks the family room and the foyer.
- The master suite boasts a 10-ft. tray ceiling, a sitting room and an opulent garden bath with a 12-ft. vaulted ceiling. Three more bedrooms, each with a walk-in closet and private bath access, complete the upper floor.

Plan FB-5347-HAST

Bedrooms: 4+	Baths: 4
Living Area:	
Upper floor	1,554 sq. ft.
Main floor	1,665 sq. ft.
Total Living Area:	**3,219 sq. ft.**
Daylight basement	1,665 sq. ft.
Garage	440 sq. ft.
Exterior Wall Framing:	2x4

Foundation Options:

Daylight basement

(All plans can be built with your choice of foundation and framing. A generic conversion diagram is available. See order form.)

BLUEPRINT PRICE CODE:	E

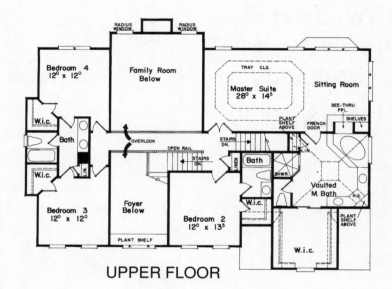

UPPER FLOOR

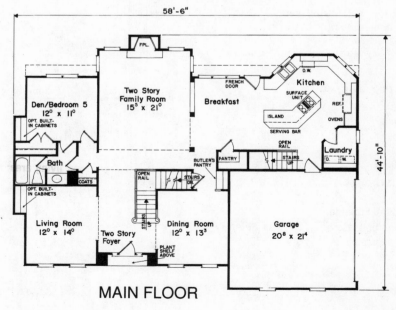

MAIN FLOOR

TO ORDER THIS BLUEPRINT, CALL TOLL-FREE 1-800-547-5570

Plan FB-5347-HAST

PRICES AND DETAILS ON PAGES 12-15

Lower Level Opens to Rear in Spacious Hillside Design

- A huge living room with fireplace and dining room with railing overlook the stairway to the lower level of this walk-out, hillside design.
- The spacious country kitchen offers an island cooktop and unique skywall.
- Three to four bedrooms, an optional hobby room, and a family room with second fireplace, wet bar and attached deck occupy the lower level.

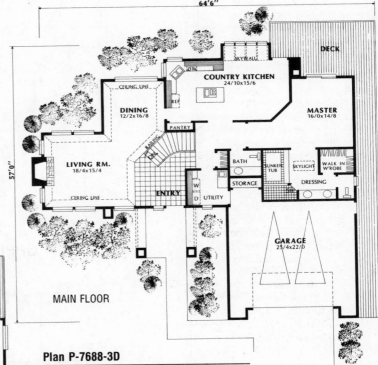

MAIN FLOOR

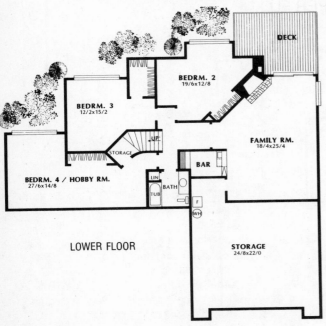

LOWER FLOOR

Plan P-7688-3D

Bedrooms: 3-4	Baths: 2½
Space:	
Main floor:	1,624 sq. ft.
Lower floor:	1,624 sq. ft.
Total living area:	3,248 sq. ft.
Garage:	557 sq. ft.
Storage:	620 sq. ft.
Exterior Wall Framing:	2x4

Foundation options:
Daylight basement.
(Foundation & framing conversion diagram available — see order form.)

Blueprint Price Code:	E

Anyone for Fun?

- A spectacular sunken game room with a corner window, vaulted ceilings, wet bar and half-wall that separates it from the family room is ideal for the active family or for those who like to entertain.
- The exciting atmosphere continues to the family room, also at a level lower than the rest of the home; here you'll find a fireplace, a rear window wall and a railing that allows a view of the adjoining vaulted nook.
- The spacious kitchen offers an island cooktop, pantry and pass-through to the game room hallway; formal, vaulted living areas are found opposite the entry.
- An upper-level bridge overlooks the game room and joins the two secondary bedrooms with the master suite and luxury, skylit master bath.

MAIN FLOOR

71'0"

PATIO

VAULTED NOOK 9/8x8/6

FAMILY RM. 18/4x13/6

VAULTED DINING 12/0x14/4

KITCHEN 17/0x14/0

42" HIGH WALL

SUNKEN VAULTED GAME RM. 24/6x16/0

PANTRY

DN TO KITCHEN

STEP

UTILITY 12/0x6/2

BAR

VAULTED LIVING RM. 14/4x16/6

ENTRY

BATH

TUB   LINEN

DW

F WH

GARAGE 32/0x22/6

DEN/ BEDRM. 4 11/0x12/0

SEAT

59'0"

UPPER FLOOR

SEAT

CEILING LINE

MASTER SUITE 18/4x13/6

SHELF   LINEN

VANITY   SKYLIGHT

SUNKEN TUB   STEP

SKYLIGHT

WALK IN WARDROBE

SKYLIGHT   RAILING

OPEN TO GAME ROOM BELOW

OPEN TO ENTRY BELOW

RAILING

BATH

TUB   LIN

SEAT

BEDRM. 2 14/8x11/0

BEDRM. 3

SEAT

ENTRY   BATH

WITH DAYLIGHT BASEMENT

Plans P-7665-3A & -3D

Bedrooms: 3-4	Baths: 3
Space:	
Upper floor	1,160 sq. ft.
Main floor	2,124 sq. ft.
Total Living Area	**3,284 sq. ft.**
Basement	2,104 sq. ft.
Garage	720 sq. ft.
Exterior Wall Framing	2x4
Foundation options:	Plan #
Daylight Basement	P-7665-3D
Crawlspace	P-7665-3A
(Foundation & framing conversion diagram available—see order form.)	
Blueprint Price Code	E

Smart Two-Story

- This simple yet classically designed two-story is functional and spacious.
- The recessed entry opens to a wide reception foyer that offers dual closets and access to each of the living areas.
- The enormous sunken living room with an optional fireplace stretches from the front of the house all the way to the back! Charming French doors open to the backyard.
- The big family room also provides easy outdoor access. A fireplace would look nice between the corner windows.
- The efficient kitchen features an island range, a work desk and a handy pantry. The adjoining breakfast area is enhanced by a lovely bay window that opens to the backyard.
- Four big bedrooms and two baths are housed on the upper floor.
- The master bedroom boasts a private sitting area and the option of a fireplace. Two walk-in closets and an elegant skylighted bath with a cathedral ceiling are also included.

Plan AX-87105

Bedrooms: 4	Baths: 2½
Living Area:	
Upper floor	1,552 sq. ft.
Main floor	1,734 sq. ft.
Total Living Area:	**3,286 sq. ft.**
Standard basement	1,734 sq. ft.
Garage	434 sq. ft.
Exterior Wall Framing:	2x4

Foundation Options:

Standard basement

(All plans can be built with your choice of foundation and framing. A generic conversion diagram is available. See order form.)

BLUEPRINT PRICE CODE:	E

UPPER FLOOR

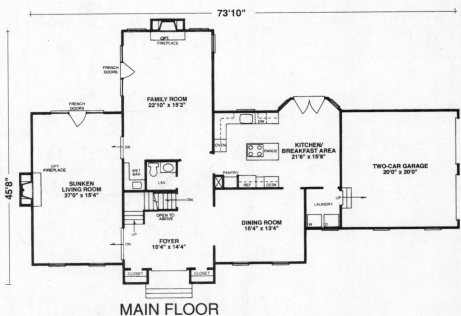

MAIN FLOOR

TO ORDER THIS BLUEPRINT,
CALL TOLL-FREE 1-800-547-5570

Plan AX-87105

PRICES AND DETAILS
ON PAGES 12-15

209

Tremendous Tri-Level Living

- Perfect for a scenic or sloping lot, this stunning home offers three levels of living space for maximum privacy and flexibility.
- At the heart of the main floor is the sunken living room, which boasts a cozy woodstove, skylights and French doors to a deluxe library.
- Just off the formal dining room is a gourmet kitchen, complete with a pantry closet, a boxed-out window and an angled snack bar overlooking the

nook. The glassed-in nook includes a built-in desk and access to the huge, wraparound backyard deck.

- Located near the garage entrance is an oversized utility room with space for a freezer, an ironing center and a laundry tub. A half-bath is nearby.
- An open stairway leads up to the very private master suite. Featured here are a raised sleeping area, a walk-in closet, a private deck and a luxurious bath with a step-up spa tub and a corner shower.
- Two more bedrooms are housed in the daylight basement, which also offers a game room, a wine cellar and a central family room with a woodstove and access to a ground-level patio.

Plan NW-855	
Bedrooms: 3	**Baths:** 2½
Living Area:	
Upper floor	549 sq. ft.
Main floor	1,388 sq. ft.
Daylight basement	1,371 sq. ft.
Total Living Area:	**3,308 sq. ft.**
Garage	573 sq. ft.
Exterior Wall Framing:	2x6

Foundation Options:

Daylight basement
(All plans can be built with your choice of foundation and framing. A generic conversion diagram is available. See order form.)

BLUEPRINT PRICE CODE: E

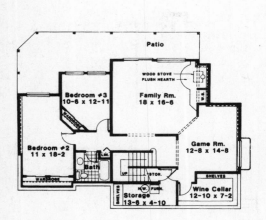

DAYLIGHT BASEMENT

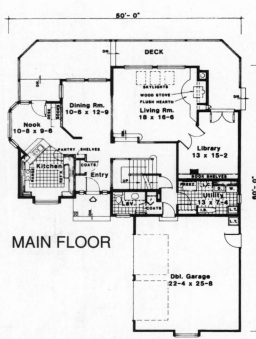

MAIN FLOOR

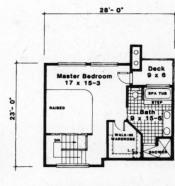

UPPER FLOOR

Plan NW-855

PRICES AND DETAILS ON PAGES 12-15

Traditional Brick Beauty

- An impressive columned entry porch invites you into the two-story foyer of this updated traditional masterpiece.
- The living and dining rooms border the foyer and feature 9-ft. ceilings and oversized bay windows.
- Pocket doors close off the living room from the family room beyond. When the doors are open, a spacious entertainment area is formed, highlighted by an 18-ft. ceiling in the family room, as well as a fireplace and double-door access to the porch.
- The large U-shaped island kitchen offers endless counter space, a walk-in pantry and a pass-through window to the porch. A bright, bayed breakfast room opens to the porch.
- A removed bedroom/den with access to the covered back porch is perfect to use as a guest room or study.
- The majestic master suite boasts a 9-ft. ceiling and private backyard access. The master bath has a huge walk-in closet, a large vanity and a spa tub extending into an exciting solarium.
- The upper floor offers three more bedrooms, another full bath and a loft area that could serve as another bedroom or a playroom or TV room.

Plan HDS-99-168

Bedrooms: 4+	Baths: 3½
Living Area:	
Upper floor	971 sq. ft.
Main floor	2,422 sq. ft.
Total Living Area:	**3,393 sq. ft.**
Garage	680 sq. ft.
Exterior Wall Framing:	2x4

Foundation Options:

Slab

(All plans can be built with your choice of foundation and framing. A generic conversion diagram is available. See order form.)

BLUEPRINT PRICE CODE: E

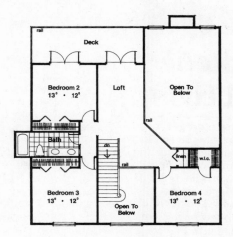

UPPER FLOOR

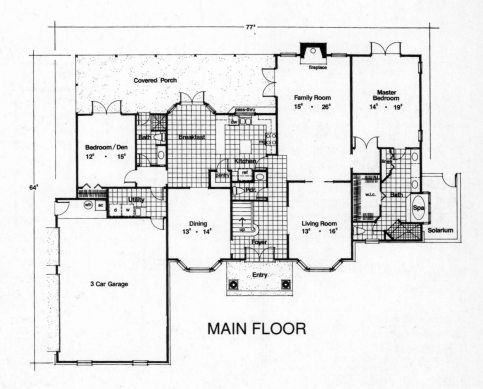

MAIN FLOOR

Stately Stone and Stucco

- This charming home combines stone and stucco to create a warm and stately appearance.
- A quaint covered porch welcomes guests into the two-story foyer. To the right, the living room features a fireplace and a 15½-ft. vaulted ceiling. On the left, columns set off the formal dining room.
- Introduced by more columns, the Great Room offers another fireplace and a convenient back stairway.
- The open kitchen includes a work island and an angled serving bar to the bayed breakfast nook. French doors open to a covered backyard porch.
- The main-floor master suite boasts a 10½-ft. tray ceiling in the sleeping area and 16-ft. vaulted ceilings in the sitting room and the luxurious garden bath.
- Ceilings in all main-floor rooms are 9 ft. high unless otherwise specified.
- Upstairs, three secondary bedrooms share two full baths. An optional bonus room is a nice extra.

Plan FB-5345-JERN

Bedrooms: 4+	Baths: 3½
Living Area:	
Upper floor	928 sq. ft.
Main floor	2,467 sq. ft.
Bonus room	296 sq. ft.
Total Living Area:	**3,691 sq. ft.**
Daylight basement	2,467 sq. ft.
Garage	531 sq. ft.
Exterior Wall Framing:	2x4

Foundation Options:

Daylight basement

(All plans can be built with your choice of foundation and framing. A generic conversion diagram is available. See order form.)

BLUEPRINT PRICE CODE:	**F**

UPPER FLOOR

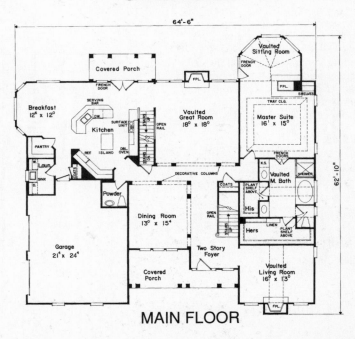

MAIN FLOOR

 Plan FB-5345-JERN *PRICES AND DETAILS ON PAGES 12-15*

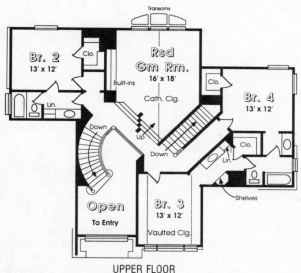

UPPER FLOOR

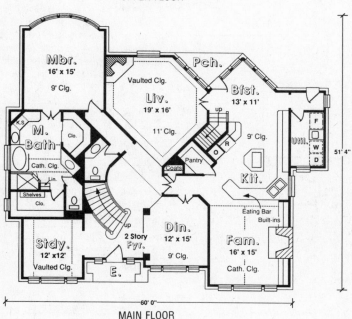

MAIN FLOOR

Dramatic Angles and Curves

- This award-winning design utilizes angular forms to create a logical and functional flow of traffic.
- Dramatic rooflines and window treatments adorn the beautiful brick exterior.
- Inside, the two-story foyer reveals the first of two stairways to the upper level; the other stairway is located in the breakfast room at the rear of the home.
- Highlights on the first floor include volume ceilings throughout and a spectacular central living room with a corner fireplace and a rear window wall overlooking the porch. A huge island kitchen boasts a sunny breakfast nook. An angled eating bar separates the kitchen from the family room, which features built-ins that flank a second fireplace.
- A spacious master bedroom on the main floor and a fantastic raised game room surrounded by three large bedrooms on the second floor complete this exciting, spacious home.

Plan KLF-921

Bedrooms: 4-5	**Baths:** 3 ½
Space:	
Upper floor	1,150 sq. ft.
Main floor	2,383 sq. ft.
Total Living Area	**3,533 sq. ft.**
Exterior Wall Framing	2x4
Foundation options:	
Slab	
(Foundation & framing conversion diagram available—see order form.)	
Blueprint Price Code	F

Room for Work and Play

- Stately columns, an arched porch and dramatic rooflines add attractive and distinguishing touches to this four-bedroom home.
- Amenities inside include a two-story foyer with a curved staircase, a two-story library with a full-length arched window, and a spacious central living room with a fireplace and adjoining patio.
- A modern island kitchen and bayed breakfast area merge with the living room for an open feel.
- The large main-floor master suite boasts a bay area with private patio access and a generous-sized personal bath with twin vanities, dual walk-in closets and a separate tub and shower.
- A large workshop off the garage is an added feature that will be appreciated by hobbyists.
- On the second floor, a versatile media room and a computer work room provide plenty of space for work and play. The upper level also has three nice-sized bedrooms and two full baths.

Plan DD-3583

Bedrooms: 4	Baths: 3½
Space:	
Upper floor	1,436 sq. ft.
Main floor	2,147 sq. ft.
Total Living Area	**3,583 sq. ft.**
Basement	2,147 sq. ft.
Garage	454 sq. ft.
Exterior Wall Framing	2x4

Foundation options:
Standard Basement
Crawlspace
Slab
(Foundation & framing conversion diagram available—see order form.)

Blueprint Price Code	F

UPPER FLOOR

75'0"

COMPUTER 11'8" x 7'4"
STOR. 8'8" x 7'4"
BEDROOM 3 13'8" x 13'4"
LIVING. BELOW
MEDIA 20'8" x 14'8"
BATH 3
BALCONY
BEDROOM 2 15'0" x 12'0"
BATH 2
BEDROOM 4 12'4" x 11'0"
FOYER BELOW
LIBRARY BELOW
42'0"

MAIN FLOOR

77'0"

PATIO
WORKSHOP 15'0" x 9'4"
UTIL.
BRKF'ST. 13'8" x 11'4"
LIVING 16'0" x 21'4"
MASTER BEDROOM 16'0" x 17'0"
KITCHEN 14'4" x 19'4"
LOGGIA
GARAGE 20'4" x 22'4"
1/2 BATH
M/BATH 14'4" x 18'0"
FOYER 10'8" x 16'4"
DINING 12'4" x 14'4"
LIBRARY 12'4" x 17'10"
PORCH
46'0"

Plan DD-3583
PRICES AND DETAILS
ON PAGES 12-15

Superb Views

- This superb multi-level home is designed to take full advantage of spectacular surrounding views.
- The two-story-high entry welcomes guests in from the covered front porch. An open-railed stairway and a 23-ft. domed ceiling are highlights here.
- The sunken living and dining rooms are defined by archways and face out to a large wraparound deck. The living room has a 13-ft. cathedral ceiling and a nice fireplace. The dining room offers a 9½-ft. domed ceiling and a wet bar.
- The octagonal island kitchen hosts a Jenn-Aire range, a sunny sink and a bayed breakfast nook. Nearby, the utility room reveals a walk-in pantry, laundry facilities and garage access.
- The quiet den boasts a second fireplace, a cozy window seat and deck access.
- The entire upper floor is occupied by the master bedroom suite, which has a spacious bayed sleeping room with a 12½-ft. cathedral ceiling. Other features include a huge walk-in closet, separate dressing areas and a private bath with a curved shower and a Jacuzzi tub.
- The exciting daylight basement has a recreation room, an exercise room and another bedroom, plus a sauna and a hot tub surrounded by windows!

Plan NW-229

Bedrooms: 2+	Baths: 2½
Living Area:	
Upper floor	815 sq. ft.
Main floor	1,446 sq. ft.
Daylight basement	1,330 sq. ft.
Total Living Area:	**3,591 sq. ft.**
Garage	720 sq. ft.
Exterior Wall Framing:	2x6

Foundation Options:
Daylight basement
(All plans can be built with your choice of foundation and framing. A generic conversion diagram is available. See order form.)

BLUEPRINT PRICE CODE: **F**

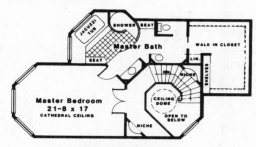

UPPER FLOOR

MAIN FLOOR

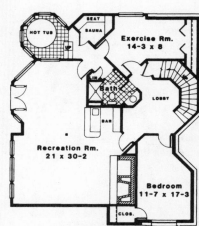

DAYLIGHT BASEMENT

TO ORDER THIS BLUEPRINT,
CALL TOLL-FREE 1-800-547-5570

Plan NW-229

PRICES AND DETAILS
ON PAGES 12-15

215

Elegant Arches

- Gracious arched windows and an entry portico create rhythm and style for this home's brick-clad exterior.
- An elegant curved staircase lends interest to the raised, two-story foyer.
- Two steps down to the left of the foyer lies the living room, with its dramatic 14-ft. cathedral ceiling. Lovely columns define the adjoining dining room. A cozy fireplace warms the entire area.
- The island kitchen overlooks the bayed breakfast room and offers a handy pass-through to the adjoining family room.
- The two-story-high family room boasts a second fireplace and a wall of windows topped by large transoms.
- The quiet master bedroom features a bay window and an 11-ft. sloped ceiling. The master bath shows off a garden tub and a separate shower.
- A sizable deck is accessible from both the breakfast room and the master suite.
- Three more bedrooms and two baths share the upper floor. A balcony bridge overlooks the foyer and family room.

Plan DD-3639

Bedrooms: 4+	Baths: 3½
Living Area:	
Upper floor	868 sq. ft.
Main floor	2,771 sq. ft.
Total Living Area:	**3,639 sq. ft.**
Standard basement	2,771 sq. ft.
Garage	790 sq. ft.
Exterior Wall Framing:	2x4

Foundation Options:

Standard basement

Crawlspace

Slab

(All plans can be built with your choice of foundation and framing. A generic conversion diagram is available. See order form.)

BLUEPRINT PRICE CODE: F

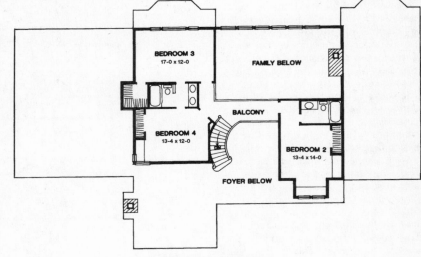

UPPER FLOOR

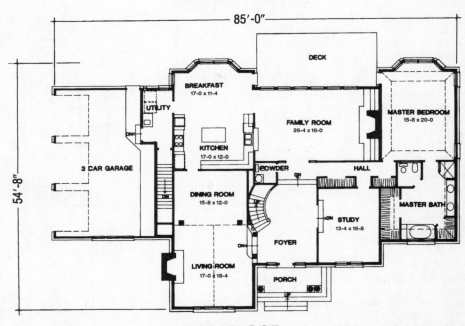

MAIN FLOOR

Ultimate Elegance

- The ultimate in elegance and luxury, this home begins with an impressive foyer that reveals a sweeping staircase and a direct view of the backyard.
- The centrally located parlor, perfect for receiving guests, has a two-story-high ceiling, a spectacular wall of glass, a fireplace and a unique ale bar. French doors open to a covered veranda with a relaxing spa and a summer kitchen.
- The gourmet island kitchen boasts an airy 10-ft. ceiling, a menu desk and a walk-in pantry. The octagonal morning room has a vaulted ceiling and access to a second stairway to the upper level.
- A pass-through snack bar in the kitchen overlooks the gathering room, which hosts a cathedral ceiling, French doors to the veranda and a second fireplace.
- Bright and luxurious, the master suite has a 10-ft. ceiling and features a unique morning kitchen, a sunny sitting area and a lavish private bath.
- The curved staircase leads to three bedroom suites upstairs. The rear suites share an enchanting deck.

Plan EOF-3

Bedrooms: 4+	Baths: 5½
Living Area:	
Upper floor	1,150 sq. ft.
Main floor	3,045 sq. ft.
Total Living Area:	**4,195 sq. ft.**
Garage	814 sq. ft.
Exterior Wall Framing:	2x6

Foundation Options:

Slab

(All plans can be built with your choice of foundation and framing. A generic conversion diagram is available. See order form.)

BLUEPRINT PRICE CODE:	**G**

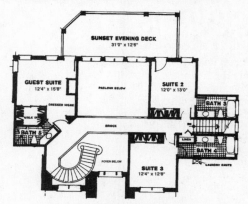

UPPER FLOOR

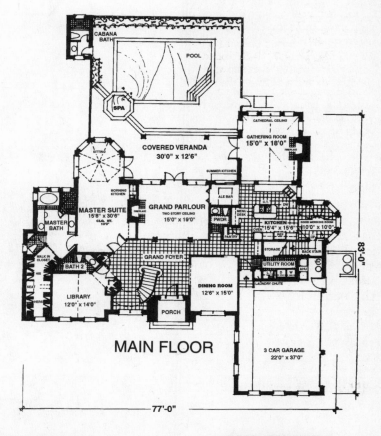

MAIN FLOOR

Design Leaves Out Nothing

- This design has it all, from the elegant detailing of the exterior to the exciting, luxurious spaces of the interior.
- High ceilings, large, open rooms and lots of glass are found throughout the home. Nearly all of the main living areas, as well as the master suite, overlook the veranda.
- Unusual features include a built-in ale bar in the formal dining room, an art niche in the Grand Room and a TV niche in the Gathering Room. The Gathering Room also features a fireplace framed by window seats, a wall of windows facing the backyard and a half-wall open to the morning room. The cooktop-island kitchen is conveniently accessible from all of the living areas.
- The delicious master suite includes a raised lounge, a three-sided fireplace and French doors that open to the veranda. The spiral stairs nearby lead to the "evening deck" above. The master bath boasts two walk-in closets, a sunken shower and a Roman tub.
- The upper floor hosts two complete suites and a loft, plus a vaulted bonus room reached via a separate stairway.

Plan EOF-61

Bedrooms: 3+	Baths: 4½
Living Area:	
Upper floor	877 sq. ft.
Main floor	3,094 sq. ft.
Bonus room	280 sq. ft.
Total Living Area:	**4,251 sq. ft.**
Garage	774 sq. ft.
Exterior Wall Framing:	2x6

Foundation Options:
Slab
(All plans can be built with your choice of foundation and framing. A generic conversion diagram is available. See order form.)

BLUEPRINT PRICE CODE: G

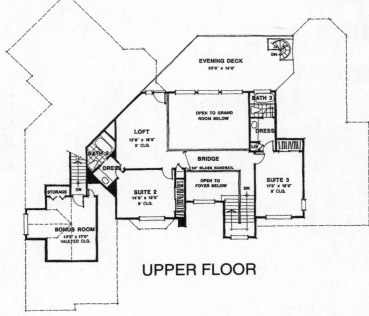

UPPER FLOOR

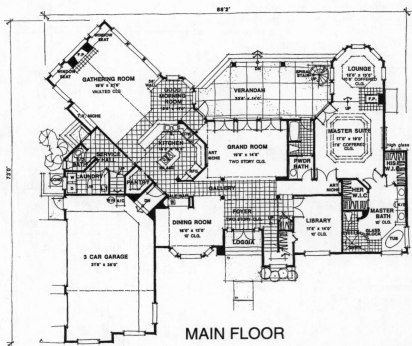

MAIN FLOOR

Plan EOF-61

PRICES AND DETAILS ON PAGES 12-15

Estate Living

- This grand estate is as big and beautiful on the inside as it is on the outside.
- The formal dining room and parlor, each with a tall window, flank the entry's graceful curved staircase.
- The sunken family room is topped by a two-story-high ceiling and wrapped in floor-to-ceiling windows. A patio door opens to the covered porch, which features a nifty built-in barbecue.
- The island kitchen and the bright breakfast area also overlook the porch, with access through the deluxe utility room.

- The master suite has it all, including a romantic fireplace framed by bookshelves. The opulent bath offers a raised spa tub, a separate shower, his-and-hers walk-in closets and a dual-sink vanity. The neighboring bedroom, which also has a private bath, would make an ideal nursery.
- The upper floor hosts a balcony hall that provides a breathtaking view of the family room below. Each of the two bedrooms here has its own bath.
- The main floor is expanded by 10-ft. ceilings, while 9-ft. ceilings grace the upper floor.

Plan DD-4300-B

Bedrooms: 4	Baths: 4½
Living Area:	
Upper floor	868 sq. ft.
Main floor	3,416 sq. ft.
Total Living Area:	**4,284 sq. ft.**
Standard basement	3,416 sq. ft.
Garage and storage	633 sq. ft.
Exterior Wall Framing:	2x4 or 2x6

Foundation Options:

Standard basement
Crawlspace
Slab

(All plans can be built with your choice of foundation and framing. A generic conversion diagram is available. See order form.)

BLUEPRINT PRICE CODE: G

MAIN FLOOR

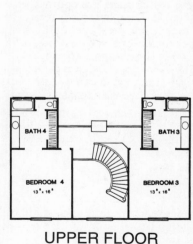

UPPER FLOOR

Extraordinary!

- For a home that is truly outstanding in style and size, this design is hard to beat! From the entry's spectacular curved stairways and 19-ft. ceiling, to the master suite's luxurious skylighted bath, elegance is found throughout.

- The spacious central living room is set off with decorative entry columns and boasts a dramatic fireplace, a 14-ft. vaulted ceiling and outdoor access.

- The gourmet kitchen is concealed behind double doors. The kitchen offers a great windowed sink area, a cooktop island, a walk-in pantry and a snack bar. The octagonal breakfast nook has a patio door to the backyard and adjoins a sunken family room with a 12-ft. ceiling and another cozy fireplace.

- Up one flight of stairs is a quiet den and an extravagant master suite. Behind dramatic double doors, the master bedroom has a romantic sitting bay and panoramic views. The skylighted bath shows off an exciting garden tub, a separate shower, a huge walk-in closet and a toilet room with a bidet.

- Up one more flight are two secondary bedrooms, each with a private bath.

Plan R-4029

Bedrooms: 3+	Baths: 4½
Living Area:	
Upper floor	972 sq. ft.
Main floor	3,346 sq. ft.
Total Living Area:	**4,318 sq. ft.**
Partial basement	233 sq. ft.
Garage	825 sq. ft.
Exterior Wall Framing:	2x6
Foundation Options:	

Partial basement

(All plans can be built with your choice of foundation and framing. A generic conversion diagram is available. See order form.)

BLUEPRINT PRICE CODE:	G

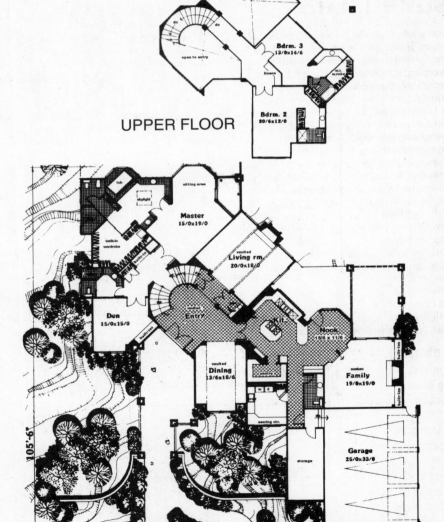

UPPER FLOOR

MAIN FLOOR

Exquisite Home

- This home's curved front steps and stately two-story-high entry introduce its exquisite interior design.
- The two-story-high foyer shows off a sweeping stairway and is flanked by the formal living areas.
- Straight ahead is the family room, with its 19-ft. vaulted ceiling, spectacular window wall and masonry fireplace.
- The roomy island kitchen includes a bayed breakfast area. A nearby wet bar is open to the dining room.
- A skylighted screened porch boasts a handy built-in barbecue grill.
- The beautiful master suite showcases a 12-ft. coffered ceiling and a spacious private bath with a huge garden tub and a curved shower.
- Upstairs, two skylighted baths serve three bedrooms, one with a window seat and the other two with 12-ft. cathedral ceilings. A balcony overlooks the foyer and family room below.
- Ceilings in all main-floor rooms are at least 10 ft. high for added spaciousness.

Plan DD-4458

Bedrooms: 4	Baths: 3½
Living Area:	
Upper floor	1,067 sq. ft.
Main floor	3,391 sq. ft.
Total Living Area:	**4,458 sq. ft.**
Standard basement	3,391 sq. ft.
Garage	774 sq. ft.
Exterior Wall Framing:	2x4

Foundation Options:

Standard basement

Crawlspace

Slab

(All plans can be built with your choice of foundation and framing. A generic conversion diagram is available. See order form.)

BLUEPRINT PRICE CODE: **G**

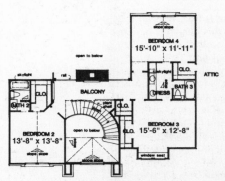

UPPER FLOOR

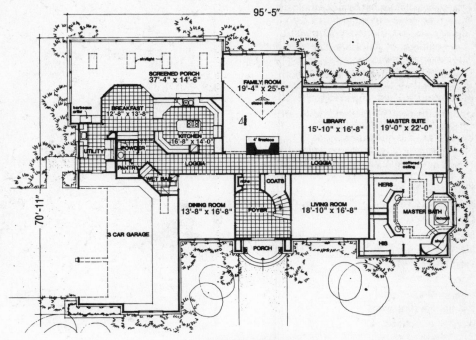

MAIN FLOOR

TO ORDER THIS BLUEPRINT,
CALL TOLL-FREE 1-800-547-5570

Plan DD-4458

PRICES AND DETAILS
ON PAGES 12-15

221

Elegance Perfected

- The grand style of this luxurious home brings elegance and grace to perfection.
- The contemporary architecture exudes an aura of grandeur, drawing the eye to its stately 2½-story entry portico.
- The interior is equally stunning with open, flowing spaces, high ceilings and decorative, room-defining columns.
- The formal zone is impressive, with a vast foyer and a sunken living room highlighted by dramatic window walls and a 20½-ft. ceiling. Round columns set off a stunning octagonal dining room with a 19-ft., 4-in. ceiling. A curved wet bar completes the effect!
- The informal areas consist of an island kitchen, a breakfast nook, a large family room and an octagonal media room. Activities can be extended to the covered back patio through doors in the breakfast nook and the family room.
- The fabulous master suite shows off a romantic fireplace, a 12-ft. ceiling, an enormous walk-in closet and a garden bath with a circular shower!
- Two more main-floor bedrooms, an upper-floor bedroom and loft area, plus two more baths complete the plan.

Plan HDS-90-819

Bedrooms: 4+	Baths: 3½
Living Area:	
Upper floor	765 sq. ft.
Main floor	3,770 sq. ft.
Total Living Area:	**4,535 sq. ft.**
Garage	750 sq. ft.
Exterior Wall Framing:	2x4

Foundation Options:

Slab
(All plans can be built with your choice of foundation and framing. A generic conversion diagram is available. See order form.)

BLUEPRINT PRICE CODE: **G**

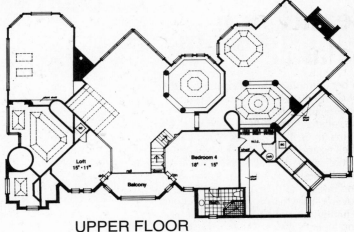

UPPER FLOOR

MAIN FLOOR

Plan HDS-90-819

PRICES AND DETAILS
ON PAGES 12-15

Beauty and Balance

- A beautiful front porch topped by a trio of dormers gives this plan its striking beauty and balance.
- A spacious foyer bisects the formal living areas, which feature built-in shelves and views of the porch.
- At the center of the home is a spacious Great Room with an inviting fireplace and three French doors that open to a covered back porch.
- A handy butler's pantry with a wet bar and a pantry closet lies between the Great Room and the Keeping Room.
- A snack bar unites the island kitchen with the sunny breakfast room and the Keeping Room, which offers a warm fireplace flanked by built-in shelves.
- The spectacular master suite boasts his-and-hers baths, two walk-in closets and a spiral staircase that leads to an upper-floor study.
- A versatile sitting room rests at the center of the upper floor, surrounded by three bedrooms, two baths and the study or optional fifth bedroom.

Plan V-4566

Bedrooms: 4+	**Baths:** 4½

Living Area:	
Upper floor	1,847 sq. ft.
Main floor	2,719 sq. ft.
Total Living Area:	**4,566 sq. ft.**
Exterior Wall Framing:	2x6

Foundation Options:

Crawlspace

(All plans can be built with your choice of foundation and framing. A generic conversion diagram is available. See order form.)

BLUEPRINT PRICE CODE: G

UPPER FLOOR

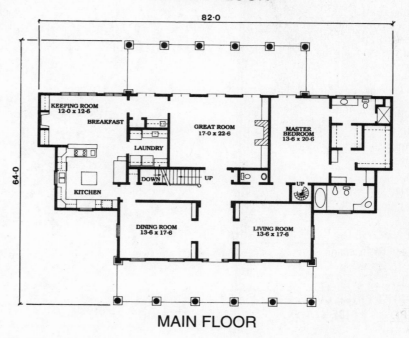

MAIN FLOOR

Spectacular Executive Estate

- The unique angular design of this executive home focuses attention on the spectacular entrance, which is enhanced by two balconies above.
- Beyond the vestibule, a 19-ft. ceiling presides over the columned Great Room and the sunny dining room. A two-story window wall overlooks the expansive backyard pool area.
- The gourmet island kitchen and breakfast nook open to a side deck and offer easy service to both the dining room and the family room.
- A nice-sized media room or library boasts two walls of built-ins.
- The master suite is a masterpiece, with its 15-ft. vaulted ceiling, romantic fireplace and sliding glass doors to a secluded sun deck and hot tub. The luxurious bath offers a whirlpool tub, a separate shower and two vanities.
- A classy, curved staircase accesses the upper floor, where three more bedrooms each have a private bath. A lounge with a window seat and a central area with outdoor balconies are other special appointments found here.

Plan B-05-85

Bedrooms: 4+	Baths: 4 full, 2 half
Living Area:	
Upper floor	1,720 sq. ft.
Main floor	3,900 sq. ft.
Total Living Area:	**5,620 sq. ft.**
Standard basement	3,900 sq. ft.
Garage	836 sq. ft.
Exterior Wall Framing:	2x6

Foundation Options:

Standard basement

(All plans can be built with your choice of foundation and framing. A generic conversion diagram is available. See order form.)

BLUEPRINT PRICE CODE:	**G**

REAR VIEW

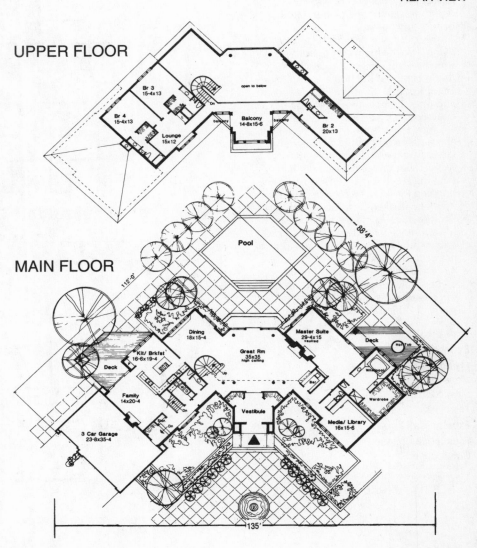

UPPER FLOOR

MAIN FLOOR

Plan B-05-85

PRICES AND DETAILS ON PAGES 12-15